ARCHITECTURE
NOW!

PROJECT COORDINATION
Caroline Keller

EDITORIAL COORDINATION
Anne Sauvadet

PRODUCTION
Thomas Grell

DESIGN
Sense/Net, Andy Disl und
Birgit Reber, Cologne

GERMAN TRANSLATION
Karin Haag

FRENCH TRANSLATION
Jacques Bosser

PRINTED IN SINGAPORE
ISBN 3–8228–4091–2

WWW.TASCHEN.COM
© **2005 TASCHEN GMBH**
Hohenzollernring 53
D – 50672 Köln

ORIGINAL EDITION
© 2001 TASCHEN GmbH

ARCHITECTURE
NOW!

Architektur heute / L'architecture d'aujourd'hui
Philip Jodidio

KÖLN LONDON LOS ANGELES MADRID PARIS TOKYO

CONTENTS

6	**INTRODUCTION**	Einleitung / Introduction
18	**TADAO ANDO**	Chicago House, *Chicago, Illinois, USA*
		Awaji Yumebutai, *Awajishima, Hyogo, Japan*
32	**ANDRESEN O'GORMAN**	Rosebery House, *Highgate Hill, Queensland, Australia*
40	**ASYMPTOTE**	Virtual Trading Floor, *New York Stock Exchange, New York, NY, USA*
		Guggenheim Virtual Museum, *New York, NY, USA*
48	**MARIO BOTTA**	Model of San Carlo alle Quattro Fontane, *Lugano, Switzerland*
54	**WILL BRUDER**	Byrne Residence, *North Scottsdale, Arizona, USA*
62	**SANTIAGO CALATRAVA**	City of Arts and Sciences, *Valencia, Spain*
72	**DALY, GENIK**	Valley Center House, *North San Diego County, California, USA*
76	**DILLER + SCOFIDIO**	The Brasserie, *Seagram Building, New York, NY, USA*
		Blur Building, *International Expo 2002, Yverdon, Switzerland*
88	**STEVEN EHRLICH**	Canyon Residence, *Los Angeles, California, USA*
94	**NORMAN FOSTER**	Greater London Authority, *London, England*
100	**FRANK O. GEHRY**	Experience Music Project, *Seattle, Washington, USA*
110	**GIGON / GUYER**	Museum Liner, *Appenzell, Switzerland*
116	**ZAHA HADID**	Landscape Formation One, *Weil am Rhein, Germany*
126	**HIROSHI HARA**	Ito House, *Chijiwa, Nagasaki, Japan*
132	**ZVI HECKER**	Palmach Museum of History, *Tel Aviv, Israel*
138	**HERZOG & DE MEURON**	House, *Leymen, France*
		Tate Modern, *London, England*
150	**STEVEN HOLL**	Cranbrook Institute of Science, *Bloomfield Hills, Michigan, USA*
156	**DAVID HOVEY**	Modular Steel House, *Glencoe, Illinois, USA*
162	**ARATA ISOZAKI**	COSI, *Columbus, Ohio, USA*
168	**JAKOB + MACFARLANE**	Centre Georges Pompidou Restaurant, *Paris, France*
176	**FRANÇOISE-HÉLÈNE JOURDA**	Mont-Cenis Academy and Municipal District Center, *Herne, Germany*
182	**REI KAWAKUBO**	Comme des Garçons Flagship Store, *Tokyo, Japan*

190	**KHRAS**	Bang & Olufsen Headquarters, *Struer, West Jutland, Denmark*
198	**WARO KISHI**	House in Suzaku, *Nara, Japan*
204	**LAMOTT ARCHITEKTEN**	Public Library, *Landau, Germany*
210	**FUMIHIKO MAKI**	Hillside West, *Tokyo, Japan* Toyama International Convention Center, *Toyama, Japan*
216	**MARMOL RADZINER**	Kaufmann House Restoration, *Palm Springs, California, USA*
226	**RICHARD MEIER**	Neugebauer House, *Naples, Florida, USA*
232	**JOSÉ RAFAEL MONEO**	Murcia Town Hall Annex, *Murcia, Spain*
238	**ERIC OWEN MOSS**	The Umbrella, *Culver City, California, USA*
246	**MVRDV**	MetaCITY/DATATOWN
258	**NEUTELINGS RIEDIJK**	Minnaert Building, *Utrecht, Netherlands* Fire Station, *Maastricht, Netherlands*
270	**JEAN NOUVEL**	Law Courts, *Nantes, France*
276	**POLSHEK PARTNERSHIP**	Rose Center for Earth and Space, American Museum of Natural History, *New York, NY, USA*
284	**CHRISTIAN DE PORTZAMPARC**	LVMH Tower, *New York, NY, USA*
290	**ELIZABETH DE PORTZAMPARC**	Les Grandes Marches Restaurant, *Paris, France*
296	**RICHARD ROGERS**	Millennium Dome, *London, England*
302	**SCHMIDT, HAMMER & LASSEN**	Extension of the Royal Library of Denmark, *Copenhagen, Denmark*
312	**ÁLVARO SIZA**	Serralves Foundation, *Porto, Portugal*
318	**EDUARDO SOUTO DE MOURA**	SILO Norte Shopping, *Matosinhos, Portugal*
324	**PHILIPPE STARCK**	St. Martin's Lane Hotel, *London, England*
330	**YOSHIO TANIGUCHI**	Tokyo National Museum, *Gallery of Horyuji Treasures, Tokyo, Japan*
336	**BERNARD TSCHUMI**	Lerner Hall Student Center, Columbia University, *New York, NY, USA*
342	**UN STUDIO**	Bascule Bridge and Bridgemaster's House, *Purmerend, Netherlands*
348	**WILLIAMS AND TSIEN**	Rifkind House, *Georgica Pond, Long Island, NY, USA*
352	**CREDITS**	

INTRODUCTION

Each new building is the result of specific circumstances, ranging from function or location to cost. Trends in taste or fashion obviously play their role in determining the appearance of architecture and its deeper meanings, though some attempt to deny such influences. "Style," the French naturalist Buffon said, "is the man himself." Perhaps, but it is also a function of the times. Despite the proliferation of new means of communication, no one style has come to dominate contemporary architecture as strongly as postwar Modernism. Currents and cross-currents ripple around the globe, often delayed by the sheer amount of time it takes to design and build a large structure. Thus, architecture in the fractured Deconstructivist style, born in the 1980s, continues to be built. So too, do the neo-Minimalist designs of the 1990s. If "style is the man himself," these buildings are logically produced by architects who fought long and hard to impose their points of view against all odds. Once their ideas have taken hold, they are not likely to move quickly onto other types of design.

While aging trends play out their existence around the world, new styles are taking hold. The new century will display a return to interest in more complex buildings, born less of the disrupted Euclidean geometry seen in the late 20th century than of computer generated volumes that seek to challenge all reference to rectilinear systems. Though some architects still feel that computers are useful only for certain tasks, others have begun to explore new frontiers such as the idea of the "virtual" building – one that will exist only on screens. Asymptote in New York have been commissioned to design a "virtual museum" for the Guggenheim, just as they have created an on-line trading environment for the New York Stock Exchange. These are spaces whose primary existence will be played out on computer screens. Some may see these efforts as being little more than an amusing result of the substantial means put into the creation of computer games like Myst or Riven. For the traditionally minded, the very heart of architecture is in its solidity or durability, admittedly relative qualities that are nonetheless completely obviated in the realm of the virtual. Others, like Hani Rashid of Asymptote, have a different idea of the future. "When speaking of an architecture for the next millennium," says Rashid, "there are two conditions to consider, the physical space of architecture as we have always known it where enclosure, form and permanence will undoubtedly persevere, and the realm of virtual architecture, now emerging from the digital domain of the Internet. Objects, spaces, buildings and institutions can now be constructed, navigated, comprehended, experienced, and manipulated across a global network. This is a new architecture of liquidity, flux and mutability predicated on technological advances and fueled by a basic human desire to probe the unknown. The inevitable path for both these architectures, the real and the virtual, will be one of convergence and merging."

This overview of recent contemporary architecture takes on the daunting task of collecting information from all over the world and attempting to make some sense of it in terms of trends and the evolution of what remains, in its most elevated expressions, a true art form. Even so, innovative architecture, which succeeds in reconciling the often contradictory limits of site, budget, and aesthetic ambition, is excessively rare as compared with the vast number of new buildings erected. Style, even in its varied guises, defines what makes architecture current, of our time. Driven by fashion or more profoundly perhaps, by the widening vistas of computer and Internet technology, will architecture become as fluid and changeable as a spring dress? Certainly not, but it is entering a time when flux and movement are more sought after than immutable monumentality.

VIRTUALLY YOURS

"The museum has become a tomb for art," declares Hani Rashid of Asymptote, "a repository where art is presented to a public presumed to be uninitiated, the pristine spaces of detached and privileged viewing or a space of cultural authority for the dissemination of ideas and the propagation of ideologies. Perhaps what still lingers and deserves to be maintained is an understanding of the space of the museum as a place that can incite provocation in both viewers and artists." Asymptote has been given the task of designing the first virtual museum, one that will exist essentially on the Internet. This "Guggenheim in Cyberspace" has the ambition to create nothing less than "a new architectural paradigm". More specifically, in the museum's terms, "The Guggenheim Virtual Museum will not only provide global access to all Guggenheim Museums including typical museum services, amenities, archives, and collections but will also provide a unique and compelling spatial environment to be experienced by the virtual visitor. In addition, the virtual museum is an ideal space for the deployment and experience of art and events created specifically for the interactive digital medium where simultaneous participation, as well as viewing, is made possible for an audience distributed around the globe. As envisioned by Asymptote and the Guggenheim, the Guggenheim Virtual Museum will emerge from the fusion of information space, art, commerce and architecture to become the first important virtual building of the 21st century." Beyond only creating an environment, one in which works of art can be agreeably viewed, Hani Rashid wants to make his virtual architecture interactive. Its use by visitors will modify its appearance, thus challenging the very solidity or immutability of architecture in general and museums in particular. Like the art it houses, the Virtual Guggenheim will be fluid, redefining itself according to circumstances. Such a project does redefine the architectural paradigm in the sense that it is subjected to almost none of the usual "real world" constraints that hamper buildings, from fire codes to access for the handicapped. It has neither to shelter nor to obey the mundane laws of mechanical engineering. Is this indeed architecture or rather a kind of electronic interior design? It certainly is new.

The taste for freely flowing or a-geometrical volumes and environments is by no means limited among younger architects to such radical approaches as that of Asymptote. Another New York group, Diller + Scofidio, is challenging the concept of traditional architecture in an entirely different way. Their "Blur Building" designed for the International Expo 2002 in Yverdon on Lake Neuchâtel in Switzerland should resemble nothing so much as a cloud. Measuring just under 100 m in length, 60 m in width and 12 m in thickness, the cloud "is made of filtered lake water shot as a fine mist through a dense array of high-pressure water nozzles integrated into a large cantilevered tensegrity structure." The public will approach the immobile cloud via a ramp that becomes glass-enclosed as it enters the water mist. Within, the architects are seeking to achieve "a near absence of stimuli, an optical 'white-out' accompanied by the 'white noise' of the mist pulse..." A panoramic video image projected on a circular screen will occupy a central darkened platform for 250 people. "Since man can no longer claim to be in the center of a controllable universe, the position of the spectator continues to be an issue of critical reflection," say the architects. Diller + Scofidio make ample use of computers in their design work, but unlike Asymptote they have chosen to make physical construction their ultimate goal. They join their New York colleagues in challenging the very principles of architecture, reaching beyond form and materials to "blur" the auditory and visual perception necessary to spatial orientation. Rather than the hierarchical spatial order imposed by almost any traditional architecture, the "Blur Building" makes nothing clear, adopting a scientific and even philosophical stance in harmony with much of contemporary thinking.

ARTS AND CRAFTS

The arts and their exhibition continue to provide one of the most exciting areas for the development of high quality contemporary architecture. For those who are only moderately interested in the idea of "virtual" museums, art and art museums constitute one of the few areas where a certain durability and immutability are considered appropriate. Nonetheless the genre is evolving rapidly, as a few selected examples prove.

Álvaro Siza's Serralves Foundation is located close to the center of Porto, Portugal, where this architect is based. The Serralves Foundation was created through a unique partnership between the Portuguese government and 50 private partners. Established in the Quinta de Serralves on a 20-hectare property including a main house built in the 1930s for the Count of Vizela, the Foundation specializes in contemporary art. Siza's structure in the park of the Foundation is both substantial in size and ambitious in scope. Using a suspended ceiling system similar to the one he devised for the Galician Center of Contemporary Art, Siza created a number of large, flexible galleries, not intended to show the permanent collection, but exclusively to facilitate temporary exhibitions. Internal courtyards and numerous windows allow the visitor to remain in contact with the very attractive park environment (3 hectares of which were created by Siza), while the interior provides all the facilities now expected of modern museums, including a gift shop, cafeteria and an auditorium. The complex is built with a visible attention to detail typical of Siza, and here he has been given the means to realize his ideas. Modernist in inspiration, the Serralves Foundation is by no means outdated in its conception. Complex despite its crisp white lines, the building is further proof that Álvaro Siza is one of the most original and powerful architects of his generation.

Born in the 1930s, like Siza, the Japanese architect Yoshio Taniguchi, recognized as a master in his own country, has emerged as a figure of international significance since he was commissioned to redesign the Museum of Modern Art in New York. His sober mastery of the Modernist vocabulary is amply demonstrated in his most recent completed work, the Gallery of Horyuji Treasures, located in the grounds of the Tokyo National Museum in Ueno Park. Since the National Museum was founded in the late 19th century as the Museum of the Imperial Household, it retains objects donated to the imperial collections in the 1870s as part of an effort to save Horyuji Temple in Nara from waves of anti-Buddhist sentiment. It was for these important items, masks, sculptures, and ritual objects made of metal that Taniguchi erected a tripartite structure. "I conceived of a building in three layers," says the architect, "an inner area walled in stone, an area outside walled in glass, and an outer area delineated by a metal canopy." The innermost box is shielded from daylight, while the entrance hall and space covered by the canopy are flooded with light. Taniguchi recalls that "the multi-layered design of the museum … is meant to symbolize the history of the precious objects it houses, which have been passed down through the ages in layers after layers of outer and inner wooden boxes that have been traditionally used to protect art treasures in Japan." Although the architect is less explicit on this point, his gallery recalls many aspects of Japanese temple design. The entry path leads the visitor toward a reflecting pool with an axial fountain, and he is required to change direction no less than four times while making his approach, thereby – typical of Japanese temples – reminding him that a significant space is being entered. He is greeted by a stone screen where he might have expected to find a door. He needs to go around this last barrier to enter the otherwise very rational exhibition space. The overall impression of extremely high quality construction is heightened by such details as the absolutely perfect alignments of every part of the building, from its innermost gallery to the outermost edges of the basin. Precise and restrained, Yoshio Taniguchi is an aristocratic master, much like his friend Fumihiko Maki. Both have found ways to blend Japanese tradition with modernity in strikingly powerful designs.

YES, BUT IS IT ART?

John Ruskin made clear his feeling that architecture could claim to be the highest of the arts, allying as it does other forms of spatial expression in a unified whole. This analysis probably has more to do with buildings dating up to the 19th century than it does with modern architecture. And yet a symbiosis does exist between the most eloquent expressions of art and architecture even today. The two continue to nourish each other and when they do meet, at that point of juncture, one is likely to find architecture that does after all suit Ruskin's definition.

Tadao Ando is the undisputed master of concrete architecture in Japan. Despite the strong geometric plans of his buildings, his sensitivity to light, and to a ritual sense of space, bring an evident spirituality to his buildings. He appears to have completed his greatest work to date on the island of Awaji. Called Yumebutai or "Dream Stage," this massive complex covers a 215 000 m² area that provided landfill for the artificial island on which the nearby Kansai Airport was built. Although it does include a hotel, a convention center and facilities for large garden shows, the "Dream Stage" is more clearly conceived as a progression of spaces where water, architecture and light meet. Its very "uselessness" affirms this work's claim to the status of pure art. Indeed, when fettered by the need for heavy security in the convention center or loaded down with the imposed interior decor of the hotel, Ando's complex is good, but not astonishing. It is in the gentle maze of courtyards and passageways that the visitor is transported to a higher plane. Fountains cascade from the hillside above, and water flows through the astonishing succession of spaces. As Tadao Ando says, "The Alhambra in Granada provides a historical model. There, water links small patios together." A million scallop shells, selected and placed by hand, line the floors of the basins, and the visitor wonders if this is indeed a dream. Commissioned by the local authorities who were concerned that tourists would bypass Awaji on the way to more seductive destinations, the complex is located near the massive new suspension bridge linking Kobe to Awaji. Not every detail of the "Dream Stage" is perfect. A small chapel in the midst of the complex is a take-off on Ando's remarkable "Church of the Light" (Ibaraki, Osaka, 1989). Rather than placing a cruciform opening behind the altar as he did in the earlier building, here he puts it in the ceiling. One of the strengths of the "Church of the Light" was its raw energy, linked to a strictly limited budget. Could it be that here almost excessive means robbed Tadao Ando of some of that energy? But this complaint is insignificant compared with the overall success of the "Dream Stage." Due to its location on Awaji, the complex has not been published as much as it deserves. Completed late in 1999, Yumebutai represents nothing less than a final statement about the art of architecture in the 20th century. This is a masterpiece.

Like Tadao Ando (with the notable exception of Yumebutai), the Swiss-Italian architect Mario Botta may be at his best in work on a smaller scale. His mountain chapels in Mogno or on the Monte Tamaro are among the most powerful small buildings of the 1990s. Botta is deeply concerned with the art of architecture, as one of his recent projects demonstrates. A series of exhibitions relating to the architecture of the Renaissance or the Baroque have brought the magnificent models of these periods to public attention. These jewels of perfection spelled out the forms imagined by their architects on a reduced scale. Mario Botta chose to create a wooden model of part of Francesco Borromini's San Carlo alle Quattro Fontane (1641) in Rome in full scale on the shore of Lake Lugano to mark a 1999 exhibition of the Italian master's work. Anchored near the entrance to Lugano's Parco Civico, this stunning "virtual monument" allied techniques and forms of the Baroque with a decidedly ephemeral, 20th-century interpretation. Intended as a signal for the exhibition and as an hommage to Borromini's talent, this work is liberated of most of the usual functional constraints of architecture. It is in a sense the essence of architecture liberated from its weighty stone, floating freely. What remains? Art?

When asked if he feels that there is a blurring of the lines between art and architecture today the architect Richard Meier replies, "No. I'm not sure there's so much of the blurring of the lines. I think it's simply that more artists want to be architects. Maybe historically more architects have wanted to be artists, but I think that today more and more artists really would like to make architecture. I think that the beginning points are usually different for an artist than an architect. The artist has an idea of what might be, and then finds someone who wants that idea. Generally an architect waits for someone to come to him with a project and then says, I have an idea for what you can do." Meier insists nonetheless that a good piece of architecture is also a work of art. Frank O. Gehry, the most sculptural of today's major architects, cites his sources with no shame. In his 1989 acceptance speech for the Pritzker Prize he said, "My artist friends, like Jasper Johns, Bob Rauschenberg, Ed Kienholz, and Claes Oldenburg, were working with very inexpensive materials – broken wood and paper – and they were making beauty. These were not superficial details, they were direct, and raised the question in my mind of what beauty was. I chose to use the craft available, and to work with craftsmen and make a virtue out of their limitations. Painting had an immediacy that I craved for in architecture. I explored the process of new construction materials trying to give feeling and spirit to form. In trying to find the essence of my own expression, I fantasized that I was an artist standing before a white canvas deciding what the first move should be."

In any case, the fate of the architecture of the new century is no longer really in the hands of architects such as Frank O. Gehry and Richard Meier. Rather it is in those of a younger generation like Toshiko Mori or Hani Rashid of Asymptote. Trailblazers like Kawakubo or even the designer Philippe Starck and many others have shown that fashion need not be a "dirty" word in architectural design. Movement and change are indeed the key to the new forms, an espousal of flux, a readiness to meet needs. This may often rule out rigid, hierarchical spaces, although the demand for the most wind-resistant of buildings, the skyscraper, defies this logic. From neo-Minimalism to a kind of messy confrontation with everyday reality and computer-generated volumes, architecture is probably changing faster today than ever before.

EINLEITUNG

Jedes neue Bauwerk ist das Ergebnis von Funktion, Standort und Kosten. Der Wandel von Geschmack oder Mode hat offenbar nicht nur Auswirkungen auf die äußere Gestaltung von Architektur, sondern auch auf ihre Bewertung und Interpretation – auch wenn dies oft geleugnet wird. »Der Stil«, sagte Buffon, »ist der Mensch selbst«. Das mag sein, aber Stil ist auch eine Zeiterscheinung. Trotz moderner Kommunikationsmittel hat keine Stilrichtung die Gegenwartsarchitektur so nachhaltig geprägt wie die Nachkriegs-Moderne. Vielmehr breiten sich unterschiedliche Strömungen und Gegenströmungen weltweit aus, oft verzögert durch lange Planungs- und Bauzeiten. So entwerfen Architekten noch heute Bauten in den gebrochenen, dekonstruktivistischen Formen der 80er oder im neo-minimalistischen Stil der 90er-Jahre. Wenn es stimmt, dass der »Stil der Mensch selbst« ist, dann bedeutet das, dass diese Gebäude von Architekten geschaffen wurden, die lange und hart kämpfen mussten, um ihre Ideen durchzusetzen und deshalb wahrscheinlich nicht so rasch den Baustil wechseln.

Während sich die Legitimation älterer Stile erschöpft, gewinnen neue an Gültigkeit. Im gerade angebrochenen Jahrhundert wird sich das Interesse vermutlich wieder zu komplexeren Bauten verlagern. Das ist jedoch weniger auf die Verwerfung der euklidischen Geometrie zurückzuführen als vielmehr auf computergenerierte Räume, die das orthogonale System hinter sich lassen. Sehen einige Architekten den Nutzen des Computers immer noch auf gewisse Aufgaben begrenzt, so haben andere begonnen, mit seiner Hilfe neues Terrain zu erkunden – etwa das Konzept des »virtuellen« Gebäudes. Die New Yorker Gruppe Asymptote etwa erhielt den Auftrag, ein »virtuelles Museum« für das Guggenheim Museum zu entwerfen, dessen Räume praktisch nur auf Computerbildschirmen existieren werden. Manch einer mag diese Arbeit als amüsante Variante von Computerspielen wie Myst oder Riven sehen. Traditionalisten sehen das Wesen der Architektur in ihrer Solidität, Stofflichkeit und Dauerhaftigkeit – relativen Eigenschaften, die im Reich des Virtuellen überflüssig werden. Andere, wie Hani Rashid von Asymptote, denken anders über die Zukunft: »Wenn wir über Architektur im neuen Jahrtausend sprechen, müssen wir zwei Bedingungen berücksichtigen. Einmal den vertrauten physischen Aspekt von Architektur, in dem es auch weiterhin räumliche Begrenzung, Form und Dauerhaftigkeit geben wird, und dann den Bereich der virtuellen Architektur, der sich im digitalen Raum des Internet entwickelt. Objekte, Räume, Gebäude und Institutionen können heute in einem weltumspannenden Netzwerk konstruiert, gesteuert, verstanden, erfahren und gestaltet werden. Dies ist eine neue Architektur der fließenden Grenzen, des beständigen Wechsels und der dauernden Veränderlichkeit. Sie basiert auf dem technischen Fortschritt und wird getrieben von dem menschlichen Grundbedürfnis, ins Unbekannte vorzustoßen. Der einzig gangbare Weg für diese beiden Architekturformen, die reale und die virtuelle, liegt darin, sich einander anzunähern und zu ergänzen.«

Der vorliegende Überblick über Architektur der Gegenwart fasst Informationen aus der ganzen Welt zusammen und bewertet sie im Hinblick auf Trends und entwicklungsgeschichtliche Perspektiven. Dabei zeigt sich: Unter den zahllosen Bauten weltweit ist innovative Architektur, die die häufig widerstreitenden Vorgaben von Standort, Budget und ästhetischem Anspruch erfolgreich miteinander in Einklang bringt, äußerst selten. Stil bestimmt die Aktualität von Architektur. Wird Architektur damit so unbeständig wie eine Frühlingsmode? Das sicher nicht. Sie tritt jedoch in ein Zeitalter ein, in dem Veränderbarkeit und Lebendigkeit wichtiger geworden sind als Unvergänglichkeit und Monumentalität.

VIRTUELLE WIRKLICHKEITEN

»Das Museum ist zu einer Art Mausoleum für die Kunst geworden«, erklärt Hani Rashid von Asymptote. »Museen sind unbelebte Orte, wo Kunst einer für unwissend gehaltenen Öffentlichkeit präsentiert wird. Es sind Tempel der distanzierten und privilegierten Betrachtung oder Domänen kultureller Autorität zur Verbreitung von Ideen und Ideologien. Daneben wird das Museum vielleicht noch – und das ist auch erhaltenswert – als Ort verstanden, der auf Besucher wie Künstler provozierend wirken kann.« Asymptote hat den Auftrag für die Gestaltung des ersten virtuellen Museums erhalten, eines Kunstraums, der nur im Internet existiert. Dieses »Guggenheim in Cyberspace« hat den Ehrgeiz, »ein neues Paradigma für die Architektur« zu schaffen. Oder, wie die Leitung des Museums konkretisiert: »Das Guggenheim Virtual Museum wird nicht nur einen weltweiten Zugang auf alle Guggenheim Museen einschließlich deren individueller Serviceleistungen, Archive und Sammlungen bieten, sondern dem virtuellen Besucher auch das Erlebnis einer einzigartigen und faszinierenden räumlichen Umgebung vermitteln. Darüber hinaus ist das virtuelle Museum der ideale Ort für das Betrachten und Erleben von Kunst und künstlerischen Events, die eigens für das interaktive digitale Medium konzipiert werden. Hier wird einem globalen Publikum die gleichzeitige Teilnahme an und Betrachtung von Kunst ermöglicht. Wie von

Asymptote und dem Guggenheim konzipiert, entsteht das »Guggenheim Virtual Museum aus der Verbindung von Information, Kunst, Handel und Architektur und wird damit zum ersten bedeutenden virtuellen Gebäude des 21. Jahrhunderts.« Hani Rashid will nicht nur eine besonders angenehme künstliche Umgebung für die Betrachtung von Kunstwerken schaffen. Ihm geht es um eine interaktive virtuelle Architektur, die sich durch die Nutzung der Besucher verändert, womit genau jene Solidität und Unvergänglichkeit unterlaufen wird, die Architektur im Allgemeinen und Museen im Besonderen zugeschrieben wird. Ebenso wie die Kunst, die es ausstellt, wird das Guggenheim Virtual Museum also ständig im Fluss sein und sich, den jeweiligen Umständen entsprechend, neu definieren. Ein solches Projekt bedeutet insofern einen Paradigmawechsel, als es keine jener Beschränkungen kennt – z. B. Feuerschutzbestimmungen –, denen die »reale« Architektur üblicherweise unterworfen ist. Ist es dann überhaupt Architektur oder eher eine Art elektronische Innenraumgestaltung? Auf jeden Fall ist es etwas Neues.

Die Vorliebe junger Architekten für freie oder nicht-euklidische Formen und Räume beschränkt sich jedoch nicht auf so radikale Lösungen wie die von Asymptote. So geht die ebenfalls in New York ansässige Gruppe Diller + Scofidio andere Wege, um die traditionelle Auffassung von Architektur zu hinterfragen. Ihr »Blur Building« (blur = verwischen, nebelhaft machen), das sie für die Expo 2002 im schweizerischen Yverdon am Neuburger See entworfen haben, soll einer Wolke ähneln. Knapp 100 m lang, 60 m breit 12 m tief, besteht diese Wolke »aus gefiltertem Seewasser, das als feiner, feuchter Nebel aus dicht angeordneten Hochdruckdüsen versprüht wird, die in eine große, freitragende Seilnetz-Konstruktion eingebettet sind.« Die Besucher betreten die unbewegliche Wolke über eine Rampe, die im Bereich des Wasserdunstes verglast ist. Im Innern streben die Architekten nach »der möglichst vollständigen Abwesenheit aller Sinnesreize; ein optisches weißes Nichts, begleitet vom weißen Rauschen der Nebeldüsen…« Ein auf eine kreisförmige Leinwand projiziertes Panoramabild umschließt eine abgedunkelte Plattform für 250 Besucher. »Da der Mensch nicht länger beanspruchen kann, der Mittelpunkt eines kontrollierbaren Universums zu sein, bleibt die Position des Betrachters Gegenstand kritischer Reflexion«, erläutern die Architekten. Diller + Scofidio machen zwar ausgiebig Gebrauch von CAD, anders als Asymptote ist ihr Ziel jedoch der Entwurf physisch-realer Konstruktionen. Einig sind sich beide Gruppen jedoch in der Herausforderung tradierter architektonischer Prinzipien, indem sie über die Gestaltung von Form und Material hinaus die akustischen und visuellen Bedingungen für die räumliche Orientierung »verwischen«. Im Gegensatz zur hierarchischen Raumfolge traditioneller Architektur macht das »Blur Building« nichts klar oder eindeutig und nimmt damit eine Position ein, die sich in Einklang mit weiten Bereichen des zeitgenössischen Denkens befindet.

KUNSTRÄUME – RÄUME FÜR KUNST

Die bildenden Künste und ihre öffentliche Präsentation bieten weiterhin eines der dankbarsten Tätigkeitsfelder für anspruchsvolle Gegenwartsarchitektur. Für jene, die nur ein begrenztes Interesse am Konzept des »virtuellen« Museums aufbringen, bilden Kunst und Ausstellungsräume einen der wenigen Bereiche, in denen eine gewisse Dauerhaftigkeit und Unveränderlichkeit nach wie vor als angemessen gelten. Dennoch hat sich auch dieses Genre rapide verändert, wie einige Beispiele belegen.

Die von Álvaro Siza entworfene Stiftung Serralves im portugiesischen Porto liegt in der Nähe des Stadtzentrums, wo auch Siza sein Büro hat. Die auf zeitgenössische Kunst konzentrierte Stiftung wurde durch eine einzigartige Zusammenarbeit der portugiesischen Regierung mit 50 Partnern aus der Wirtschaft ins Leben gerufen. Ihr Sitz in der Quinta de Serralves erstreckt sich über ein Gelände von 20 ha, einschließlich eines in den 1930er-Jahren für den Grafen von Vizela erbauten Haupthauses. Sizas Bau im Park der Stiftung ist in Ausmaß und Anspruch ein groß angelegtes Unternehmen. Unter Verwendung einer Hängedeckenkonstruktion, ähnlich jener, die er für das Galicische Zentrum für Zeitgenössische Kunst entworfen hat, gestaltete Siza eine Reihe großer, flexibler Galerien für Wechselausstellungen. Innenhöfe und Fenster bieten dem Besucher ständigen Ausblick auf den Park (von dem Siza 3 ha gestaltete); im Innern befinden sich zudem ein Museumsshop, ein Café und ein Vortragssaal. Der ganze Bau ist von einem augenfälligen Gespür für Details geprägt, das typisch für Siza ist. Hierfür hat man ihm alle erdenklichen Mittel zur Verfügung gestellt. Von der klassischen Moderne inspiriert, ist die Stiftung Serralves in ihrer Anlage keineswegs überholt. Trotz ihrer klaren weißen Linien eher komplex in der Formensprache, beweist sie ein weiteres Mal, dass Álvaro Siza einer der kreativsten und kraftvollsten Architekten seiner Generation ist.

Der japanische Architekt Yoshio Taniguchi wurde ebenso wie Siza in den 30er-Jahren geboren. Im eigenen Land ist er seit langem ein anerkannter Meister, und mit dem Auftrag für den Umbau des Museum of Modern Art in New York hat er auch internationale Bedeutung erlangt. Seine souveräne Beherrschung des Stilvokabulars der Moderne zeigt sich besonders deutlich in seinem letzten Bau, den Räumen der Horyuji-Schatzkammern im Untergeschoss des Tokioter Nationalmuseums im Ueno Park. Diese Institution wurde im späten 19. Jahrhundert als Museum des kaiserlichen Hofs gegründet und enthält Kunstobjekte, die der kaiserlichen Sammlung in den 1870er-Jahren als Schenkung überlassen wurden, um den Bestand des Horyuji-Tempels in Nara vor der damals aufflackernden anti-buddhistischen Stimmung zu retten. Für diese bedeutenden Ausstellungsstücke wie Masken, Skulpturen und rituelle Gegenstände aus Metall hat Taniguchi eine dreiteilige Konstruktion errichtet. Der Architekt über seinen Entwurf: »Ich hatte die Vorstellung eines Gebäudes, das aus drei Schichten besteht: einem von einer Steinmauer umgebenen inneren, einem von einer Glaswand umschlossenen mittleren und einem durch ein überhängendes Schutzdach aus Metall definierten äußeren Bereich.« Der innere Raum ist vom Tageslicht abgeschirmt, während die Eingangshalle und der von dem Schutzdach überdeckte Bereich von Licht durchflutet werden. Taniguchi führt weiter aus, dass die mehrschichtige Konzeption des Museums »die Geschichte seiner kostbaren Ausstellungsstücke symbolisieren soll, die Jahrhunderte lang in den zahllosen Fächern hölzerner Kisten, die im alten Japan zur Aufbewahrung von Kunstschätzen verwendet wurden, auf uns gekommen sind«. Obgleich der Architekt weniger ausführlich auf diesen Punkt eingeht, erinnert seine Museumsgestaltung auch an viele Aspekte der japanischen Tempelarchitektur. Der Zugangsweg führt die Besucher auf ein spiegelndes Wasserbecken mit einem symmetrisch angeordneten Springbrunnen hin, dabei muss man nicht weniger als viermal die Richtung wechseln. Diese Gestaltung stellt einen für japanische Tempel typischen Zugang dar, der die Besucher daran erinnert, dass sie einen bedeutungsvollen Ort betreten. Anstelle einer Eingangstür passiert der Besucher dann einen steinernen Wandschirm, bevor er das sonst sehr zweckmäßig angelegte Gebäude betritt. Der allgemeine Eindruck eines qualitativ äußerst anspruchsvollen Bauwerks wird noch verstärkt durch Details wie eine absolut perfekte Übereinstimmung sämtlicher Gebäudeteile, von der innersten Galerie bis zum äußersten Rand des Wasserbeckens. Mit seiner präzisen und beherrschten Formensprache ist Taniguchi ein aristokratischer Meister seiner Kunst, ganz ähnlich wie sein Freund Fumihiko Maki. Beide haben in ihren eindrucksvollen, inhaltsreichen Entwürfen ganz eigene Wege gefunden, um die japanische Tradition harmonisch mit der Moderne zu verbinden.

ARCHITEKTUR ALS KUNST?

John Ruskin vertrat die Ansicht, die Architektur könne beanspruchen, die höchste Kunstform zu sein, da sie andere räumliche Ausdrucksformen zu einem einheitlichen Ganzen verbindet. Diese Einschätzung lässt sich wahrscheinlich eher auf Bauwerke beziehen, die vor dem Ende des 19. Jahrhunderts entstanden sind als auf die moderne Architektur. Und dennoch existiert sogar heute noch eine Symbiose zwischen den überzeugendsten Werken der Kunst und der Architektur. Weiterhin befruchten beide Bereiche einander, und an dem Punkt, an dem sie sich treffen, kann man auf eine Form von Architektur stoßen, die der Definition von Ruskin durchaus entspricht.

Tadao Ando ist der unbestrittene Meister der Betonarchitektur in Japan. Sein sensibler Umgang mit Licht und sein rituelles Raumgefühl geben Andos geometrisch-strengen Bauten eine spürbare Spiritualität. Auf der Insel Awaji scheint er sein bislang größtes Werk vollendet zu haben. Der umfangreiche Komplex mit dem Namen Yumebutai oder »Dream Stage« (Traumbühne) nimmt eine Fläche von 215 000m² ein, die Schüttmaterial für die künstliche Insel lieferte, auf welcher der nahegelegene Flughafen Kansai erbaut wurde. Obwohl es ein Hotel, ein Kongresszentrum und Anlagen für Gartenbauausstellungen umfasst, ist »Dream Stage« eher eine Abfolge von Räumen, in denen sich Wasser, Architektur und Licht begegnen. Gerade in seinen scheinbar zweckfreien Elementen bestätigt die Anlage ihren Anspruch auf den Status eines reinen Kunstwerks. In Bereichen wie dem Kongresszentrum und dem Hotel dagegen wirkt Yumebutai zwar gelungen, aber keineswegs verblüffend. Es ist vielmehr das sanft verwirrende Labyrinth aus Innenhöfen und Durchgängen, das den Besucher seiner Alltagswelt enthebt. Wasserfälle stürzen von Hängen und Wasserläufe strömen durch eine erstaunliche Vielzahl von Räumen. Tadao Ando meint dazu: »Die Alhambra in Granada, wo das Wasser kleine Patios miteinander verbindet, lieferte ein historisches Vorbild.« Eine Million Muschelschalen bedecken die Böden der Wasserbecken, und der Besucher fragt sich, ob das alles nicht eigentlich ein Traum sei. In Auftrag gegeben wurde der Komplex von den örtlichen Behörden, die besorgt waren, dass die Touristen Awaji auf ihrem Weg zu verlockenderen Reisezielen übersehen könnten. Er liegt zudem nicht weit von der eindrucksvollen neuen Hängebrücke entfernt, die Kobe mit Awaji verbindet. Allerdings ist nicht jedes Detail von »Dream Stage« perfekt. Eine kleine Kapelle in der Mitte der Anlage ist ein Abklatsch von Andos außergewöhnlicher »Church of the Light« (Kirche des Lichts) in Ibaraki, Osaka (1989). Statt wie hier eine kreuzförmige Öffnung hinter den Altarraum zu platzieren, verlegt Ando sie nun an die Decke. Eine der Stärken seiner »Church of the Light« ist ihre kraftvolle Energie; und dabei hatte Ando für dieses Projekt nur ein relativ geringes Budget. Könnte es sein, dass Ando wegen der fast grenzenlosen Mittel, die ihm für »Dream Stage« zur Verfügung standen, etwas von dieser Energie eingebüßt hat? Dieser Einwand scheint jedoch nebensächlich angesichts des erfolgreichen Konzepts von »Dream Stage«. Aufgrund seiner Lage auf Awaji hat der Komplex nicht die Publizität erlangt, die er verdient. Yumebutai wurde Ende 1999 vollendet und ist nichts Geringeres als ein abschließendes Statement zur Kunst der Architektur im 20. Jahrhundert. Es ist in der Tat ein Meisterwerk.

Wie Tadao Ando (mit der rühmlichen Ausnahme von Yumebutai) zeigt sich auch Mario Botta aus dem Tessin in kleineren Projekten von seiner besten Seite. Seine Bergkapellen in Mogno und auf dem Monte Tamaro gehören zu den kraftvollsten kleineren Bauten der 1990er-Jahre. Für Botta ist der künstlerische Aspekt von Architektur sehr wichtig, wie eines seiner jüngsten Projekte demonstriert. Aus Anlass der Francesco Borromini-Ausstellung 1999 errichtete Botta am Ufer des Luganer Sees das originalgroße Holzmodell eines Teils von Borrominis Kirche San Carlo alle Quattro Fontane (1641) in Rom. Dieses großartige »virtuelle Denkmal« verband Bautechniken und -formen des Barock mit einer bewusst flüchtigen Interpretation des 20. Jahrhunderts. Zugleich ist Bottas Hommage an den großen Barockarchitekten von den funktionalen Beschränkungen befreit, denen Architektur meist unterliegt.

Auf die Frage, ob er der Meinung sei, dass sich die Grenzen zwischen Kunst und Architektur gegenwärtig verwischen, antwortete der amerikanische Architekt Richard Meier: »Nein, ich glaube nicht, dass die Grenzen sich so sehr verwischen. Eher denke ich, dass es einfach mehr Künstler gibt, die auch Architekten sein wollen. Vielleicht wollten in der Vergangenheit mehr Architekten Künstler sein. Aber ich glaube, heute würden sich immer mehr Künstler wirklich gerne als Architekten betätigen... Die Ausgangspunkte sind meiner Meinung nach für Künstler und Architekten unterschiedlich. Der Künstler hat eine Idee von dem, was sein könnte, und dann findet er jemanden, der diese Idee verwirklicht haben will. Ein Architekt dagegen wartet in der Regel darauf, dass jemand mit einem Projekt auf ihn zukommt, und dann entwickelt er eine Idee für dieses Projekt.« Dennoch betont Meier, dass ein gelungenes Bauwerk immer auch ein Kunstwerk ist. Frank O. Gehry, der am stärksten plastisch gestaltende unter den bedeutenden zeitgenössischen Architekten, zitiert ohne Scheu die Quellen seiner künstlerischen Inspiration. 1989 sagte er in seiner Dankesrede zur Verleihung des Pritzker Prize: »Meine Künstlerfreunde wie Jasper Johns, Bob Rauschenberg, Ed Kienholz und Claes Oldenburg arbeiteten mit sehr billigen Materialen – Holzstücken und Papier –, und sie schufen Schönheit. Diese Materialien waren keine oberflächlichen Details, sie waren bewusst eingesetzt und weckten in mir die Frage, was Schönheit sei. Ich entschied mich für das Handwerk, das mir zur Verfügung stand, und dafür, aus dessen Begrenzungen eine Tugend zu machen. Malerei hat eine Unmittelbarkeit, nach der ich mich in der Architektur sehnte. Ich erforschte die Entwicklung neuer Baustoffe und versuchte, die Form mit Gefühl und Geist zu füllen. In dem Bemühen, den wahren Kern meines eigenen Ausdrucks zu finden, stellte ich mir vor, ich sei ein Maler, der vor einer weißen Leinwand steht und sich den ersten Arbeitsschritt überlegt.«

Letztlich liegt das Schicksal der Architektur des neuen Jahrhunderts jedoch nicht in den Händen von Architekten wie Frank O. Gehry und Richard Meier. Ihr Weg wird vielmehr von den Vertretern einer jüngeren Generation wie Toshiko Mori oder Hani Rashid von Asymptote bestimmt. Bahnbrechende Pioniere wie Rei Kawakubo oder Philippe Starck und viele andere haben gezeigt, dass Mode im Kontext architektonischer Gestaltung kein Schimpfwort sein muss. Lebendigkeit und Veränderung sind Kernbegriffe für die neuen Bauformen, ebenso wie das Zulassen eines beständigen Wechsels und die Bereitschaft, wechselnden Bedürfnissen zu entsprechen. Oft mag das streng gegliederte Räume ausschließen, obgleich die anhaltende Nachfrage nach dem wohl am stärksten hierarchisierten Gebäude, dem Wolkenkratzer, dieser Logik widerspricht. Vom Neo-Minimalismus über die ungeordnete Konfrontation mit der alltäglichen Lebenswirklichkeit bis zu virtuellen Bauwerken: Die Architektur verändert sich gegenwärtig wohl so rasch wie nie zuvor.

INTRODUCTION

Chaque réalisation architecturale naît de circonstances spécifiques liées à sa fonction, à son site, à son budget. Le goût, voire la mode jouent évidemment leur rôle dans la détermination de l'aspect du bâti et même dans sa signification profonde, même si certains tentent de nier ce type d'influences. Buffon disait « Le style, c'est l'homme ». C'est peut-être exact, mais le style est aussi fonction du temps. Malgré la prolifération des nouveaux moyens de communication, aucun mouvement stylistique n'a réussi à s'imposer en architecture contemporaine avec autant de force que le modernisme dans la période de l'après-guerre. Des courants et sous-tendances se répandent sur le globe, souvent ralentis par la durée nécessaire à la conception et à la réalisation d'une œuvre importante. Ainsi, des projets de style déconstructiviste apparus dans les années 1980 continuent à être réalisés. Il en va de même pour le néo-minimalisme des années 1990. Si le style est l'homme, ces bâtiments sont les produits d'architectes qui se sont longtemps battus pour imposer leur point de vue dans le passé. Une fois que leurs idées semblent triompher, on ne peut attendre d'eux qu'ils s'orientent immédiatement vers une démarche différente.

Alors que des tendances surannées terminent leur existence par un tour du monde, d'autres styles apparaissent. Le XXIe siècle assistera à un renouveau de l'intérêt pour des constructions plus complexes, moins liées à la géométrie euclidienne – passablement bousculée à la fin du siècle précédent – qu'aux recherches par ordinateur qui s'efforcent de remettre en question les références aux systèmes rectilignes. Bien que certains architectes pensent encore que l'ordinateur n'est utile qu'à certaines tâches, d'autres ont commencé à explorer de nouvelles frontières comme ce concept de « bâtiment virtuel » qui n'existerait que sur écran. A New York, l'agence Asymptote, qui a été retenue pour concevoir un musée virtuel pour Guggenheim, vient de créer un environnement de marchés en ligne pour le New York Stock Exchange. Il s'agit d'espaces dont l'existence première se déroulera sur l'écran de l'ordinateur. On peut penser que ces efforts ne vont guère plus loin que les importants moyens investis dans la création de jeux vidéo comme « Myst » ou « Riven ». Pour un esprit traditionaliste, l'essence même de l'architecture réside dans sa solidité ou sa permanence, qualités assez relatives faut-il le préciser, mais qui n'en sont pas moins entièrement éliminées de l'univers virtuel. D'autres, comme Hani Rashid d'Asymptote ont une vision différente du futur. « Lorsque l'on parle de l'architecture du millénaire à venir », explique Rashid, « il faut prendre en compte deux conditions, l'espace physique de l'architecture tel que nous l'avons toujours connu, dont l'enveloppe, la forme et la permanence subsisteront sans aucun doute, et le domaine de l'architecture virtuelle qui émerge aujourd'hui de l'espace numérique de l'Internet. Objets, volumes, espaces, immeubles et institutions peuvent désormais être édifiés, transmis, appréhendés, expérimentés et manipulés sur le réseau global. C'est une nouvelle architecture de fluidité, de flux et de mutabilité, qui repose sur des avances technologiques, nourrie d'un désir humain fondamental d'affronter l'inconnu. La voie inévitable de ces deux architectures, la réelle et la virtuelle, sera la convergence et la fusion. »

Ce survol de l'architecture contemporaine récente s'efforce de remplir une tâche audacieuse : réunir des informations venues du monde entier et tenter de trouver quelque sens en termes de tendances et d'évolution dans ce qui reste, à travers ses expressions les plus élevées, une authentique forme d'art. Même ainsi, l'architecture novatrice, celle qui réussit à réconcilier les limites souvent contradictoires d'un site, d'un budget et d'une ambition esthétique, reste excessivement rare comparée à l'énorme masse de ce qui se construit à chaque instant. Le style, même sous ses différents atours, fait l'architecture du moment, de notre temps. Animée par la mode ou, plus profondément peut-être, par les perspectives plus vastes qu'ouvrent l'ordinateur et l'Internet, l'architecture deviendra-t-elle aussi fluide et changeante qu'une petite robe de printemps ? Certainement pas, mais elle fait néanmoins son entrée dans une époque où le flux et le mouvement seront des valeurs plus recherchées que la monumentalité et l'immuabilité.

VIRTUELLEMENT VOTRE

« Le musée est devenu le tombeau de l'art », affirme Hani Rashid d'Asymptote « une châsse dans laquelle l'art est présenté à un public présumé non initié, dans les espaces splendides d'une vision détachée et privilégiée d'un lieu d'autorité culturelle au service de la diffusion d'idées et de la propagation d'idéologies. Ce qui subsiste encore et mérite d'être maintenu est peut-être la compréhension de l'espace du musée, lieu qui peut inciter à la provocation, chez les spectateurs comme chez les artistes. » Asymptote s'est vu confier la tâche de concevoir le premier musée virtuel qui existera essentiellement sur Internet. Ce « Guggenheim du cyberespace » possède l'ambition de créer rien de moins qu'un « nouveau paradigme architectural ». Plus spécifiquement, « le Guggenheim

Virtual Museum donnera non seulement accès à tous les musées Guggenheim, y compris aux services, archives et collections caractéristiques d'un musée, mais offrira également un environnement exclusif et convaincant que pourra expérimenter le visiteur virtuel. Par ailleurs, le musée virtuel est l'espace idéal pour le déploiement et la connaissance de l'art et d'événements spécifiquement créés pour un médium numérique qui permet en même temps à un public dispersé dans le monde entier de visiter et d'intervenir sur le site. Pour Asymptote et le Guggenheim, le Guggenheim Virtual Museum, né de la fusion d'un espace d'information, de l'art, du commerce et de l'architecture, deviendra le premier bâtiment virtuel important du XXIe siècle. » En plus de créer un environnement dans lequel les œuvres d'art pourront être facilement regardées, Hani Rashid veut que son architecture virtuelle soit interactive. Son utilisation par les visiteurs modifiera son apparence et remettra en cause la solidité ou l'immuabilité même de l'architecture en général et des musées en particulier. Comme l'art qu'il accueillera, le Guggenheim virtuel sera fluide, se redéfinissant de lui-même en fonction des circonstances. Un tel projet remet en question le paradigme architectural dans le sens où il n'est soumis pratiquement à aucune des contraintes du « monde réel » qui entravent la construction, comme les réglementations de sécurité ou l'accès des handicapés. Il ne doit ni protéger ni obéir aux lois communes de l'ingénierie. Architecture ou aménagement intérieur électronique ? En tout cas, cette orientation est la dernière nouveauté.

Dans la jeune génération d'architectes, le goût pour les volumes ou environnements libres et fluides, voire non géométriques, ne se limite pas à l'approche radicale d'Asymptote. Une autre agence new-yorkaise, Diller + Scofidio, remet ainsi en question le concept d'architecture traditionnelle de façon entièrement différente. Leur « Blur Building » (bâtiment flou) conçu pour l'International Expo 2002 d'Yverdon-les-Bains (au bord du lac de Neuchâtel, Suisse) devrait ressembler à rien de moins qu'à un nuage. Avec près de 100 m de long, 60 de large et 12 d'épaisseur, ce nuage « se matérialisera grâce à l'eau du lac filtrée et projetée en brouillard par un réseau serré de jets sous haute-pression dans une vaste sculpture en porte-à-faux. Le public s'approchera de cette masse gazeuse immobile par une rampe prise dans une structure de verre à l'endroit où elle pénètre dans le brouillard. A l'intérieur, les architectes cherchent à obtenir une quasi-absence de stimuli, une sorte de ‹ blanc › optique accompagné du seul bruit — tout aussi blanc — de la brume. Une image vidéopanoramique projetée sur écran circulaire occupera la plate-forme centrale conçue pour 250 personnes. Comme l'homme ne peut plus prétendre être au centre d'un univers qu'il maîtriserait, la position du spectateur est l'enjeu de réflexions critiques », expliquent les architectes. Diller + Scofidio utilisent abondamment les ordinateurs dans leur travail de conception, mais à la différence d'Asymptote, leur objectif final est toujours de construire. Il se rapprochent de leurs collègues new-yorkais dans la remise en cause des principes mêmes de l'architecture, allant au-delà de la forme et des matériaux pour « rendre flous » les repères visuels et auditifs nécessaires à l'orientation spatiale. Plutôt que l'ordre spatial hiérarchique imposé par presque toutes les architectures traditionnelles, le Blur Building n'apporte aucune solution claire, mais adopte une attitude scientifique et même philosophique en harmonie avec une bonne partie de la pensée contemporaine.

ARTS AND CRAFTS

Les arts, et leur exposition, restent l'un des champs d'élection de l'architecture contemporaine de haute qualité. Pour tous ceux qui ne s'intéressent que modérément aux musées virtuels, l'art et les musées d'art constituent l'un des domaines dans lesquels une certaine immuabilité et durabilité semble appropriée. Le genre évolue néanmoins rapidement comme le montrent les quelques exemples choisis ici.

La Fondation Serralves d'Alvaro Siza (Porto, Portugal) se situe non loin du centre de la ville de Porto, base de son agence. La Fondation a été créée grâce à un partenariat d'un type unique entre le gouvernement portugais et 50 entreprises du secteur privé. Edifiée dans le parc de la Quinta de Serralves — propriété de 20 ha comprenant une résidence construite dans les années 1930 pour le comte de Vizela —, elle se consacre à l'art contemporain. Le projet de Siza est très ambitieux. A partir d'un principe de plafonds suspendus similaires à ceux mis au point pour le Centre d'Art Contemporain de Galice, l'architecte a créé un certain nombre de grandes galeries aux aménagements souples, non pas destinées à une collection permanente, mais à des expositions temporaires. Des cours intérieures et de nombreuses baies permettent au visiteur de rester en contact avec le merveilleux parc aménagé sur 3 ha par Siza lui-même. L'intérieur offre toutes les facilités que l'on attend aujourd'hui d'un musée, entre autres une boutique, une cafétéria et un auditorium. L'ensemble est réalisé avec un soin visible du détail, attitude typique de l'architecte qui, pour une fois, a disposé d'un budget conséquent. D'inspiration moderniste, la Fondation Serralves n'en est pas pour autant de conception dépassée. Complexe en dépit de ses lignes nettes et tendues, elle démontre une fois encore qu'Alvaro Siza est l'un des architectes les plus originaux et les plus créatifs de sa génération.

Né dans les années 1930, comme Siza, l'architecte japonais Yoshio Taniguchi, considéré comme un maître dans son propre pays, a accédé à la réputation internationale lorsqu'il a été choisi pour rénover le Museum of Modern Art de New York. La sobriété majestueuse de son vocabulaire moderniste se retrouve dans son œuvre la plus récente, la Galerie des Trésors Horyuji, située dans l'enceinte du Musée National de Tokyo au parc Ueno. Depuis sa fondation à la fin du XIXe siècle, comme Musée de la maison impériale, cette institution conserve les objets offerts aux collections de l'Empereur dans les années 1870. Elle visait à préserver le contenu du temple Horyuji de Nara des agissements d'un mouvement anti-bouddhiste. C'est pour exposer ces importantes œuvres d'art en métal que Taniguchi a érigé un bâtiment en trois parties. « J'ai conçu un bâtiment en trois strates : une zone intérieure aux murs de pierre, une aire périphérique aux murs de verre et une zone extérieure délimitée par un auvent métallique. » La boîte centrale est protégée de la lumière naturelle, tandis que le hall d'entrée et l'espace sous auvent sont baignés de lumière. Taniguchi se rappelle que « cette conception symbolise l'histoire des précieux objets que le bâtiment abrite, objets transmis au cours des âges dans ces boîtes gigognes en bois qui, au Japon, servent traditionnellement à protéger les trésors. » Bien que l'architecte soit moins explicite sur ce point, sa galerie évoque également de multiples aspects des temples japonais. Le visiteur qui suit le cheminement prévu tombe d'abord sur un bassin à fontaine axiale ; ensuite, il doit changer au moins quatre fois de direction avant d'atteindre l'entrée. Ce parcours typique des temples japonais rappelle au passant qu'il pénètre dans un espace chargé de sens. Un écran de pierre l'accueille là où il s'attendrait à trouver une porte. Il faut contourner cette ultime barrière pour pénétrer dans le musée lui-même, d'organisation par ailleurs très rationnelle. L'impression générale est celle d'une construction de grande qualité, mise en valeur par des détails de finition comme l'alignement absolument parfait de chaque partie du bâtiment et de la galerie intérieure en fonction des contours extérieurs du bassin. La précision et la rigueur de Yoshio Taniguchi font de lui un maître possédant la même noblesse que son ami Fumihiko Maki. Tous deux savent comment unir la tradition japonaise à la modernité dans des créations d'une grande force.

OUI, MAIS EST-CE BIEN DE L'ART ?
Pour John Ruskin, il était évident que l'architecture pouvait prétendre au titre d'art suprême, puisqu'elle associait de multiples formes d'expression et de conceptions spatiales en un tout unifié. Cette analyse concernait sans doute davantage les constructions de son époque que l'architecture moderne. Une symbiose existe cependant entre l'architecture contemporaine et les expressions artistiques les plus éloquentes. Elles continuent à se nourrir mutuellement et lorsqu'elles se rencontrent, il est permis de penser qu'après tout l'architecture répond bien à la définition qu'en donnait Ruskin.

Tadao Ando est sans conteste le grand maître de l'architecture en béton au Japon. Aussi puissante l'articulation géométrique de ses plans puisse-t-elle être, sa sensibilité à la lumière et à la ritualisation de l'espace enrichit ses réalisations d'une indéniable spiritualité. C'est sur l'île d'Awaji, qu'il vient de mettre la dernière main à son chef-d'œuvre. Appelé, Yumebutai ou « Scène de rêve », ce complexe imposant recouvre 215 000m² d'un terrain dont la terre a servi à créer l'île artificielle de l'aéroport voisin de Kansai. Bien qu'elle comprenne un hôtel, un centre de congrès et des installations pour de grandes expositions horticoles, cette « Scène » est essentiellement un cheminement d'un espace à l'autre ; l'eau, l'architecture et la lumière jouent de concert. Son « inutilité » lui permet de revendiquer le statut d'œuvre d'art. En fait, entravé par les exigences de sécurité du centre de congrès et gêné par le décor imposé de l'hôtel, le complexe d'Ando est intéressant, sans être bouleversant. C'est dans le délicat labyrinthe de cours et d'allées que le visiteur se sent transporté à un niveau plus élevé. Des cascades descendent de la colline et l'eau court à travers une étonnante succession d'espaces. Ando s'explique : « L'Alhambra de Grenade m'a fourni un modèle historique. Là-bas, l'eau relie les petits patios. » Un million de coquilles Saint-Jacques, choisies et disposées à la main, bordent les bassins et le visiteur peut se demander s'il ne rêve pas. Commandé par les autorités locales qui craignaient que les touristes ne sautent Awaji en se rendant vers des destinations plus séduisantes, le complexe est situé près de l'énorme pont suspendu qui relie l'île à Kobe. Tous les détails ne sont pas parfaits. La petite chapelle centrale est une reprise de la remarquable «Eglise de lumière» (Ibaraki, Osaka, 1989) d'Ando. L'ouverture cruciforme est ici découpée dans le plafond et non dans le mur derrière l'autel. L'un des intérêts de l'église d'Ibaraki résidait dans son énergie brute, due en partie à son budget limité. L'excès de moyens a-t-il privé Ando de cette énergie? Néanmoins cette critique est mineure face à la réussite de cette «Scène de rêve» qui, du fait de sa localisation, n'a pas bénéficié des publications qu'elle mérite. Achevé fin 1999, Yumebutai ne représente rien moins qu'une date marquante de l'art architectural du XXᵉ siècle. C'est un chef-d'œuvre.

Comme Tadao Ando, l'architecte suisse Mario Botta se sent particulièrement à l'aise dans les réalisations de dimensions plus intimes. Ses chapelles de montagne à Mogno ou au sommet du Monte Tamaro comptent parmi les plus impressionnantes constructions de dimensions réduites des années 1990. La profonde sensibilité architecturale de Botta transparaît dans un de ses plus récents projets. Une série d'expositions sur l'architecture de la Renaissance et de la période baroque ont attiré l'attention sur les superbes maquettes datant de cette période. Mario Botta a choisi de recréer en maquette grandeur nature et en bois une partie de l'église romaine de Francesco Borromini, San Carlo alle Quattro Fontane (1641), sur les rives du lac de Lugano pour annoncer une exposition sur l'œuvre du maître italien. Ancré près de l'entrée du Parco Civico de Lugano, cette étonnant «monument virtuel» allie les techniques et les formes du baroque à une interprétation éphémère du XXᵉ siècle. L'œuvre est affranchie de la plupart des contraintes fonctionnelles de l'architecture. Elle représente l'essence de celle-ci, libérée de son carcan de pierre, flottant librement. Qu'en reste-t-il? L'art?

Lorsqu'on lui demande si les barrières entre l'art et l'architecture s'estompent, l'architecte Richard Meier réplique: «Non. Je ne pense pas que le problème se pose ainsi. Je crois simplement que davantage d'artistes veulent être architectes. Mais peut-être qu'il y a eu dans l'histoire encore plus d'architectes ayant voulu être artistes. Je pense qu'aujourd'hui de plus en plus d'artistes souhaiteraient faire de l'architecture. Les points de départ de l'artiste et de l'architecte sont généralement différents. L'artiste a une idée de ce qui pourrait être, puis il trouve une personne intéressée par cette idée. Généralement, un architecte attend que quelqu'un vienne vers lui avec un projet avant de dire: j'ai une idée de ce que vous pourriez faire.» Meier insiste néanmoins sur le fait qu'une grande réalisation architecturale est aussi une œuvre d'art. Frank O. Gehry, le plus sculptural des grands architectes contemporains cite ses sources sans honte. Dans son discours prononcé lors de la remise du Prix Pritzker en 1989, il déclarait: «Mes amis artistes, comme Jasper Johns, Bob Rauschenberg, Ed Kienholz et Claes Oldenburg travaillaient à partir de matériaux très bon marché – morceaux de bois et papier – et ils en faisaient naître la beauté. Il ne s'agissait pas de détails superficiels, leur approche était directe et soulevait en moi la question même de la beauté. Je choisis d'utiliser ce qui était alors disponible, de travailler avec des artisans, et de faire de leurs limites une vertu. La peinture offrait ce caractère immédat que j'enviais pour l'architecture. J'explorais les nouveaux matériaux de construction pour essayer de donner un esprit et un sentiment à la forme. En tentant de trouver l'essence de ma propre expression, je m'imaginais comme un artiste devant sa toile blanche, et qui va décider de ce que sera son premier mouvement.»

De toutes façons, le destin de l'architecture du siècle qui commence n'est plus vraiment entre les mains d'architectes comme Frank O. Gehry ou Richard Meier. Il est plutôt entre celles d'une génération plus jeune, celle de Toshiko Mori ou d'Hani Rashid d'Asymptote. Trail Balzer comme Kawakubo ou même le designer Philippe Starck et tant d'autres ont montré que la mode n'est pas forcément un mot «vulgaire» en matière de conception architecturale. Le mouvement et le changement sont bien la clé des formes nouvelles, le mariage des tendances, une disponibilité à répondre aux besoins. Ceci peut souvent rendre obsolèts les espaces rigides et hiérarchisés, bien que la demande pour le type d'immeuble le plus résistant au vent, le gratte-ciel, défie cette logique. Entre le minimalisme et une sorte de confrontation brouillonne avec la réalité de tous les jours et les volumes créés par ordinateur, l'architecture change probablement aujourd'hui plus vite qu'elle ne l'a jamais fait.

TADAO ANDO

Tadao Ando Architect & Associates
5-23, Toyosaki 2-chome
Kita-ku, Osaka 531-0072
Japan

Chicago House ▶

Born in Osaka in 1941, **TADAO ANDO** is self-educated as an architect, largely through his travels in the United States, Europe and Africa (1962-69). He founded Tadao Ando Architect & Associates in Osaka in 1969. He has received the Alvar Aalto Medal, Finnish Association of Architects (1985), Medaille d'or, French Academy of Architecture (1989), the 1992 Carlsberg Prize and the 1995 Pritzker Prize. He has taught at Yale (1987), Columbia (1988) and Harvard (1990). Notable buildings include: Rokko Housing (Kobe, 1981-93), Church on the Water, Hokkaido (1988), Japan Pavilion Expo '92 (Seville, Spain, 1992), Forest of Tombs Museum (Kumamoto, Japan, 1992), and the Suntory Museum (Osaka, 1994). Recent work includes the Awaji Yumebutai (Awajishima, Hyogo, Japan, 1997-2000), Modern Art Museum of Fort Worth, Texas (1999-2002), and Pulitzer Foundation for the Arts (St. Louis, Missouri, 1999-2001).

TADAO ANDO, geboren 1941 in Osaka, erlernte den Beruf des Architekten als Autodidakt, vorwiegend auf Reisen durch Nordamerika, Europa und Afrika (1962-69). 1969 gründete er das Büro Tadao Ando Architect & Associates in Osaka. Er wurde mit der Alvar-Aalto-Medaille des Finnischen Architektenverbands (1985), der Medaille d'or der Académie Française d'Architecture (1989), dem Carlsberg-Preis (1992) und dem Pritzker Prize (1995) ausgezeichnet. Ando lehrte an den Universitäten Yale (1987), Columbia (1988) und Harvard (1990). Zu seinen bekanntesten Bauten zählen die Rokko Wohnanlage in Kobe, Japan (1981-93), die Kirche auf dem Wasser in Hokkaido (1988), der Japanische Pavillon für die Expo '92 in Sevilla (1992), das Forest of Tombs Museum in Kumamoto, Japan (1992) und das Suntory Museum in Osaka (1994). Neuere Projekte sind das Modern Art Museum of Fort Worth, Texas (1999-2002) und die Pulitzer Foundation for the Arts in St. Louis, Missouri (1999-2001).

Né à Osaka en 1941, **TADAO ANDO** est un architecte autodidacte, formé en grande partie lors de ses voyages aux U.S.A., en Europe et en Afrique (1962-69). Il fonde Tadao Ando Architects & Associates à Osaka en 1969. Titulaire de la Médaille Alvar Aalto de l'Association finlandaise des architectes (1985), de la Médaille d'or de l'Académie Française d'Architecture (1989), du Prix Carlsberg 1992, et du Pritzker Prize 1995. Il a enseigné à Yale (1987), Columbia (1988) et Harvard (1990). Parmi ses réalisations les plus notoires : immeuble d'habitation Rokko, Kobé (1982-83) ; église sur l'eau, Hokkaido (1988) ; pavillon japonais pour Expo '92, Séville, Espagne (1992) ; Musée de la forêt des tombes, Kumamoto (1992) ; Musée Suntory, Osaka (1994). Parmi ses réalisations récentes : le Awaji Jumebutai, Awajishima, Hyogo, Japon (1997-2000), le Modern Art Museum of Fort Worth, Texas (1999-2002) et le Pulitzer Foundation for the Arts, St. Louis, Missouri (1999-2001).

CHICAGO HOUSE

Chicago, Illinois, USA, 1992-97

Planning: 5/92-12/94. Construction: 12/93-12/97.
Client: withheld. Floor area: 835 m².

Located in a quiet residential area near Lincoln Park, the **CHICAGO HOUSE** (total floor area 835 m²) consists of a 12 x 12 m – unit on the south side containing the private family quarters, while a rectangular unit half its size on the north side includes more public areas for receiving guests. A long, narrow living room links these two basic forms. A terrace and lower-level pool create a spectacular reception space that brings to mind the concept of some of Ando's smaller museums in Japan. The design takes into account the natural setting in particular one poplar tree that the owners are fond of. This is Tadao Ando's first residential project in the United States. It is, in fact, his first completed building in North America.

Das **CHICAGO HOUSE,** ein Privathaus mit einer Gesamtnutzfläche von 835 m², liegt in einer ruhigen Wohngegend unweit des Lincoln Park. Es besteht aus einem 12 x 12 m großen Bauteil auf der Südseite, in dem sich die Privaträume der Familie befinden und einem halb so großen rechteckigen Bauteil, der mehrere Räume für den Empfang und die Unterbringung von Gästen besitzt. Ein langgestreckter, schmaler Wohnraum verbindet diese beiden Bereiche. Die Terrasse und der unterhalb davon angelegte Swimmingpool bilden einen spektakulären Eingangsbereich, der an das Baukonzept einiger von Ando ausgeführter kleinerer Museen in Japan erinnert. Der Entwurf bezieht die natürliche Umgebung mit ein, speziell eine Pappel, die den Eigentümern besonders am Herzen liegt. Bei diesem Projekt handelt es sich um Tadao Andos erstes fertiggestelltes Bauwerk in Nordamerika.

Située dans un tranquille quartier résidentiel, près de Lincoln Park, la **MAISON CHICAGO** de 835 m² se compose d'un élément de 12 x 12m au sud contenant les pièces privées tandis que le volume rectangulaire de moitié moins important au nord est réservé à la réception. Ces deux formes géométriques élémentaires sont reliées par une longue et étroite salle-de-séjour. Une terrasse et une piscine en contrebas déterminent un vaste espace de réception qui rappelle certains petits musées édifiés par Ando au Japon. Le projet tient compte du cadre naturel, en particulier d'un peuplier qu'aimaient les propriétaires. C'est la première maison signée par l'architecte aux Etats-Unis, et en fait sa première réalisation achevée dans ce pays.

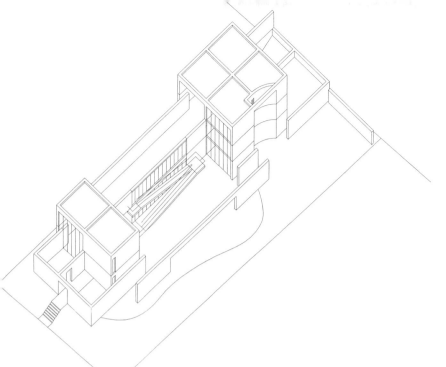

With its large pond and inclined stairway, the Chicago House brings to
mind certain Japanese buildings of
Ando such as the Nariwa Municipal
Museum (Nariwa-cho, Okayama,
1993-94).

Mit seinem großen Wasserbecken
und der geneigten Treppe erinnert
dieses Wohnhaus an andere in Japan
entstandene Bauten des Architekten,
wie etwa sein 1994 fertiggestelltes
Nariwa Municipal Museum in Nariwa-
cho, Okayama.

Par son grand plan d'eau et sa
rampe inclinée, la Maison Chicago
rappelle certaines créations de Ando
au Japon, dont le Musée municipal
de Nariwa (Nariwa-cho, Okayama,
1993-94).

AWAJI YUMEBUTAI

Awajishima, Hyogo, Japan, 1995-2000/03

Planning: 2/95-7/97. Construction: 10/97-2000/03.
Client: Hyogo Prefecture. Floor area: 93 500 m2.

AWAJI YUMEBUTAI, in many ways Tadao Ando's most ambitious project,covers a site area of 215 000 m² that had been used to obtain landfill for the Kansai International Airport, built on an artificial island. Named Yumebutai or "A Stage for Dreams," the complex includes a hotel and a conference center, but its most striking feature is a succession of fountains and internal courtyards. Tadao Ando has said, "The basic framework of this project is round universes and square universes, which are connected by walkways. Rather than depending solely on geometry, I experimented with using the spaces created by the irregular topography that remained. In addition, I tried to create a new style of garden combining the traditional Japanese tour garden with Western tour gardens, whose framework is much less ambiguous."

AWAJI YUMEBUTAI ist in vielerlei Hinsicht Tadao Andos ehrgeizigstes Werk. Es bedeckt eine Fläche von 215 000 m² und liegt in der Nähe des auf einer künstlichen Insel erbauten internationalen Flughafens Kansai. »Yumebutai« oder »Eine Bühne für Träume« getauft, umfaßt der Komplex ein Hotel und ein Konferenzzentrum, sein auffälligstes Merkmal ist aber wohl eine Abfolge von Brunnen und offenen Innenhöfen. Tadao Ando erklärte dazu:»Die Grundidee für dieses Projekt ist die Verbindung von runden und quadratischen Einheiten durch Gehwege. Statt mich ausschließlich von der Geometrie bestimmen zu lassen, experimentierte ich mit der Gestaltung von Räumen, die sich durch die unregelmäßige topografische Beschaffenheit des Standorts ergaben. Darüber hinaus wollte ich einen Garten neuen Stils kreieren, indem ich den traditionellen japanischen Garten mit westlichen Gärten kombinierte, deren Anlage wesentlich klarer ist.«

A de nombreux égards projet le plus ambitieux de Tadao Ando, le complexe **AWAJI YUMEBUTAI** s'étend sur un terrain de 215 000 m² dont la terre a été prélevée pour créer l'île artificielle de l'aéroport international de Kansai. Appelé « Yumebutai » ou « Une scène pour les rêves », l'ensemble comprend un hôtel et un centre de conférence. Son intérêt tient cependant surtout à une succession de fontaines et de cours intérieures. Tadao Ando précise que : « La base de ce projet repose sur des univers ronds et des univers carrés, reliés par des allées. Plutôt que de m'appuyer exclusivement sur la géométrie, je me suis servi des espaces générés par les irrégularités de la topographie. J'ai essayé de créer un nouveau style de jardin qui combine le traditionnel jardin de promenade japonais et les modèles occidentaux, dont la trame est beaucoup moins ambiguë. »

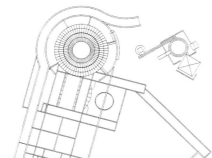

Tadao Ando was asked to create a complex series of buildings, gardens and fountains on this seaside plot, located near the Kobe-Awaji Bridge.

Tadao Ando erhielt den Auftrag, für das Grundstück am Meer, nahe der Kobe-Awaji Brücke, eine komplexe Folge von Gebäuden, Gärten und Brunnen zu entwerfen.

Sur ce terrain en bord de mer, proche du pont Kobé-Awaji, le programme consistait en un ensemble d'immeubles, de jardins et de fontaines.

Left: an aerial view of the vast site located on the island of Awaji, used to provide landfill for the neighboring Kansai Airport.

Links: Luftaufnahme des riesigen, für den benachbarten Flughafen Kansai künstlich angelegten Geländes auf der Insel Awaji.

A gauche : vue aérienne de la vaste zone de l'île d'Awaji, creusée pour fournir la terre nécessaire à la construction de l'île artificielle de l'aéroport voisin de Kansai.

Hundreds of thousands of scallop shells recovered from a canning facility in Northern Japan were placed by hand in the concrete of the ponds and waterfalls of the complex.

Hunderttausende von Muschelschalen aus einer nordjapanischen Konservenfabrik wurden von Hand in den Beton der Brunnen und Wasserfälle eingesetzt.

Des centaines de milliers de coquilles saint-jacques récupérées dans une conserverie du Nord du Japon furent pressées à la main dans le béton des bassins et des cascades du complexe.

Both visually and in terms of the sound of falling water, the Awaji Yumebutai complex is based on a series of cascades. Stairs, fountains and flowers are arranged in a geometric progression not unlike a musical composition.

Stufen, Brunnen und Pflanzen bilden, ähnlich einer musikalischen Komposition, in Kaskaden angeordnet, sowohl optisch als auch akustisch den zentralen Aspekt des Awaji Yumebutai-Komplexes.

La conception visuelle et sonore du complexe d'Awaji Yumebutai repose sur une série de cascades. Des escaliers, des fontaines et des fleurs sont disposés en une progression géométrique qui évoque une composition musicale.

Ando's powerful sense of architectural drama finds expression in these images. Vast areas of the Awaji Yumebutai complex serve no specific purpose, but lead visitors to a heightened awareness of space, light, sound and architecture.

Andos ausgeprägtes Gefühl für architektonische Dramatik wird an diesen Bauten spürbar. Große Teile des Awaji Yumebutai-Komplexes dienen allein dazu, den Besuchern ein höheres Bewusstsein für Architektur, Raum, Licht und Akustik zu vermitteln.

Le sens du spectacle architectural dont fait souvent preuve Ando s'exprime dans ces images. Si de vastes parties du Awaji Yumebutai ne répondent à aucune fonction précise, elles suscitent chez le visiteur une conscience aiguë de l'espace, de la lumière, du son et de l'architecture.

ANDRESEN O'GORMAN

Andresen O'Gorman Architects
The Studio, 9 Ormond Terrace
Indooroopilly
Queensland 4068
Australia

Tel: +61 7 3878 5855
Fax: +61 7 3878 4900
e-mail: B.Andresen@mailbox.uq.edu.au

BRIT ANDRESEN received her degree in architecture at the Norges Tekniske Høgskole in Trondheim, Norway. She had her own firm, Brit Andresen Architect (1970-76), and worked in association with Barry Gasson and John Meunier for the Burrell Museum in Glasgow (1971-76) before her association with **PETER O'GORMAN**. O'Gorman received his B.Arch. degree from Queensland University. He had his own practice, Peter O'Gorman Architect, from 1965 to 1980. He taught at Queensland University from 1968 to 1998. Brit Andresen has taught at Cambridge (1970-76), the Architectural Association in London (1971-76), Queensland University (1977-2000), and at the University of California, Los Angeles (1981-83). Together, they have worked on private residences in Australia, such as the Mooloomba House (North Stradbroke Island, 1995-99), the Ocean View House (Mount Mee, 1993-95), and the Tomsgate Way House (Mount Nebo, 1988-90).

BRIT ANDRESEN schloss ihr Architekturstudium an der Norges Tekniske Høgskole im norwegischen Trondheim ab. Bevor sie sich mit **PETER O'GORMAN** zusammenschloss, war sie von 1970 bis 1976 in ihrem eigenen Büro tätig und arbeitete zusammen mit Barry Gasson und John Meunier für das Burrell Museum in Glasgow (1971-76). Sie lehrte in Cambridge (1970-76), an der Architectural Association in London (1971-76), der Queensland University (1977-2000) und der University of California, Los Angeles (1981-83). Peter O'Gorman erwarb seinen Bachelor of Architecture an der Queensland University und arbeitete von 1965 bis 1980 in seinem eigenen Büro Peter O'Gorman Architect. Von 1968 bis 1998 lehrte er an der Queensland University. Zu den von Andresen und O'Gorman gemeinsam ausgeführten Wohnbau-Projekten in Australien gehören das Mooloomba House auf North Stradbroke Island (1995-99), das Ocean View House, Mount Mee (1993-95) und das Tomsgate Way House, Mount Nebo (1988-90).

BRIT ANDRESEN est diplômée d'architecture du Norges Tekniske Nøgskole norvégien. Elle crée sa propre agence, Brit Andresen Architect (1970-76) et travaille en association avec Barry Gasson et John Meunier pour le Burrell Museum de Glasgow (1971-76) avant de s'associer à **PETER O'GORMAN**. Elle a enseigné à Cambridge (1970-76), à l'Architectural Association de Londres (1971-76), à Queensland University (1977-2000) et à l'UCLA (1981-83). Peter O'Gorman est diplômé d'architecture de Queensland University. Il dirige son agence, Peter O'Gorman Architect, de 1965 à 1980. Il enseigne à Queensland University de 1968 à 1988. Ils ont travaillé ensemble sur des résidences privées en Australie entre autres pour Mooloomba House (North Stradbroke Island, 1995-99), Ocean View House (Mount Mee, 1993-95) et Tomsgate Way House (Mount Nebo, 1988-90).

ROSEBERY HOUSE

Highgate Hill, Queensland, Australia, 1995-97

Planning: 1995-96. Construction: 1997. Client: withheld.
Floor area: c. 280 m². Costs: US$132 000.

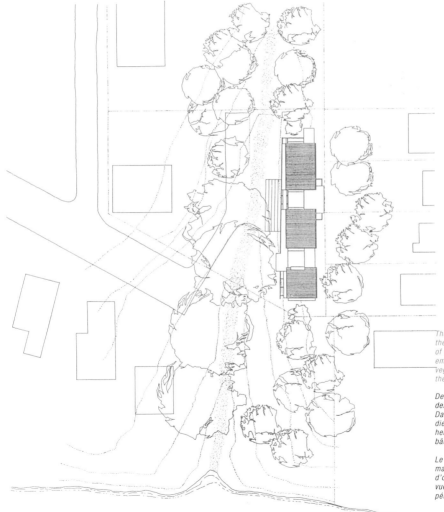

The site plan shows a division of
the house into three parts. A sense
of openness of the house (right) is
emphasized in this image, where the
vegetation almost seems to enter
the architecture.

Der Geländeplan zeigt die Gliederung
des Hauses in drei Bauteile. Rechts:
Das Bild, in dem die Natur beinahe in
die Architektur einzudringen scheint,
hebt den offenen Charakter des Gebäudes hervor.

Le plan au sol montre la division de la
maison en trois parties. L'impression
d'ouverture est accentuée dans cette
vue (à droite) où la végétation semble
pénétrer l'architecture.

Seen from certain angles (below, left) the house seems to constitute a linear whole. It is the timber-battened screen on the western side that gives this feeling of unity.

Aus bestimmten Blickwinkeln scheint das Haus eine geradlinige Einheit zu bilden (unten links). Auf der Westseite des Gebäudes wird dieser Eindruck durch die mit Holz verschalte Schutzwand erzeugt.

Sous certains angles (ci-dessous à gauche) la maison donne l'impression de se développer en ligne droite. Côté Ouest, un écran de bois à claire-voie confirme ce sentiment d'unité.

Situated in a hilly, overgrown gully in Brisbane, the US$132 000 **ROSEBERY HOUSE** is essentially composed of three pavilions connected by decks. Because of the subtropical climate, the decks are neither exclusively interior nor exterior elements, an impression heightened by the use of corrugated polycarbonate for the roofs of the eastern deck area. The division of the house into three parts (bedrooms, kitchen/dining room, and printmaking studio/laundry) was at least partially intended to bring light into the different areas. A timber-battened screen on the western side brings together the entire composition. Built of Australian eucalyptus, the house is not atypical in an area that favors light wooden houses. With its relaxed style and sensitivity to its natural environment, the house fits into the local traditions, even though it improves them technically by several steps.

Das in einer überwachsenen Geländefurche in Brisbane gelegene, für 132 000 US$ erbaute **ROSEBERY HOUSE** besteht im Wesentlichen aus drei Pavillons, die durch Plattformen miteinander verbunden sind. Wegen des subtropischen Klimas sind diese Plattformen weder reine Innen- noch reine Außenräume, was optisch durch die Verwendung von gewelltem Polycarbonat für die Dächer des östlichen Bereichs unterstrichen wird. Die Aufteilung des Hauses in drei Teile (Schlafzimmer, Küche/Esszimmer, Grafikatelier/Waschküche) entspricht den unterschiedlichen Lichtanforderungen der verschiedenen Wohnbereiche. Eine holzverschalte Wand auf der Westseite fügt die Komposition zu einem Ganzen zusammen. Das aus australischem Eukalyptus gebaute Haus ist nicht untypisch für diese Gegend, in der leichte Holzhäuser bevorzugt werden. Mit seiner schlichten Architektur, die Rücksicht auf die umgebende Natur nimmt, fügt sich der Bau in lokale Traditionen ein, auch wenn er diese in technischer Hinsicht um ein Vielfaches übertrifft.

Située dans un ravin à la végétation luxuriante au milieu des collines de Brisbane, le **ROSEBERY HOUSE** dont le budget s'est élevé à US$ 132 000 se compose de trois pavillons réunis par des terrasses. Sous ce climat subtropical, les terrasses n'appartiennent vraiment ni au dedans ni au dehors, impression renforcée par l'emploi de polycarbonate ondulé pour les toits qui protègent la terrasse ouest. La division de la maison en trois parties (chambres, cuisine/salle-à-manger et atelier d'impression/buanderie) devait permettre de profiter au mieux de la lumière naturelle. L'écran en lattis de bois sur la façade ouest unifie la composition. Construite en eucalyptus d'Australie, cette maison n'est pas atypique dans une région qui apprécie les constructions légères en bois. Son style décontracté et sa sensibilité à l'environnement naturel, renvoient aux traditions locales qu'elle fait techniquement progresser de plusieurs pas.

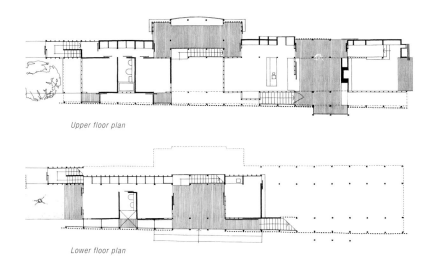

Upper floor plan

Lower floor plan

The penetration of the natural sur-
roundings and light into the interior
of the house is clear in these images.

Natur und Licht scheinen fließend
in die Innenbereiche des Hauses
überzugehen.

La pénétration de l'environnement
naturel et de la lumière est évident
dans l'intérieur de la maison.

ASYMPTOTE

Asymptote Architecture
561 Broadway, 5A
New York, NY 10012
United States

Tel: +1 212 343 7333
Fax: +1 212 343 7099
e-mail: info@asymptote.net
Web: www.asymptote-architecture.com

LISE ANN COUTURE (right) was born in Montreal in 1959. She received her B.Arch. degree from Carleton University, Ottawa, Canada, and her M.Arch. degree from Yale. She has been a Design Critic in the Master of Architecture program at Parsons School of Design, New York. **HANI RASHID** (left) received his M.Arch. degree from the Cranbrook Academy of Art, Bloomfield Hills, Michigan. They created Asymptote in 1989. Projects include the 1988 prize-winning commission for the Los Angeles West Coast Gateway, a commissioned housing project for Brig, Switzerland (1991), and their participation in the 1993 competition for an Art Center in Tours, France. They have also built a theater festival structure in Århus, Denmark in 1997. Presently Asymptote is designing a Edutainment Center in Kyoto, Japan and the Guggenheim Virtual Museum, published here in an initial version.

LISE ANN COUTURE (rechts), 1959 in Montreal geboren, erwarb ihren Bachelor of Architecture an der Carleton University in Kanada und ihren Master of Architecture an der Yale University. Anschließend war sie im Rahmen des Master of Architecture-Programms als Designkritikerin an der Parsons School of Design in New York tätig. **HANI RASHID** (links) machte seinen Master of Architecture an der Cranbrook Academy of Art, Bloomfield Hills, Michigan. Gemeinsam riefen sie 1987 Asymptote ins Leben. Zu ihren Projekten gehören der preisgekrönte Entwurf für den Los Angeles West Coast Gateway (1988), die Ausarbeitung eines Wohnhausprojekts für Brig in der Schweiz (1991) und ihr Wettbewerbsbeitrag für ein Kunstzentrum im französischen Tours (1993). Außerdem haben sie 1997 einen Bau für das Theaterfestival in Århus, Dänemark ausgeführt. Derzeit arbeiten Couture und Rashid an der Planung eines Technikmuseums in Kioto und am Guggenheim Virtual Museum, das hier in einer ersten Version vorgestellt wird.

LISE ANN COUTURE (à droite), née à Montréal en 1959, est Bachelor of Architecture de la Carleton University, Canada, et Master of Architecture de Yale. Elle a été « Design Critic » du programme de maîtrise en architecture de la Parsons School of Design, New York. **HANI RASHID** (à gauche) est Master of Architecture de la Cranbrook Academy of Art, Bloomfield Hills, Michigan. Ils créent Asymptote en 1989. Parmi leurs travaux : le projet primé de la West Coast Gateway (Los Angeles, 1988), un projet de logements (Brig, Suisse, 1991), leur participation au concours de 1993 pour un Centre d'art à Tours, France (1993), une structure pour un festival de théâtre (Århus, Danemark, 1997). Actuellement, Asymptote travaille à un Musée des Technologies pour Kyoto et sur le projet du Guggenheim Virtual Museum, publié ici dans sa version initiale.

VIRTUAL TRADING FLOOR

New York Stock Exchange, New York, NY, USA, 1998-99

Asymptote created two related projects for the New York Stock Exchange (NYSE). The first, the **3DTF** (Three Dimensional Trading Floor), is a "data-scape" that brings together information flow, data and correlation models into a single seamless three-dimensional architectural model. The 3DTF is intended to provide real-time information on the movements of the stock markets, and is an experiment in the gradual transfer of trading to a completely virtual environment. Before moving to that phase, however, Asymptote has also created the Advanced Trading Floor Operations Center off the main floor of the NYSE, a similarly inspired design that includes 60 high-resolution flat screen LCD monitors and an LED message board.

Asymptote schuf zwei miteinander verbundene Entwürfe für die New Yorker Börse (NYSE). Bei dem **3DTF** (Three Dimensional Trading Floor) genannten Projekt handelt es sich um eine »Daten-Landschaft«, die Informationsflüsse, Daten und Korrelationsmodelle zu einer zusammenhängenden, dreidimensionalen architektonischen Raumgestaltung zusammenführt. 3DTF ist für die Erfassung von Echtzeit-Informationen über alle Vorgänge auf dem Aktienmarkt konzipiert und stellt einen weiteren, experimentellen Schritt in der allmählichen Verlagerung des Börsenhandels auf ein vollständig virtuelles Environment dar. Zuvor hat Asymptote in einem ähnlich inspirierten Entwurf auch das »Advanced Trading Floor Operations Center« neben dem Hauptbörsenparkett der NYSE gestaltet, das mit 60 hochauflösenden Flachbildschirmen und einer LED-Anzeigentafel ausgestattet ist.

Asymptote est à l'origine de deux projets conjoints pour le New York Stock Exchange (NYSE). Le premier, appelé **3DTF** (Three Dimensional Trading Floor), est un « datascape » qui réunit des flux d'information, des modèles de données et de corrélations en un modèle architectural unique et tridimensionnel. Le 3DTF fournit en temps réel des informations sur les mouvements des marchés boursiers. C'est une expérimentation de transfert graduel du trading vers un environnement totalement virtuel. Avant d'en arriver là, Asymptote a par ailleurs conçu le Advanced Trading Floor Operations Center un peu à l'écart du plateau principal du NYSE, projet d'inspiration similaire qui comprend 60 écrans plats haute-résolution et un panneau d'affichage LED.

A "virtual" trading area that gives
real-time data on the ebb and flow of
stock prices, is placed in juxtaposition
with an actual space (left) designed
by Asymptote at the edge of the NYSE
trading floor.

Das virtuelle Börsenparkett übermit-
telt Echtzeit-Informationen über den
aktuellen Stand der Aktienkurse und
ist einem realen Raum (links) gegen-
übergestellt, den Asymptote für die
New Yorker Börse (NYSE) gestaltet
hat.

L'aire de marchés virtuelle qui fournit
des informations en temps réel sur
les variations et les flux des actions,
est juxtaposée à une salle réelle
(à gauche) conçue par Asymptote
à côté de la salle des marchés du
New York Stock Exchange.

GUGGENHEIM VIRTUAL MUSEUM

New York, NY, USA, 1999-2002

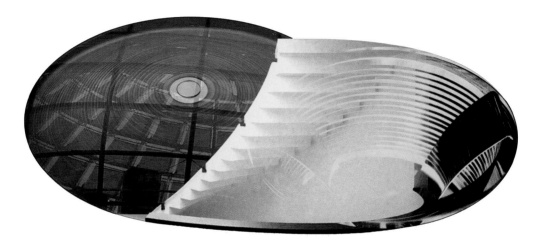

As part of a larger project intended to commission Internet-based works of art, the Guggenheim Museum in New York has asked Asymptote to create the "first important virtual building of the 21st Century," a fusion of "information space, art, commerce and architecture." This ambitious plan, calling for "navigable three-dimensional spatial entities accessible on the Internet as well as a real-time interactive component installed at the various Guggenheim locations," imagines a virtual architecture that would change according to visitor preferences or uses. In this sense, the **GUGGENHEIM VIRTUAL MUSEUM** will be in constant flux, corresponding, according to the architects, to the real requirements of truly contemporary art and art appreciation.

Als Teil eines größeren Projekts zur Vermittlung von Kunstwerken im Internet hat das Guggenheim Museum Asymptote mit der Gestaltung des »ersten bedeutenden virtuellen Gebäudes des 21. Jahrhunderts« beauftragt. Dieser ehrgeizige Plan hat die Verbindung von »Information, Kunst, Handel und Architektur« zum Ziel und erfordert »ein dreidimensionales, interaktives Environment für das Internet sowie eine interaktive Echtzeit-Komponente, die in den verschiedenen Guggenheim Einrichtungen installiert werden soll.« Die zugrunde liegende Idee ist eine virtuelle Architektur, die sich mit den Vorlieben oder Bedürfnissen der Benutzer verändert. In diesem Sinne wird sich das **GUGGENHEIM VIRTUAL MUSEUM** ständig im Fluß befinden und damit, nach Aussage der Architekten, den realen Anforderungen einer wirklich aktuellen Kunst und Kunstbetrachtung entsprechen.

Elément d'un important projet de commandes d'œuvres d'art par Internet, le Guggenheim Museum de New York a demandé à Asymptote de créer le premier grand « batiment virtuel » du XXIe siècle, fusion « d'espaces d'information, de l'art, du commerce et de l'architecture. » Ce plan ambitieux, qui fait appel à des « entités spatiales accessibles par Internet ainsi qu'à des échanges interactifs en temps réel entre les diverses implantations du Guggenheim, » imagine une architecture virtuelle modifiable selon les préférences ou les besoins du visiteur. En ce sens, le **GUGGENHEIM VIRTUAL MUSEUM** apparaîtra comme un flux constant de données, ce qui correspond, pour les architectes, aux attentes concrètes de l'art réellement contemporain et à son appréciation.

Asymptote displayed their designs
for the Guggenheim Virtual Museum
at TZ Art and Henry Urbach Galleries.

Asymptotes Entwürfe für das Guggenheim Museum wurden in der TZ Art
und Henry Urbach Galerie ausgestellt.

Asymptote a exposé ses projets pour le
Guggenheim Virtual Museum dans la
TZ Art et Henry Urbach galerie.

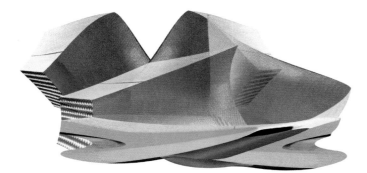

Unlike any existing traditional building, the Guggenheim Virtual Museum
could change its form to correspond
to visitor patterns, for example.

Im Gegensatz zu gebauten Museen
kann das Guggenheim Virtual Museum
jederzeit seine Form verändern, um
sich den Bedürfnissen der Besucher
anzupassen.

A la différence des constructions
traditionnelles, le Guggenheim virtuel
peut changer de forme en fonction
du profil des visiteurs.

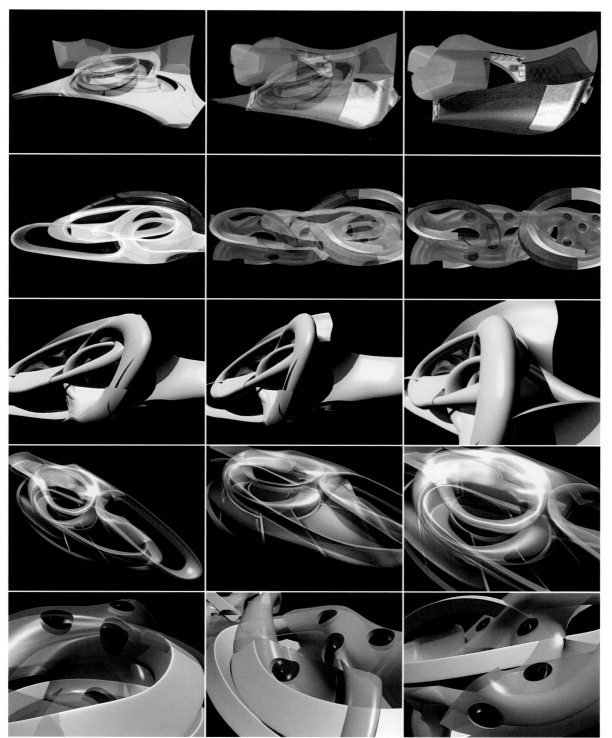

MARIO BOTTA

Mario Botta
Via Ciani 16
6904 Lugano
Switzerland

Tel: +41 91 972 8625
Fax: +41 91 970 1454
e-mail: mario.botta@botta.ch

Born in Mendrisio, Switzerland (1943), **MARIO BOTTA** left school at 15 to become an apprentice in an architectural office in Lugano. A year later, he designed his first house. During the studies at the University Institute of Architecture (IUAV) in Venice, where he graduated with Carlo Scarpa and Giuseppe Mazzariol, he worked briefly in the offices of Le Corbusier and Louis I. Kahn. He built private houses in the Ticino (Cadenazzo, 1970-71, Riva San Vitale, 1971-73, Ligornetto, 1975-76, and Stabio, 1980-82). Major buildings include Mediathèque (Villeurbanne, 1984-88), Malraux Cultural Center (Chambéry, 1982-87), Evry Cathedral (1988-95), all in France, San Francisco Museum of Modern Art (1992-95), and Chapel (Monte Tamaro, 1992-96), Museum Jean Tinguely (Basel, 1993-96), Church of St. John the Baptist (Mogno, 1986-98), all in Switzerland, the Municipal Library (Dortmund, Germany, 1995-99), and the recently completed Friedrich Dürrenmatt Center (Neuchâtel, Switzerland, 1992/97-2000). Current projects are the design for a church at Malpensa Airport (2000), and the Museum of Modern and Contemporary Art and Cultural Center (Rovereto, Italy, 1993-). In 1996 he founded the new Academy of Architecture in Mendrisio.

MARIO BOTTA, geboren 1943 im schweizerischen Mendrisio, verließ mit 15 Jahren die Schule und begann eine Lehre in einem Architekturbüro in Lugano. Dort entwarf er 1959 sein erstes Wohnhaus. Während seiner Studien am Istituto Universitario di Architettura (IUAV) in Venedig, die er bei Carlo Scarpa und Giuseppe Mazzariol abschloss, arbeitete er zeitweilig bei Le Corbusier und Louis I. Kahn. Danach baute er Einfamilienhäuser im Tessin (Cadenazzo, 1970-71, Riva San Vitale, 1971-73, Ligornetto, 1975-76 und Stabio, 1980-82). Zu Bottas Großprojekten gehören die Mediathèque in Villeurbanne (1984-88), das Malraux Kulturzentrum in Chambéry (1982-87) und die Kathedrale in Evry (1988-95), alle in Frankreich; das San Francisco Museum of Modern Art (1992-95), eine Kapelle auf dem Monte Tamaro (1992-96), das Museum Jean Tinguely in Basel (1993-96) und die Kirche Johannes der Täufer in Mogno (1986-98), alle in der Schweiz; die Stadtbibliothek in Dortmund (1995-99) sowie das erst kürzlich vollendete Friedrich Dürrenmatt Zentrum in Neuchâtel (Schweiz, 1992/97-2000). Seine jüngsten Projekte sind der Entwurf für eine Kirche für den Flughafen Malpensa (2000) sowie das Museum für Moderne und Zeitgenössische Kunst und Kulturzentrum in Rovereto, Italien (seit 1993). 1996 gründete er die neue Architektur-Akademie in Mendrisio.

Né à Mendrisio, Suisse, en 1943, **MARIO BOTTA** quitte l'école à 15 ans pour faire son apprentissage dans une agence d'architecture de Lugano. Il dessine sa première maison l'année suivante. Pendant ses études à l'University Institute of Architecture (IUAV) à Venise, qu' il a terminé chez et Carlo Scarpa et Giuseppe Mazzariol, il a brièvement travaillé dans l'entourage de Le Corbusier et Louis I. Kahn. Il a construit des villas en Suisse à Cadenazzo (1970-71), à Riva San Vitale (1971-73), à Ligornetto (1975-76) et à Stabio (1980-82). Parmi ses principales réalisations : la mediathèque de Villeurbanne (1984-88), le Centre culturel André Malraux (Chambéry, 1982-87), la cathédrale d'Evry (1988-95), le San Francisco Museum of Modern Art (1992-95), la chapelle de Tamaro (Monte Tamaro, Suisse, 1992-96), le musée Tinguely (Bâle, 1993-96), la chapelle de Saint Jean-Baptiste (Mogno, Suisse, 1986-98), la bibliothèque municipale (Dortmund, Germany, 1995-99) et le centre Friedrich Dürrenmatt (Neuchâtel, Suisse, 1992/97-2000). Parmi ses projets récents : la chapelle pur l'aéroport de Malpensa (2000) et le Musée d'art moderne et contemporain – Centre culturel de Rovereto (Italie, 1993-).

MODEL OF SAN CARLO ALLE QUATTRO FONTANE

Lugano, Switzerland, 1999

Promotors: Università della Svizzera italiana, Accademia di architettura. Planning: 2/99.
Construction: 3/99-8/99. Timber cut: 400 m³. Mounted panels: 491.

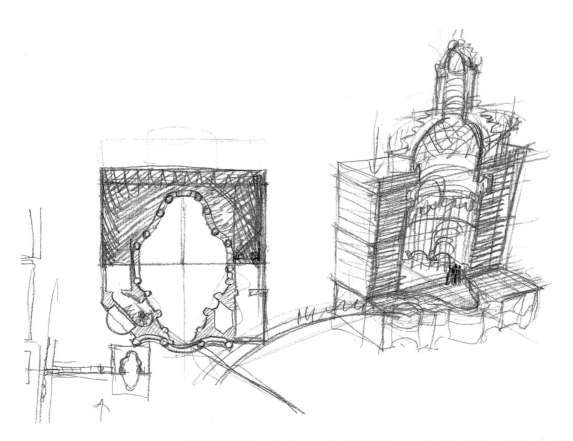

Mario Botta's drawings show the model's open, hollowed-out form. Baroque architects often created elaborate wooden models, but never at full scale. Botta's model is a masterpiece of craftsmanship.

Oben: Bottas Zeichnungen zeigen die offene Hohlform des Modells. Rechts: Die Architekten des Barock fertigten zwar häufig kunstvolle Holzmodelle ihrer Bauwerke an, aber nie im Maßstab 1:1. Bottas Arbeit ist ein Meisterwerk der Handwerkskunst.

Ci-dessus : Les dessins de Mario Botta montrent la maquette ouverte, en creux. A droite : Les architectes baroques créaient souvent des maquettes élaborées, mais jamais à échelle réelle. Celle de San Carlo est un chef d'œuvre de réalisation.

Mario Botta designed a 33 m-high full-scale wooden model of **SAN CARLO ALLE QUATTRO FONTANE** and the exhibition at the Museo Cantonale d'arte di Lugano to mark the 400th anniversary of the birth of architect Francesco Borromini. Set on a 22 m²-platform anchored a few meters off the shore-line in the lake near the entrance to the Parco Ciani, the model is made up of 35 000 planks, each 4.5 cm thick. Held together by steel cables, the whole structure is attached to a 100-ton steel frame. Based on a survey of Borromini's church by Professor Sartor in Rome, the model was built thanks to the efforts of the Swiss Italian University, Accademia di architettura, Mendrisio, and realized on a work-creation scheme involving unemployed people, architects, designers, carpenters and craftsmen working under Mario Botta's supervision.

Mario Botta entwarf ein 33 m hohes, originalgroßes Modell der Kirche **SAN CARLO ALLE QUATTRO FONTANE** in Rom für die im Museo Cantonale d'arte di Lugano veranstaltete Ausstellung zum 400. Geburtstag des italienischen Baumeisters Francesco Borromini. Das Modell steht auf einer 22 m² großen Plattform, die einige Meter vor dem Ufer und in der Nähe des Eingangs zum Parco Ciani im See verankert wurde. Es besteht aus 35 000, jeweils 4,5 cm dicken Holzplanken. Durch Stahlseile zusammengehalten, hängt die gesamte Konstruktion an einem 100 t schweren Stahlrahmen. Der Entwurf des Modells beruht auf dem Aufmaß von Borrominis Kirche durch Professor Sartor in Rom und wurde dank der Bemühungen der italienisch-schweizerischen Universität Accademia di architettura in Mendrisio unter Mario Bottas Leitung von arbeitslosen Architekten, Designern, Zimmerleuten und Handwerkern realisiert.

Mario Botta a conçu cette reproduction grandeur nature de 33 m de haut de l'église de **SAN CARLO ALLE QUATTRO FONTANE** et l'exposition du Musée cantonal d'art de Lugano pour le 400ème anniversaire de la naissance de l'architecte Francesco Borromini. Posée sur une plate-forme de 22 m² ancrée à quelques mètres de la rive du lac près de l'entrée du Parc Ciani, elle a nécessité 35 000 planches de 4,5 cm d'épaisseur. Maintenue par des câbles d'acier, elle repose sur une ossature d'acier de 100 t. Réalisée grâce aux efforts de l'université italo-helvétique Accademia di architettura de Mendrisio, d'après une étude de l'église de Borromini par le Professeur Sartor à Rome, elle a été construite par des chômeurs, des architecte, des designers, des charpentiers et des artisans travaillant sous le contrôle de Mario Botta.

WILL BRUDER

william p. bruder-architect, ltd
1314 West Circle Mountain Road
New River, Arizona 85087
United States

Tel: +1 623 465 7399
Fax: +1 623 465 0109
e-mail: bruder@netwest.com

Byrne Residence ▶

Born in Milwaukee, Wisconsin in 1946, **WILL BRUDER** has a B.F.A. degree in sculpture from the University of Wisconsin-Milwaukee, and is self-trained as an architect. He apprenticed under Paolo Soleri and Gunnar Birkerts. He obtained his architecture license in 1974 and created his own studio the same year. In 1987, he was a fellow at the American Academy in Rome for six months. He has taught and lectured at Massachusetts Institute of Technology (MIT), ASU and the "cable works" in Helsinki. His most important built work is the Phoenix Central Library in Phoenix, Arizona (1989-95). Recent projects include the Teton County Library and Riddell Advertising, Jackson, Wyoming, Temple Kol Ami, Scottsdale, Arizona, the Deer Valley Rock Art Center, Phoenix, Arizona, and residences in Boston, Colorado, Arizona, Canada and Australia, as well as a restaurant in Manhattan.

WILL BRUDER, geboren 1946 in Milwaukee, Wisconsin, erwarb den Bachelor of Fine Arts (B.F.A.) in Bildhauerei, als Architekt ist er Autodidakt. Er ging bei Paolo Soleri und Gunnar Birkerts in die Lehre, bevor er 1974 die Zulassung als Architekt erhielt und sein eigenes Büro gründete. 1987 war er ein halbes Jahr an der American Academy in Rom tätig. Gelehrt hat Will Bruder am Massachusetts Institute of Technology (MIT), der ASU und bei »cable works« in Helsinki. Sein bedeutendster Bau ist die Phoenix Central Library in Phoenix, Arizona (1989-95). Zu seinen neueren Projekten gehören die Teton County Library und Riddell Advertising in Jackson, Wyoming, die Kol Ami-Synagoge in Scottsdale, Arizona, das Deer Valley Rock Art Center in Phoenix, Arizona, ein Restaurant in Manhattan sowie Wohnhäuser in Boston, Colorado, Arizona, Kanada und Australien.

Né à Milwaukee, Wisconsin en 1946, **WILL BRUDER** est diplômé de sculpture de l'Université de Wisconsin-Milwaukee et architecte autodidacte. Il fait son apprentissage auprès de Paolo Soleri et de Gunnar Birkerts. Licencié en architecture en 1974, il crée son propre atelier la même année, puis étudie à l'American Academy de Rome pendant six mois en 1987. Il enseigne et donne des conférences au MIT à l'ASU et à « cable works » (Helsinki). Son œuvre la plus importante aux Etats-Unis est la Phoenix Central Library (Phoenix, Arizona, 1988-95). Parmi ses projets récents : la Teton County Library, l'agence Riddell Advertising (Jackson, Wyoming), le Temple Kol Ami (Scottsdale, Arizona), le Valley Rock Art Center (Phoenix, Arizona) et des résidences à Boston, dans le Colorado, l'Arizona, au Canada et en Australie, ainsi qu'un restaurant à Manhattan.

BYRNE RESIDENCE

North Scottsdale, Arizona, USA, 1994-98

Design: 1994-95. Construction: 1996-98. Client: Bill and Carol Byrne. Floor area: 250m².

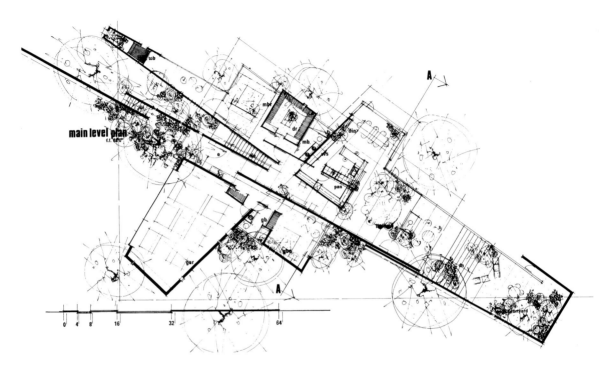

main level plan

The architect describes the **BYRNE RESIDENCE** very well, "The sculptural design concept of this residence is one of creating a metaphorical series of abstract canyon walls of concrete masonry, emerging like geological gestures from the home's natural desert site." This 250-m² house is located on a 2-hectare lot roughly 80 km north of Phoenix. Its angled surfaces evoke the sandstone surfaces of the area, and the architect has respected the clients' request for an energy-efficient and "organic" type of architecture. Will Bruder refers to Frank Lloyd Wright's Price House (1954, Phoenix) as an indirect source of inspiration for his design, and the two residences do in fact share, among other features, the idea of concrete-block walls.

Der Architekt selbst beschreibt die **BYRNE RESIDENCE** so: »Das bildhauerische Gestaltungskonzept dieses Wohnhauses bestand darin, eine metaphorische Serie stilisierter Felswände aus Betonmauerwerk zu schaffen, die wie geologische Formationen aus der natürlichen Wüstenumgebung des Hauses erwachsen.« Das Gebäude mit einer Nutzfläche von 250 m² liegt auf einem 2 ha großen Grundstück ca. 80 km nördlich von Phoenix. Seine schrägen Außenwände, die dem Wunsch der Bauherren nach einem energiesparenden und »organischen« Bautypus nachkommen, erinnern an die für diese Gegend typischen Sandsteinformationen. Will Bruder nennt Frank Lloyd Wrights Price House in Phoenix (1954) als indirekte Inspirationsquelle für seine Gestaltung, und tatsächlich haben die beiden Wohnhäuser, neben anderen Merkmalen, die Idee der Wände aus Betonformstein gemeinsam.

Le descriptif de la **BYRNE RESIDENCE** de Will Bruder est précis : « Le concept sculptural de cette résidence repose sur la création d'une succession de parois métaphoriques formant une sorte de ‹canyon› abstrait en maçonnerie de béton qui émerge du site désertique environnant à la manière de plissements géologiques. » La maison de 250 m² s'élève sur un terrain de 2 ha à 80 km environ au nord de Phoenix. Les surfaces anguleuses évoquent le paysage minéral de la région. L'architecte a respecté les souhaits du client qui voulait un projet « organique » et économe en énergie. Will Bruder cite la Price House de Frank Lloyd Wright (Phoenix, Arizona, 1954) parmi ses sources d'inspiration indirectes. D'ailleurs, les murs en parpaings de béton sont une caractéristique commune à les deux résidences.

Despite its apparent sophistication, this design calls on the idea of the ephemeral shelter, thus differentiating itself from the more deeply anchored architecture of Frank Lloyd Wright for example.

Trotz seines raffinierten Entwurfs erinnert das Gebäude in der Ausführung eher an Behelfsbauten. Dadurch unterscheidet es sich beispielsweise von der massiveren Architektur eines Frank Lloyd Wright.

La sophistication apparente de ce projet repose en fait sur l'idée d'abri temporaire, ce qui le différencie, entre autres, des architectures solidement ancrées dans le sol de Frank Lloyd Wright.

As the topographical plan to the left indicates, the house draws part of its inspiration from the very lay of the land (below left). It is intended to be in harmony with its spectacular natural setting.

Inspirationsquellen für die Gestaltung waren sowohl die geographischen Gegebenheiten (unten links) als auch die spektakuläre Landschaft, in die die Byrne Residence harmonisch eingefügt ist.

Comme le montre le plan du site (en bas à gauche), la maison tire en partie son inspiration de la forme même du terrain et s'harmonise avec son spectaculaire environnement naturel.

Will Bruder is one of the recognized masters of contemporary architecture in the Southwestern United States. Open to its environment, this house shows a mastery of form that is more than regional.

Will Bruder ist einer der anerkanntesten Vertreter zeitgenössischer Architektur im Südwesten der USA. Die Offenheit gegenüber der Umgebung und die ungewöhnliche Formensprache machen seine Byrne Residence zu einem Meisterwerk von überregionaler Bedeutung.

Will Bruder est l'un des maîtres reconnus de l'architecture contemporaine dans le Sud-Ouest américain. Ouverte à son environnement, cette maison témoigne d'un traitement des formes qui n'est pas seulement d'inspiration régionale.

SANTIAGO CALATRAVA

Santiago Calatrava, S. A.
Höschgasse 5
8008 Zurich
Switzerland

Tel: +41 1422 7500
Fax: +41 1422 5600
www.calatrava.com

City of Arts and Sciences ►

Born in Valencia in 1951, **SANTIAGO CALATRAVA** studied art and architecture at the Escuela Técnica Superior de Arquitectura in Valencia (1969-74) and engineering at the Eidgenössische Technische Hochschule in Zurich (doctorate in technical science, 1981). He opened his own architecture and civil engineering office the same year. His built work includes Gallery & Heritage Square, BCE Place (Toronto, 1987), the Bach de Roda Bridge (1985-87) and the Torre de Montjuic (1989-92) in Barcelona, the Kuwait Pavilion and the Alamillo Bridge at Expo '92, Seville, and the Lyon-Satolas TGV Station (1989-94). He recently completed the Oriente Station in Lisbon. He was a finalist in the competition for the Reichstag in Berlin. His most recently completed project is the City of Arts and Sciences in Valencia, published here.

SANTIAGO CALATRAVA, geboren 1951 in Valencia, studierte an der dortigen Escuela Técnica Superior de Arquitectura Kunst und Architektur (1969-74) sowie Ingenieurbau an der Eidgenössischen Technischen Hochschule (ETH) in Zürich, wo er 1981 promovierte. Im selben Jahr gründete er sein eigenes Büro für Architektur und Bauingenieurwesen. Zu Calatravas Bauten gehören Gallery & Heritage Square, BCE Place in Toronto (1987), die Bach de Roda-Brücke (1985-87) und die Torre de Montjuic (1989-92) in Barcelona, der Kuwait-Pavillon und die Alamillo-Brücke für die Expo '92 in Sevilla sowie der TGV-Bahnhof Lyon-Satolas (1989-94). Kürzlich vollendete er den Oriente-Bahnhof in Lissabon. Calatravas Entwurf für den Reichstag in Berlin kam in die Endauswahl. Sein jüngstes Projekt ist das hier vorgestellte Wissenschaftsmuseum in Valencia.

Né à Valence, Espagne, en 1951, **SANTIAGO CALATRAVA** étudie l'art et l'architecture à la Escuela Técnica Superior de Arquitectura de Valencia (1969-74) et l'ingénierie à l'ETH (Zurich) dont il est docteur en sciences techniques, en 1981, date à laquelle il ouvre son agence d'architecture et d'ingénierie. Parmi ses réalisations : la Gallery & Heritage Square, BCE Place (Toronto, 1987), le pont Bach de Roda (Barcelone, 1985-87), la Torre de Montjuic (Barcelone, 1989-92), le pavillon du Koweit à Expo '92 (Séville), le pont Alamillo pour la même manifestation, ainsi que la gare TGV de Lyon-Satolas (1989-94). Il a récemment achevé la gare de l'Oriente à Lisbonne. Finaliste du concours pour le Reichstag, à Berlin, il vient d'achever le Musée des sciences de Valence.

CITY OF ARTS AND SCIENCES

Valencia, Spain, 1991-

Planetarium: Planning: 1991-95. Construction: 1996-98. Floor area: 2 561 m². Costs: Ptas 3 000 000 000.
Museum: Planning: 1991-95. Construction: 1996-2000. Floor area: 41 530 m². Cost estimate: Pts 10 400 000 000.
Opera: Planning: 1995-97. Construction: 1997-. Floor area: 44 150 m². Cost estimate: Pts 11 380 000 000.
Client: Generalitat Valenciana.

Part of a long-standing effort of the government of Valencia to rehabilitate an area at the eastern periphery of the city, lodged between a large highway and the dried-up bed of the Turia River, Calatrava's **CITY OF ARTS AND SCIENCES** took almost ten years to be completed. A native of Valencia, he won the 1991 competition for the project that, at the time, included a telecommunications tower resting on three elongated feet. Rising to a height of 327 m, the tower would have been the most visible element of the whole complex. Changes in the city's government led to a replacement of the tower in 1996 by a music center and an Opera, the Palacio de las Artes. The Planetarium, with its eye-shaped plan and hemispheric dome with movable ribbed covering, was built on an area of almost 2 561 m² between 1996 and 1998. The 241 m-long, 41 530-m² Museum of Science is based on an asymmetrical repetition of tree- and rib-like forms filled with glass to admit ample daylight. The Palacio de las Artes (under construction since 1997) will eventually complete the composition.

Calatravas **STADT DER KÜNSTE UND WISSENSCHAFTEN**, deren Fertigstellung beinahe zehn Jahre erforderte, ist das Ergebnis der langjährigen Bemühungen der Provinzregierung von Valencia, das am östlichen Stadtrand zwischen einer großen Autobahn und dem ausgetrockneten Flussbett des Turia liegende Gebiet zu sanieren. Calatrava, selbst aus Valencia gebürtig, gewann 1991 den Wettbewerb für das Projekt, das zum damaligen Zeitpunkt noch einen Telekommunikationsturm auf drei spitz zulaufenden Pfeilern einschloss. Mit einer Höhe von 327 m wäre dieser Turm zu der beherrschende Element des gesamten Komplexes geworden. Veränderungen innerhalb der Stadtverwaltung führten dazu, dass der Turm 1996 durch den Palacio de las Artes, der eine Oper, ein Theater und ein Musik- und Tanzzentrum umfaßt, ersetzt wurde. Das Planetarium mit seinem, an ein Auge erinnernden Grundriss und seiner Kuppel in Form einer Halbkugel unter einer Verkleidung aus beweglichen Rippen wurde zwischen 1996 und 1998 auf einer Fläche von 2 561 m² errichtet. Die Anlage des 241 m langen und 41 530 m² umfassenden Wissenschaftsmuseums basiert formal auf einer asymmetrischen Wiederholung verästelter- oder rippenartiger Formen, die mit Glas ausgefüllt wurden, durch das reichlich Tageslicht einfällt. Der seit 1997 im Bau befindliche Palacio de las Artes wird schließlich die Komposition vervollständigen.

Dans le cadre d'un vaste effort du gouvernement de la région de Valence pour réhabiliter une zone de la périphérie est de la ville, entre une importante autoroute et le lit asséché du fleuve Turia, il a fallu presque dix ans pour mener à bien le projet de cette **CITÉ DES ARTS ET DES SCIENCES.** Né à Valence, Calatrava avait remporté le concours lancé pour ce projet en 1991. Le concours comprenait alors une tour de télécommunications de 327 m de haut, appuyée sur trois pieds allongés. Elle fut remplacée en 1996 par un centre de musique et un opéra, le Palacio de las Artes. Le Planétarium et son dôme hémisphérique en forme d'œil à couverture mobile et nervuré a été édifié sur un terrain de 2 561 m² de 1996 à 1998. Le Musée des Sciences de 41 530 m² et 241 m de long est une répétition asymétrique de formes végétales et de nervures réunies par une verrière qui favorise un généreux éclairage naturel. Dans l'avenir, le Palacio de las Artes (en construction depuis 1997) complétera la composition.

Set at the eastern fringe of Valencia, near the end of the long green belt formed by the Turia River gardens (designed by Ricardo Bofill), the City of Arts and Sciences presents a ribbed design not unlike a gigantic thoracic cage.

Die Gestaltung der am Ostrand von Valencia und am Ausläufer des von Ricardo Bofill entworfenen Turia Park- und Grüngeländes gelegenen Stadt der Künste und Wissenschaften ähnelt mit ihrer Reihung breiter Rippen einem riesigen Brustkorb.

A la limite est de la commune de Valence et vers l'extrémité de la longue ceinture verte des jardins de la Turia (dessinés par Ricardo Bofill), la Cité des Arts et des Sciences et son squelette nervuré font penser à une gigantesque cage thoracique.

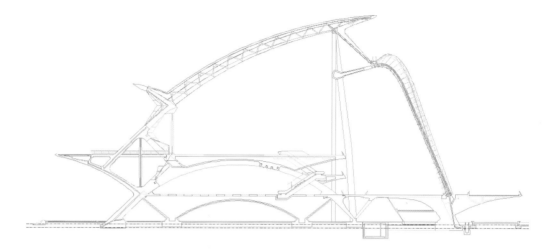

The 240 m-long atrium space of the City of Sciences brings to mind Calatrava's BCE Place, Galleria & Heritage Square (Toronto, Canada, 1987-92), with its six story-high 115 m-long gallery.

Die 240 m lange Vorhalle des Wissenschaftsmuseums erinnert an Calatravas BCE Place, Galleria & Heritage Square in Toronto (1987-92), mit seiner sechsgeschossigen, 115 m langen Galerie.

L'atrium de 240 m de long rappelle une autre réalisation de Calatrava : la galerie de 115 m de long et six étages de haut de BCE Place, Galleria & Heritage Square (Toronto, Canada, 1987-92).

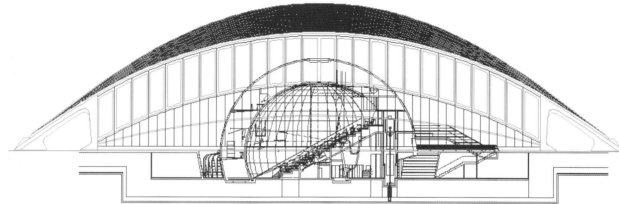

The Planetarium, which was the first part of the complex to reach completion, clearly resembles an eye – and even includes a moving "eyelid." The hemispheric form of the theater naturally lends itself to this interpretation, but Calatrava often uses the form of the eye in his work.

Das Planetarium, das als erstes Gebäude der Anlage fertiggestellt wurde, erinnert mit seinem halbkugelförmigen Kuppelsaal an ein Auge, und hat sogar ein bewegliches »Augenlid«. Calatrava hat die Form des Auges bereits in früheren Arbeiten verwendet.

Le Planétarium, première partie du complexe achevée, ressemble à un œil, « paupière » mobile comprise. La forme hémisphérique de la salle se prête à cette interprétation, d'ailleurs l'architecte a souvent utilisé la forme de l'œil dans ses créations.

DALY, GENIK

Daly, Genik
1558 10th Street
Santa Monica, California 90401
United States

Tel: +1 310 656 3180
Fax: +1 310 656 3183
email: kevin@dalygenik.com or
chris@dalygenik.com
Web: www.dalygenik.com

Valley Center House ▶

KEVIN DALY received his M.Arch. degree at Rice University and his B.Arch. at the University of California at Berkeley. He has participated in the studio faculty of the Southern California Institute of Architecture (1992-99). Before becoming a principal of Daly, Genik in 1989, he worked at the Design Build Studio in Berkeley (1980-85), with Hodgetts & Fung (1985-86), and as an associate in the office of Frank O. Gehry (1986-90). **CHRIS GENIK** received his B.Arch. degree from Carleton University, Ottawa (1983) and his M.Arch. from Rice University, Houston, Texas (1985). Following graduate school, he formed a partnership with Rice University professor Peter Waldman and undertook a series of institutional, residential, and theoretical projects. While practicing, he held a teaching position at the University of Houston, Texas. He moved to Los Angeles to create **DALY, GENIK** in 1989.

KEVIN DALY erwarb seinen Bachelor of Architecture an der Rice University, Houston, Texas und seinen Master of Architecture an der University of California in Berkeley. Von 1992 bis 1999 lehrte er am Southern California Institute of Architecture (SCI-Arc). Bevor er 1989 einer der Leiter von **DALY, GENIK** wurde, war Kevin Daly Mitarbeiter im Design Studio in Berkeley (1980-85), bei Hodgetts & Fung (1985-86) und im Büro von Frank O. Gehry (1986-90). **CHRIS GENIK** erwarb 1983 den Bachelor of Architecture an der Carleton University und 1985 den Master of Architecture an der Rice University. Nach seinem Graduiertenstudium bildete er eine Partnerschaft mit dem an der Rice University als Professor tätigen Peter Waldman und führte eine Reihe praktischer und theoretischer Projekte durch. Daneben unterrichtete er an der University of Houston. 1989 zog er nach Los Angeles und gründete zusammen mit Kevin Daly das Architekturbüro Daly, Genik.

KEVIN DALY est Bachelor of Architecture de l'University of California de Berkeley et Master of Architecture de la Rice University. Il a enseigné au Southern California Institute of Architecture (1992-99). Avant de s'associer à Chris Genik, il avait travaillé pour l'agence Design Build Studio de Berkeley (1980-85), chez Hodgetts & Fung (1985-86) et comme associé chez Frank O. Gehry (1986-90). **CHRIS GENIK** est diplômé en architecture de la Carleton University (1983) et Master of Architecture de la Rice University, Houston, Texas (1985). Associé à un professeur de Rice University, Peter Waldman, il réalise une série de projets institutionnels, résidentiels et théoriques. En même temps, il enseigne à l'Université de Houston, Texas. Il s'installe à Los Angeles où il crée **DALY, GENIK** en 1989.

VALLEY CENTER HOUSE

North San Diego County, California, USA, 1998

Construction: 1998. Client: withheld at owner's request. Floor area: 265 m2.

Located at an altitude of 550 m above sea level near a citrus and avocado ranch 70 km northeast of San Diego, the **VALLEY CENTER HOUSE** was intended to replace a residence destroyed by a wildfire in November 1996. Laid out in a skewed "U" form, the house offers 265 m² of space, and features large perforated aluminum screens attached to aluminum tube frames that can swing down to shield the house from the sun or offer privacy at night. The screens also protect the residence in case of another wildfire. The bare concrete floors and reinforced concrete fireplace inside the structure are designed to survive earthquakes. The combination of aluminum and concrete gives the house an almost industrial look that seems inspired by temporary housing or shipping containers.

Das **VALLEY CENTER HOUSE** liegt 550 m über dem Meeresspiegel, in der Nähe einer Zitronen- und Avocado-Farm, 70 km nordöstlich von San Diego. Es ersetzt ein Wohnhaus, das im November 1996 bei einem Waldbrand zerstört wurde. Das Gebäude ist in Form eines angeschrägten »U« geschnitten und hat eine Wohnfläche von 265 m². Es ist mit großen Blendschirmen aus perforiertem Aluminium ausgestattet, die ausschwenkbar sind, um die Bewohner tagsüber vor der Sonne zu schützen und nachts die notwendige Privatsphäre zu bieten. Darüber hinaus dienen die Blenden als Feuerschutz. Die nackten Betonböden und der Kamin aus Stahlbeton im Hausinneren sind erdbebensicher konstruiert. Während die Kombination von Aluminium und Beton an Industriebauten erinnert, scheint die Form des Gebäudes von Behelfsbauten oder Schiffscontainern inspiriert zu sein.

Située à 70 km au nord-est de San Diego et 550 m d'altitude, en bordure d'une plantation de citronniers et d'avocatiers, le **VALLEY CENTER HOUSE** remplace une précédente résidence détruite par un incendie de forêt en novembre 1996. Ses 265 m² se répartissent selon un plan en U en biais. Elle présente d'importants écrans d'aluminium perforé fixés sur une structure en tube d'aluminium, qui se rabattent pour protéger la maison du soleil ou des regards pendant la nuit. Ils jouent également un rôle de protection en cas d'incendie. Les sols en béton nu sont antisismiques. La combinaison d'aluminium et de béton donne à la maison une allure presque industrielle qui semble inspirée des abris temporaires ou des conteneurs de transport.

The swinging perforated aluminum screens allow the house to be almost completely open to its environment or, on the contrary, completely closed.

Durch die ausschwenkbaren Blendschirme aus perforiertem Aluminium lässt sich das Gebäude entweder zu seiner Umgebung hin öffnen oder von ihr abschirmen.

Des écrans d'aluminium perforé pivotants permettent à la maison de s'ouvrir sur son environnement ou de se refermer totalement sur elle-même.

DILLER + SCOFIDIO

Diller + Scofidio
36 Cooper Square
New York, NY 10003
United States

Tel: +1 212 260 7971
Fax: +1 212 260 7924
e-mail: disco2@flashcom.net

ELIZABETH DILLER is an Associate Professor at Princeton University, and RICARDO SCOFIDIO is a Professor of Architecture at The Cooper Union in New York. According to their own description, "DILLER + SCOFIDIO is a collaborative, interdisciplinary studio involved in architecture, the visual arts and the performing arts. The team is primarily involved in thematically-driven experimental work that takes the form of architectural commissions, temporary installations and permanent site-specific installations, multimedia theater, electronic media, and print." Their recent work includes Slither, 100 units of social housing in Gifu, Japan (under construction), and Moving Target, a collaborative dance work with Charleroi/Danses, Belgium, as well as The Brasserie in the Seagram Building, New York, published here. Installations by Diller + Scofidio have been seen at the Fondation Cartier in Paris (Master/Slave, 1999), the Museum of Modern Art in New York and the Musée de la Mode in Paris.

ELIZABETH DILLER ist außerordentliche Professorin in Princeton, RICARDO SCOFIDIO Professor an der Cooper Union School of Architecture in New York. Ihrer eigenen Beschreibung zufolge ist »DILLER + SCOFIDIO ein interdisziplinäres Gemeinschaftsprojekt, das sich mit Architektur, den bildenden und den darstellenden Künsten beschäftigt. Das Team führt hauptsächlich experimentelle Arbeiten durch, die sich auf der Grundlage von Architektur, Installation, Multimediaveranstaltung, elektronischen Medien und Druckgrafik mit bestimmten Themen auseinandersetzen.« Zu ihren jüngsten Projekten gehören Slither, 100 Einheiten des sozialen Wohnungsbaus in Gifu, Japan (im Bau), Moving Target, eine Tanztheaterproduktion in Zusammenarbeit mit der belgischen Tanzgruppe Charleroi/Danses sowie das hier vorgestellte Restaurant The Brasserie im Seagram-Building, New York. Installationen von Diller + Scofidio wurden in der Fondation Cartier in Paris (Master/Slave, 1999), im Museum of Modern Art in New York und im Musée de la Mode in Paris gezeigt.

ELIZABETH DILLER est professeur associé à Princeton, RICARDO SCOFIDIO Professeur d'architecture à la Cooper Union, New York. Selon leur présentation: « DILLER + SCOFIDIO est une agence interdisciplinaire coopérative qui se consacre à l'architecture, aux arts plastiques et aux arts du spectacle. L'équipe travaille essentiellement sur des recherches thématiques expérimentales qui se concrétisent sous forme de commandes architecturales, d'installations temporaires, d'installations permanentes adaptées au site, théâtre multimédia, médias électroniques et imprimés. » Parmi leurs projets récents : Slither, 100 logements sociaux à Gifu, Japon (en construction) et Moving Target, une œuvre chorégraphique en collaboration avec Charleroi/Danses, Belgique, ainsi que The Brasserie dans le Seagram Building, New York, publiée ici. Les installations de Diller + Scofidio ont été présentées à la Fondation Cartier à Paris (Master/Slave, 1999) au Museum of Modern Art de New York et au Musée de la mode à Paris.

THE BRASSERIE

Seagram Building, New York, NY, USA, 1998-2000

Planning: 1998-2/99. Construction: 3/99-1/2000. Client: Restaurant Associates
Floor area: 650 m². Costs: withheld at owner's request.

THE BRASSERIE is one of the best-known restaurants in New York. Originally designed by Philip Johnson at the same time as the Four Seasons Restaurant, it is located in Mies van der Rohe's Seagram Building. Set in a 650-m² underground space, the Diller + Scofidio project (completed with Charles Renfro and Deane Simpson) started out by "removing all traces of Philip Johnson's interior," that had been severely damaged by fire some time ago. Seating 230 guests, the restaurant is built with sensitivity to the apparent transparency of the Seagram Building, contrasting here with the windowless underground space. Each guest who comes in is videotaped, and his or her image is projected on 15 monitors above the bar. A long glass stairway descends into the middle of the main room, allowing arriving guests to be viewed by the seated patrons. Other features include a 15 m-long lenticular glass wall that partially blurs the vision from most angles. Pear wood is used for some of the ceiling surfaces and the madrone on the floor. Dining room tables are made of poured resin formed around stainless steel structural supports.

THE BRASSERIE in Mies van der Rohes Seagram Building ist eines der bekanntesten Restaurants in New York. Sie wurde wie auch das Four Seasons Restaurant ursprünglich von Philip Johnson gestaltet. Diller + Scofidio begannen ihr Projekt (zusammen mit Charles Renfro und Deane Simpson) für den 650 m² umfassenden Bereich im Untergeschoss damit, »alle Spuren von Philip Johnsons Innenausstattung zu entfernen«, wobei hinzugefügt werden muß, dass das Restaurant vor einiger Zeit durch ein Feuer stark beschädigt worden war. Das für 230 Gäste ausgelegte Restaurant wurde mit viel Gespür für die Transparenz des Seagram Building gestaltet, der die Architekten einen fensterlosen unterirdischen Raum entgegensetzten. Jeder der eintretenden Gäste wird mit einer Videokamera aufgenommen, woraufhin ihr oder sein Bild auf 15 über der Bar hängenden Monitoren erscheint. Eine lange Glastreppe führt in die Mitte des Hauptraums, so werden neuankommende Gäste für die an den Tischen Sitzenden bereits beim Hinabsteigen sichtbar. Zu den weiteren Gestaltungsmitteln gehört eine 15 m lange linsenförmige Glaswand, die für eine teilweise verschwommene Sicht sorgt. Teile der Deckentäfelung sind aus Birnbaum, die Böden aus Madrone. Die Esstische bestehen aus gegossenen Kunstharzplatten, die plastisch um Stützkonstruktionen aus Edelstahl geformt wurden.

THE BRASSERIE est l'un des plus célèbres restaurants new yorkais. Conçu à l'origine par Philip Johnson au même moment que celui des Four Seasons, il est installé dans le Seagram Building de Mies van der Rohe. Le projet de 650 m² en sous-sol de Diller + Scofidio (avec la collaboration de Charles Renfro et de Deane Simpson) a consisté dans un premier temps à « supprimer toute trace des aménagements de Philip Johnson, » d'autant plus qu'un incendie avait ravagé les lieux quelque temps plus tôt. Conçue pour 230 couverts, la salle n'est pas sans rendre hommage à la transparence du Seagram Building, même dans cet espace souterrain sans fenêtre. Chaque client est enregistré en vidéo à son arrivée et son image se retrouve projetée sur 15 moniteurs disposés au-dessus du bar. Un long escalier de verre descend jusqu'au milieu de la salle principale, ce qui permet à chacun de voir les nouveaux arrivants. Le restaurant comporte également un mur de verre lenticulaire de 15 m de long qui brouille partiellement la vision sous la plupart des angles. Certains plafonds sont revêtus de poirier et le sol de madrone. Les tables sont en résine coulée sur une structure en acier inoxydable.

Diller + Scofidio radically transformed one of New York's most famous restaurant interiors, the original Brasserie, designed by Philip Johnson, although the basic below-grade volume was necessarily maintained.

Diller + Scofidio gestalteten den Innenraum des berühmten, von Philip Johnson entworfenen New Yorker Restaurants radikal um. Die Grundform des Untergeschosses blieb jedoch erhalten.

Diller + Scofidio ont radicalement transformé l'un des plus célèbres décors de restaurant de New York, créé à l'origine par Philip Johnson. Ils ont dû néanmoins respecter les proportions de ce grand volume en sous-sol.

BLUR BUILDING

International Expo 2002, Yverdon, Switzerland, 1998-2002

Planning: 1998-2000. Construction: 2000-5/2002. Client: EXPO 02 by Extasia.
Dimensions: 100 x 60 x 12 m (fog structure). Budget: $7 500 000.

The **BLUR BUILDING**, realized in collaboration with the Extasia-Team, is designed to appear like a cloud hovering above Lake Neuchâtel. 100 m wide, 60 m deep, and 12 m thick, it rises up to a height of 25 m above the water. The "cloud" effect will be achieved through the use of filtered lake water "shot as a fine mist through a dense array of high-pressure water nozzles integrated into a large cantilevered tensegrity structure." A ramp will lead into the cloud where visitors will experience a kind of sensory deprivation due to the "white-out" accompanied by "white noise" produced by mist projectors. A "black-out shell" in the center of the structure will be used to project a panoramic image in the round for 250 visitors at a time. Omnimax movies would be used to "twist spatial conventions to challenge geographical continuity and linear time."

Das **BLUR BUILDING**, in Zusammenarbeit mit dem Extasia-Team realisiert, ist so gestaltet, dass es wie eine über dem Neuburger See schwebende Wolke aussieht. Bei einer Länge von 100 m, einer Breite von 60 m und einer Tiefe von 12 m erhebt es sich 25 m über dem Wasserspiegel. Der »Wolken-Effekt« wird durch den Einsatz gefilterten Seewassers erzielt, das »als feiner Nebel aus einer dichten Anordnung von Hochdruck-Wasserdüsen versprüht wird, die in eine große, freitragende Seilnetz-Konstruktion eingebaut sind.« Die Besucher gelangen über eine Rampe in das Innere der Wolke, wo sie aufgrund eines optischen »weißen Nichts«, begleitet vom »weißen Rauschen« der Nebelapparate eine Art sensorischen Entzug erleben. Im Zentrum der Konstruktion befindet sich eine muschelförmige »black-out« Plattform für bis zu 250 Besucher, auf der ein Panoramabild auf eine kreisförmige Leinwand projiziert wird. Dazu werden Omnimax-Filme eingesetzt, die »die räumlichen Sehgewohnheiten verzerren und so die geographische Kontinuität und zeitliche Linearität infragestellen«.

Le **BLUR BUILDING**, un collaboration avec le Extasia-Team, est conçu pour donner l'impression d'un nuage suspendu au-dessus du lac de Neuchâtel. De 100 m de large, 60 de profondeur et 12 d'épaisseur, il s'élèvera jusqu'à 25 m au-dessus du niveau de l'eau. L'effet de nuage sera obtenu « au moyen d'eau du lac filtrée et projetée en brume par un réseau serré de jets haute pression intégrés à une vaste structure suspendue ». Une rampe conduira les visiteurs à l'intérieur du nuage où ils éprouveront une sensation de privation due à un « blanc optique » renforcé par le « bruit blanc » produit par les projecteurs de brume. Une « coquille d'isolement » au centre de la structure servira de salle de projection panoramique circulaire pour 250 visiteurs. Des films Omnimax seront projetés « qui perturberont les conventions spatiales et remettront en jeu la continuité géographique et la linéarité du temps. »

The almost surreal idea of a stationary cloud that is in fact a building challenges all existing notions of facade, volume and relation to the earth in architecture.
Because it is actually intended to be built, this is a fundamentally radical design.

Die fast surreal anmutende Idee eines Gebäudes in Form einer Wolke, die beständig an einem Ort schwebt, stellt sämtliche in der Architektur bestehenden Vorstellungen von Fassade, Rauminhalt und Bezug zum Boden in Frage und ist damit ein von Grund auf radikaler Entwurf.

L'idée presque surréaliste d'un bâtiment en forme de nuage remet en question toutes les notions architecturales de façade, de volume et de relations au sol. Ce projet radical a néanmoins été étudié pour être réalisé.

DILLER + SCOFIDIO

The so-called "Glass Box" within the structure is a space where visitors, surrounded by glass on six sides, will experience a "sense of physical suspension only heightened by an occasional opening in the fog."

Die sogenannte »Glass Box« ist ein sechsseitig verglaster Raum im Gebäudeinneren, in dem die Besucher ein Gefühl des Schwebens verspüren, das sich noch verstärkt, wenn sich der Nebel gelegentlich lichtet.

La « Boîte de verre » à l'intérieur de la structure est un espace dans lesquels les visiteurs, entourés de verre sur six côtés, expérimenteront « le sentiment physique d'être en suspension, renforcé à l'occasion par une percée dans le brouillard. »

The Angel Bar deck is set above the
fog, offering a panoramic view of
the landscape and the lake. It serves
only mineral water from a variety
of international sources.

Die »Angel Bar« liegt auf einer Plattform über dem Nebel und bietet einen
Rundblick über die Landschaft und
den See. Es wird dort nur Mineral-
wasser aus vielen verschiedenen
Ländern serviert.

La terrasse du Bar des Anges, qui
ne propose que des eaux minérales
venues du monde entier, se trouve
au dessus du brouillard. Elle offre
une vue panoramique sur le paysage
et le lac.

STEVEN EHRLICH

Steven Ehrlich Architects
10865 Washington Blvd.
Culver City, California 90232
United States

Tel: +1 310 838 9700
Fax: +1 310 838 9737
e-mail: inquire@s-ehrlich.com
web: www.s-ehrlich.com

Canyon Residence ▶

Born in New York in 1946, **STEVEN EHRLICH** received his B.Arch. degree from the Rensselaer Polytechnic Institute in Troy, New York (1969). He studied indigenous vernacular architecture in North and West Africa from 1969 to 1977. He has completed numerous private residences, including the Friedman Residence (1986), the Ehrman-Coombs Residence (1989-1991, Santa Monica), and the Shulman Residence (Brentwood, 1989-1992) all in the Los Angeles area. Other built work includes the Shatto Recreation Center (Los Angeles, 1991); Sony Music Entertainment Campus (Santa Monica, 1993); Child Care Center for Sony, Culver City (1993-95); Game Show Network, Culver City (1995) as well as the Robertson Branch Library (Los Angeles, 1996). More recently, he has worked on the DreamWorks SKG Animation Studios, Glendale, California, 1998; the Orange Coast Collage Art Center, Costa Mesa, 2000; and the Biblioteca Latinoamericana & Washington Youth Center, San Jose, 1999. A recent widely published project was his House Extension (Santa Monica, California, 1996-98) for Richard Neutra's 1938 Lewin House.

STEVEN EHRLICH, 1946 in New York geboren, erwarb 1969 den Bachelor of Architecture am Rensselaer Polytechnic Institute in Troy, New York. Von 1969 bis 1977 studierte er die Architektur der Eingeborenen Nord- und Westafrikas. Ausgeführt hat er zahlreiche Privathäuser, darunter das Haus Friedman (1986), das Haus Ehrmann-Coombs in Santa Monica (1989-91) und das Haus Shulman in Brentwood (1989-92), die alle in der Region Los Angeles liegen. Zu seinen weiteren realisierten Bauten gehören das Shatto Recreation Center in Los Angeles (1991), der Sony Music Entertainment Campus in Santa Monica (1993), das Child Care Center für Sony (1993-95) und das Game Show Network (1995), beide in Culver City, sowie die Robertson Branch Library in Los Angeles (1996). Seine jüngsten Arbeiten sind die Dream-Works SKG Animation Studios in Glendale, Kalifornien (1998), das Orange Coast College Art Center in Costa Mesa (2000) sowie die Biblioteca Latinoamericana und das Washington Youth Center in San Jose (1999). Große Beachtung fand seine Erweiterung von Richard Neutras 1938 erbauten Haus Lewin in Santa Monica, Kalifornien (1996-98).

Né à New York en 1946, **STEVEN EHRLICH** est Bachelor of Architecture du Rensselaer Polytechnic Institute de Troy, New York (1969). Il étudie ensuite l'architecture vernaculaire indigène d'Afrique du Nord et de l'Ouest de 1969 à 1977. Il a construit de nombreuses résidences privées dont la Friedman Residence (1986), la Ehrman-Coombs Residence (Santa Monica, 1989-1991) et la Shulman Residence (Brentwood, 1989-1992), toutes trois dans la région de Los Angeles en Californie. Parmi ses autres réalisations : le Shatto Recreation Center (Los Angeles, 1991), le Sony Music Entertainment Campus (Santa Monica, 1993), le Child Care Center Sony (1993-95) et le Game Show Network (1995) à Culver City ainsi que la Robertson Branch Library (Los Angeles, 1996). Plus récemment, il a réalisé les Dreamworks SKG Animation Studios (Glendale, Californie, 1998), le Orange Coast Collage Art Center (Costa Mesa, 2000), ainsi que la Biblioteca Latinoamericana et le Washington Youth Center (San Jose, 1999). Une des ses interventions souvent publiée est l'extension de la Lewin House de Richard Neutra (1938) à Santa Monica, Californie (1996-98).

CANYON RESIDENCE

Los Angeles, California, USA, 1996-98

Planning and construction: 1996-98. Floor area: 687 m².
Client: withheld at owner's request.

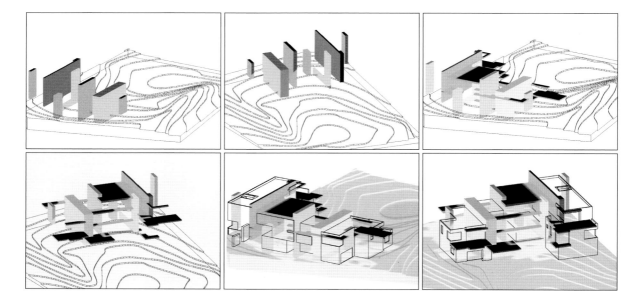

In this 687-m² house, the architect uses a series of vertical masses in stucco to house fireplaces, stairway, service cores and storage. Their counterpoint is a set of horizontal canopies clad in copper. Set on a sloping site, the **CANYON RESIDENCE** steps down the hillside, never exceeding a height of two stories, but permitting a living room height that approaches 6 m. The living room divides the two-story bedroom area from the "family-kitchen zone." Designed around large trees, the house is meant to be closely connected to its natural environment. Architecture critic Joseph Giovannini has likened the composition of this house to that of the De Stijl artists, and more specifically to the lines of Mondrian's "Boogie Woogie" paintings.

Das 687 m² umfassende Wohnhaus ist stufenförmig auf einem Hanggrundstück errichtete. Es geht nicht über eine Höhe von zwei Geschossen hinaus, wobei das Wohnzimmer eine Deckenhöhe von annähernd 6 m hat. Dieser Wohnraum trennt den zweistöckigen Schlafzimmertrakt vom Essbereich und der Küche. Bei der **CANYON RESIDENCE** kontrastiert eine Serie von vertikalen, mit Gips verputzten Baukörpern, die der Unterbringung von Kaminen, Treppenaufgang, Versorgungsschächten und Speicher dienen, mit einer Reihe horizontaler, kupferbeschichteter Schutzdächer. Das Haus wurde bewusst um große Bäume herum angelegt, um eine enge Verbindung mit seiner natürlichen Umgebung herzustellen. Der Architekturkritiker Joseph Giovannini hat die Gestaltung dieses Bauwerks mit der Formensprache der De Stijl-Künstler, insbesondere mit den Linien von Mondrians »Boogie Woogie«-Gemälden verglichen.

Pour cette maison de 687 m², l'architecte a imaginé une succession de masses verticales en stuc qui abritent les cheminées, l'escalier, les locaux techniques et de rangement. Des dais horizontaux revêtus de cuivre viennent en contrepoint. La **CANYON RESIDENCE** descend en escalier la pente de la colline sans jamais dépasser deux niveaux, la hauteur du séjour approchant cependant 6 m. Ce séjour sépare les deux chambres de la zone «famille-cuisine». Dessinée autour de grands arbres existants, le projet cherche à créer un lien étroit avec son cadre naturel. Le critique d'architecture Joseph Giovannini a comparé sa composition à celles d'artistes du groupe De Stijl et en particulier aux peintures de la série «Boogie-Woogie» de Mondrian.

Right: Calling both on local architectural tradition, such as the houses of Richard Neutra, and on modern painting as inspiration, Steven Ehrlich integrates this design into the lush Southern California vegetation.

Rechts: Steven Ehrlich integriert seinen sowohl von lokaler Architekturtradition – wie den Häusern von Richard Neutra – als auch von modernen Gemälden inspirierten Entwurf in die üppige Vegetation Südkaliforniens.

A droite : S'appuyant à la fois sur les traditions architecturales locales, comme les maisons de Richard Neutra, et sur la peinture moderne, Steven Ehrlich a cherché à intégrer son projet dans la luxuriante végétation de Californie du Sud.

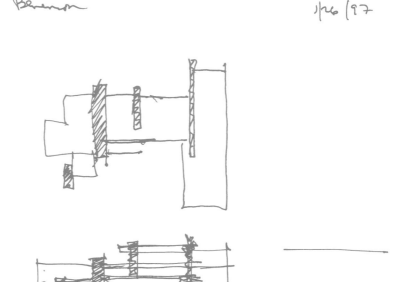

Benson 1/26/97

o VERTICAL MASS (COLORED PLASTER)

o VOID (GLASS to OPEN)

o ~~STUCCO~~ MASS (WHITE STUCCO)

o FLOATING PLANES — (steel or copper clad planes)

The architect's own reference to voids and floating planes (above) in the drawing above becomes apparent in the interior views of the house, where openings and perspectives penetrate the volumes, particularly in the generous space of the living room (above left).

Die vom Architekten skizzierten Hohlräume und freischwebenden Flächen (oben) sind im Inneren des Hauses, besonders im großzügig bemessenen Wohnraum, in Form von Öffnungen und Ausblicken, die den Baukörper durchdringen, umgesetzt (oben links).

Les vides et les plans flottants esquissés par l'architecte (dessins ci-dessus) se retrouvent dans les vues intérieures de la maison, où des ouvertures et des perspectives pénètrent les volumes, en particulier dans le généreux espace du séjour (en haut à gauche).

NORMAN FOSTER

Foster and Partners
Riverside Three
22 Hester Road
London SW11 4AN
England

Tel: +44 20 7738 0455
Fax: +44 20 7738 1107/08
e-mail: enquiries@fosterandpartners.com
Web: www.fosterandpartners.com

Born in Manchester in 1935, **NORMAN FOSTER** studied architecture and city planning at Manchester University (1961). Awarded the Henry Fellowship to Yale University, he received the M.Arch. degree, and met Richard Rogers, with whom he created Team 4. He received the Royal Gold Medal for Architecture (1983) and the American Institute of Architects Gold Medal for Architecture (1994). He was knighted in 1990 and made a life peer in 1999. Norman Foster has built the IBM Pilot Head Office (Cosham, 1970-71), Sainsbury Centre for Visual Arts and Crescent Wing, University of East Anglia (Norwich, 1976-77; 1989-91), Hong Kong and Shanghai Banking Corporation Headquarters (Hong Kong, 1981-86), London's third airport, Stansted (1987-91), the Faculty of Law of Cambridge University (1993-95), and the Commerzbank Headquarters (Frankfurt, Germany, 1994-97). Recent projects include the Hong Kong International Airport (1995-98), the new Reichstag (Berlin, 1993-99), and the British Museum Redevelopment (London, 1997-2000).

NORMAN FOSTER, geboren 1935 in Manchester, studierte bis 1961 Architektur und Stadtplanung an der Manchester University. Er wurde mit dem Henry Fellowship der Yale University ausgezeichnet und schloss dort seine Studien mit dem Master of Architecture ab. In Yale lernte er Richard Rogers kennen, mit dem er Team 4 gründete. 1983 wurde Foster mit der Royal Gold Medal for Architecture ausgezeichnet und 1990 geadelt. 1994 wurde ihm die Gold Medal for Architecture des American Institute of Architects verliehen, 1999 wurde er zum Lord ernannt. Zu seinen Bauten gehören das IBM Pilot Head Office in Cosham (1970-71), das Sainsbury Centre for Visual Arts und der Crescent Wing der University of East Anglia in Norwich (1976-77; 1989-91), der Sitz der Hong Kong and Shanghai Bank in Hongkong (1981-86), Londons dritter Flughafen, Stansted (1987-91), die Juristische Fakultät der University of Cambridge (1993-95) und die Commerzbank-Zentrale in Frankfurt am Main (1994-97). Zu seinen jüngsten Projekten gehören der Internationale Flughafen Hongkong (1995-98), der Umbau des Reichstags in Berlin zum neuen Sitz des Deutschen Bundestags (1993-99) und die Modernisierung des British Museum in London (1997-2000).

Né à Manchester en 1935, **NORMAN FOSTER** étudie l'architecture et l'urbanisme à la Manchester University (1961). Titulaire d'un Henry Fellowship de la Yale University, il passe son Master of Architecture à Yale (1963), où il rencontre Richard Rogers avec lequel il crée Team 4. Il est titulaire de la Royal Gold Medal for Architecture (1983) et de l'American Institute of Architects Gold Medal for Architecture (1994). Fait chevalier en 1990, Norman Foster est nommé pair à vie en 1999. Parmi ses réalisations : le siège pilote d'IBM (Cosham, Grande-Bretagne, 1970-71), le Sainsbury Centre for Visual Arts et la Crescent Wing de l'Université d'East Anglia (Norwich, Grande-Bretagne, 1976-77, 1989-91), la tour de la Hong Kong and Shanghai Bank (Hongkong, 1981-86), le terminal de l'aéroport de Stansted, Grande-Bretagne (1987-91), la faculté de droit de Cambridge (1993-95), le siège de la Commerzbank (Francfort, Allemagne, 1994-97), l'aéroport international de Hongkong (1995-98), le Reichstag (Berlin, 1993-99) et la rénovation du British Museum (Londres 1997-2000).

GREATER LONDON AUTHORITY

London, England, 1999-2002

Planning: 2/99-2/2000. Construction: 3/1999-2002 (scheduled).
Client: CIT Group. Floor area: ca. 17 187 m². Budget: £65 000 000.

Located on the Thames near the Tower Bridge, directly opposite the Tower of London, these new 10-story headquarters for the **GREATER LONDON AUTHORITY** will provide about 17 000 m² of available floor space and be built at a cost of approximately £65 million. An office for the Mayor of London and the Cabinet will be located on the eighth floor of the "flask-like form." An exhibition or function room on the ninth floor has been dubbed "London's Living Room" and can accommodate about 200 people. The unusual spherical shape of the building "has been generated as a result of thorough scientific analysis, aiming to reduce both solar gain and heat loss via the building's skin, thus reducing the building's energy needs." More specifically, energy consumption is to be reduced to 25% of a typical air-conditioned office building.

Der Entwurf dieses am Themse-Ufer, nahe der Tower Bridge und direkt gegenüber dem Tower of London gelegenen neuen Sitzes der **GREATER LONDON AUTHO-RITY** sieht eine Gesamtnutzfläche von ca. 17 000 m² auf zehn Geschossen vor und ist mit ca. 65 Millionen Pfund veranschlagt. In der achten Etage des »glaskolbenförmi-gen« Gebäudes wird ein Büro für den Bürgermeister von London und sein Kabinett eingerichtet. Ein Ausstellungs- oder Empfangssaal im neunten Stock, der den Namen »Londons Wohnzimmer« erhalten hat, kann etwa 200 Personen fassen. Die ungewöhnliche, kugelförmige Gestalt des Gebäudes »beruht auf gründlichen wissenschaftli-chen Untersuchungen, die zum Ziel hatten, den Verlust an Sonnenenergie und Wärme durch die Außenhaut des Gebäudes und damit den Energiebedarf zu minimieren«. Dadurch wird der Energieverbrauch auf 25% eines typischen Bürogebäudes mit Klimaanlage gesenkt.

Situé au bord de la Tamise, près de Tower Bridge, juste en face de la Tour de Londres sur l'autre rive, le nouveau siège de la **GREATER LONDON AUTHORITY** offrira environ 17 000 m² de surface brute sur 10 niveaux pour un coût estimé à £65 millions. Le bureau du Maire de Londres et son cabinet seront installés au huitième niveau de cet immeuble « en forme de bocal ». Une salle d'exposition ou de réception au neuvième niveau a déjà été surnommée le « London Living Room », et pourra rece-voir 200 personnes. La forme sphérique inhabituelle de l'immeuble vient d'une analyse scientifique visant à réduire l'effet du soleil et la déperdition de chaleur et donc de diminuer les besoins énergétiques du bâtiment au moyen de son enveloppe. La consommation d'énergie devrait être de 25% inférieure à celle d'un immeuble climatisé classique.

As in many of his recent designs, Norman Foster is most attentive to problems of solar gain and heat flow, doing the utmost to give the building a large degree of energy self-suffi-ciency.

Wie in vielen seiner neueren Entwürfe hat sich Norman Foster auch hier besonders mit der Nutzung von Son-nenenergie und Wärmestrom aus-einandergesetzt, um den Energie-verbrauch des Gebäudes möglichst gering zu halten.

Comme dans beaucoup de ses projets récents, Foster, particulièrement attentif aux problèmes de l'exposition solaire et des flux de chaleur, s'est efforcé d'assurer au projet un degré élevé d'autonomie énergétique.

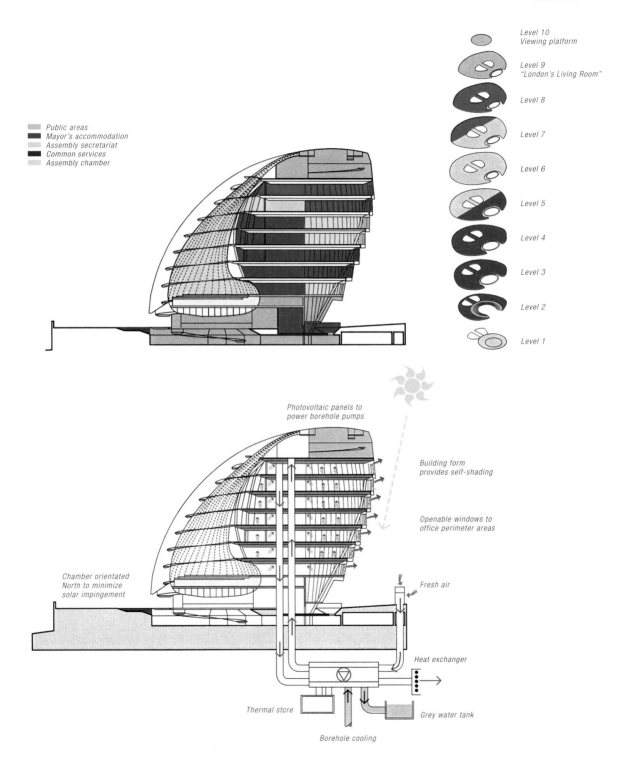

Level 10
Viewing platform

Level 9
"London's Living Room"

Level 8

Level 7

Level 6

Level 5

Level 4

Level 3

Level 2

Level 1

Public areas
Mayor's accommodation
Assembly secretariat
Common services
Assembly chamber

Photovoltaic panels to power borehole pumps

Building form provides self-shading

Openable windows to office perimeter areas

Chamber orientated North to minimize solar impingement

Fresh air

Heat exchanger

Thermal store

Grey water tank

Borehole cooling

Calling on CAD-design to work out the complex curves in this structure, the architect has placed an emphasis on the building's transparency.

Die komplexen Windungen des Gebäudes sind mit CAD-Programmen ausgearbeitet. Foster hat viel Betonung auf die Transparenz des Gebäudes gelegt.

Utilisant la CAO pour mettre au point les courbes complexes de la structure, l'architecte a mis l'accent sur la transparence.

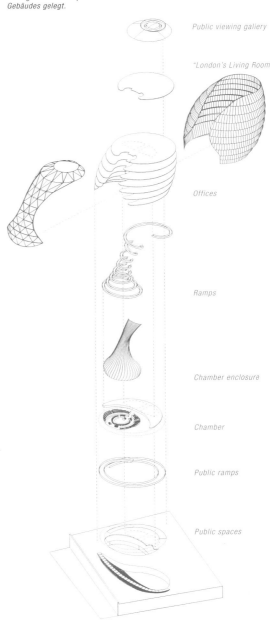

Public viewing gallery

"London's Living Room"

Offices

Ramps

Chamber enclosure

Chamber

Public ramps

Public spaces

FRANK O.GEHRY

Frank O. Gehry & Associates, Inc.
1520-B Cloverfield Boulevard
Santa Monica, California 90404
United States

Tel.: +1 310 828 6088
Fax: +1 310 828 2098

Experience Music Project ▶

Born in Toronto, Canada in 1929, **FRANK O. GEHRY** studied at the University of Southern California, Los Angeles (1949-51), and at Harvard (1956-57). Principal of Frank O. Gehry and Associates, Los Angeles, since 1962, he received the 1989 Pritzker Prize. Among his notable projects are the Loyola Law School, Los Angeles, California (1981-84); the Norton Residence, Venice, California (1983); the California Aerospace Museum, Los Angeles, California (1982-84); the Schnabel Residence, Los Angeles, California (1989); the Festival Disney, Marne-la-Vallée, France (1989-92); the University of Toledo Art Building, Toledo, Ohio (1990-92); the American Center, Paris, France (1993); the Disney Concert Hall, Los Angeles, California (construction temporarily halted); the Nationale-Nederlanden Building, Prague, Czech Republic (1994-96); the Guggenheim Bilbao, Spain (1993-97); Pariser Platz 3, Berlin, Germany (1994-2001) and the Experience Music Project, Seattle, Washington (1996-2000). Gehry is recognized as one of the most creative and influential architects of the latter part of the 20th century.

FRANK O. GEHRY, geboren 1929 in Toronto, studierte von 1949 bis 1951 an der University of Southern California (USC) in Los Angeles und von 1956 bis 1957 in Harvard. Seit 1962 ist er Leiter von Frank O. Gehry and Associates in Los Angeles und erhielt 1989 den Pritzker Prize. Zu seinen bekanntesten Bauten gehören die Loyola Law School in Los Angeles (1981-84), das Haus Norton in Venice (1983), das California Aerospace Museum (1982-84) und das Haus Schnabel in Los Angeles (1989), das Festival Disney im französischen Marne-la-Vallée (1989-92), das University of Toledo Art Building in Toledo, Ohio (1990-92), das Amerikahaus in Paris (1993), die Disney Concert Hall, Los Angeles (die Bauarbeiten wurden vorübergehend eingestellt), das Nationale Nederlanden-Gebäude in Prag (1994-96), das Guggenheim Bilbao, Spanien (1993-97), das Gebäude Pariser Platz 3 in Berlin (1994-2000) und das hier vorgestellte Experience Music Project in Seattle, Washington (1996-2000). Gehry ist anerkanntermaßen einer der kreativsten und einflussreichsten Architekten des ausgehenden 20. Jahrhunderts.

Né à Toronto (Canada) en 1929, **FRANK O. GEHRY** étudie à l'University of Southern California, Los Angeles (1949-51) et à Harvard (1956-57). A la tête de Frank O. Gehry and Associates, Los Angeles, depuis 1962, il se voit attribuer le Prix Pritzker en 1989. Parmi ses projets les plus remarqués : la Loyola Law School, Los Angeles, Californie (1981-84) ; la Norton Residence, Venice, Californie (1983) ; le California Aerospace Museum, Los Angeles, Californie (1982-84) ; la Schnabel Residence, Los Angeles (1989) ; Festival Disney, Marne-la-Vallée, France (1989-92) ; l'Art Building, University of Toledo, Ohio (1990-92) ; l'American Center, Paris, France (1993) ; le Disney Concert Hall, Los Angeles (construction provisoirement interrompue) ; l'immeuble Nationale Nederlanden, Prague, République Tchèque (1994-96) ; le Guggenheim Bilbao, Espagne (1993-97) ; Pariser Platz 3, Berlin, Allemagne (1994-2000) et l'Experience Music Project, Seattle, Washington (1996-2000). Il est considéré comme l'un des architectes les plus créatifs et les plus influents de la dernière partie du XXᵉ siècle.

EXPERIENCE MUSIC PROJECT

Seattle, Washington, USA, 1995-2000

Planning: 1995-97. Construction: 1997-2000. Client: Experience Music Project.
Floor area: 13 006 m². Costs: $240 000 000.

One of the most surprising and ambitious of Frank O. Gehry's recent buildings, the 13 000 m² **EXPERIENCE MUSIC PROJECT** was financed largely by Microsoft co-founder Paul Allen. Built at a cost of $240 million, it became a constructive response to I. M. Pei's Rock and Roll Hall of Fame in Cleveland, Ohio (1995), although it was originally intended to house only Allen's collection of Jimi Hendrix memorabilia. Clad in aluminum and stainless steel panels, an unusual feature of the building is the use of color not typical of Gehry's work. The choice of colors is inspired by rock and roll or guitar themes: blue for the Fender, gold for Les Paul and purple for Jimi Hendrix (inspired by his song Purple Haze). Gehry adds that the red passages are a tribute to the faded old trucks rock and roll stars used to drive. One source of inspiration for the forms was the idea of a shattered 1960s Fender Stratocaster guitar, but for the most part the project consists of abstract, sculptural volumes similar to those used in the Guggenheim Bilbao. In both projects, Gehry uses computer-assisted design on a large scale, feeding images of guitars into the imaging software and morphing them almost beyond recognition. Each of the building's 21 000 panels has a unique shape and size, and is cut and bent to fit its specific location. Gehry insists on the conviviality of the design, saying "With its folds, the building is intended to be huggable, like a mother cradling a baby in her arms against the folds of her garment."

Eines der erstaunlichsten und anspruchsvollsten unter Frank O. Gehrys jüngsten Bauwerken ist das 13 000 m² umfassende **EXPERIENCE MUSIC PROJECT,** das hauptsächlich von Microsoft-Mitbegründer Paul Allen finanziert wurde. Obwohl das Gebäude ursprüglich nur Allens Sammlung von Jimi Hendrix-Memorabilien beherbergen sollte, beliefen sich die Gesamtbaukosten schließlich auf 240 Millionen Dollar; es wurde zu einer architektonischen Replik der 1995 von I. M. Pei erbauten Rock and Roll Hall of Fame in Cleveland, Ohio. Ein besonderes Merkmal dieses mit Aluminium- und Edelstahltafeln verkleideten Gebäudes ist die Verwendung von Farben, die eher untypisch für Gehrys Arbeiten ist. Die Farbwahl wurde von Themen aus dem Bereich Rock and Roll und Gitarrenmusik inspiriert: Blau steht für die Fender-Gitarre, Gold für Les Paul und Purpur für Jimi Hendrix (angeregt durch sein Lied Purple Haze). Gehry fügt hinzu, dass die rotgestrichenen Gänge ein Tribut an die alten, abgewetzten Trucks sind, in denen die Rock and Roll Stars früher gerne herumfuhren. Die Form wurde von einer zertrümmerten Fender Stratocaster E-Gitarre aus den 60er-Jahren inspiriert. Zum größten Teil setzt sich das Gebäude jedoch aus abstrakten, plastisch geformten Baukörpern zusammen, ähnlich denen, die Gehry für das Guggenheim Bilbao verwendet hat. Wie dort hat Gehry auch bei diesem Projekt mit einer CAD-Software gearbeitet. Für den Entwurf des Experience Music Project hat er Bilder von E-Gitarren in das Programm eingespeist und diese anschließend fast bis zur Unkenntlichkeit umgestaltet. Jede der 21 000 Tafeln, mit denen das Gebäude verkleidet ist, wurde individuell gefertigt und hat eine ihrem jeweiligen Platz entsprechende Form und Größe. Gehry betont die heitere Ausstrahlung des Designs und sagt: »Mit seinen Falten soll der Bau zum Umarmen einladen und an eine Mutter denken lassen, die ihr Baby auf dem Arm hält und es schützend in den Falten ihrer Kleidung birgt.«

Ce **EXPERIENCE MUSIC PROJECT** de 13 000 m² est l'une des plus surprenantes et ambitieuses réalisations récentes de Frank O. Gehry. Il a été en grande partie financé par le cofondateur de Microsoft, Paul Allen. Pour un coût de $240 millions, il est une réponse au Rock and Roll Hall of Fame de I. M. Pei à Cleveland (Ohio, 1995). A l'origine il devait simplement abriter la collection de souvenirs de Jimi Hendrix réunis par Allen. Habillé de panneaux d'aluminium et d'acier inoxydable, il se distingue par une utilisation de la couleur peu fréquente dans l'œuvre de Gehry. Le choix chromatique a été inspiré par des thèmes de guitare ou de Rock'n roll : bleu pour Fender, or pour Les Paul et pourpre pour Jimi Hendrix (inspiré de sa chanson, Purple Haze). Gehry ajoute que les passages en rouge sont un hommage aux vieux camions rouge délevé que les stars du rock avaient l'habitude de conduire. Une des sources formelles est une vieille guitare Fender Stratocaster des années 1960, mais pour l'essentiel, le projet se compose de volumes abstraits et sculpturaux similaires à ceux du Guggenheim Bilbao. Ici, Gehry a en abondamment secours à la CAO, alimentant les logiciels d'images de guitares soumises à un traitement de morphing à la limite de la reconnaissance. Le bâtiment est recouvert de 21 000 panneaux de taille et de forme différentes, chacun ayant été découpé et façonné en fonction de sou emplacement. Gehry insiste sur la convivialité de ce projet : «Avec ses plis et ses replis, le bâtiments est plein de tendresse, comme une mère berçant un bébé dans ses bras contre les plis de son vêtement. »

Although its extravagant, sculptural forms are not unfamiliar to those who know his work, Gehry's Experience Music Project makes use on a large scale of strong colors.

Während die extravaganten skulpturalen Formen des Experience Music Project den Kennern von Gehrys Arbeiten durchaus vertraut sind, setzt er hier zusätzlich eine ungewöhnlich breite Palette kräftiger Farben ein.

Si les formes sculpturales et extravagantes de l'Experience Music Project n'étonnent plus chez Gehry, le recours aux couleurs fortes à grande échelle surprend.

Though obviously not contradictory
with the ebb and flow of rock and roll,
Gehry's architecture again underlines
his position as a sculptural master,
redefining architecture at a level that
brings it closer to art.

Gehry unterstreicht mit diesem Bau-
werk, das den Rhythmus des Rock and
Roll formal umsetzt, abermals seine
Position als Meister der bildhaueri-
schen Gestaltung. Damit rückt er die
Architektur an die Grenze zur Kunst.

Dans l'esprit du rock and roll, l'intervention de Gehry met une fois encore
en valeur sa maîtrise de la sculpture
et des formes qui élève son architecture à un niveau proche de la création
artistique.

Here, as in the Guggenheim Bilbao, the surprising architectural forms of the exterior of the building are an integral part of the conception of the interior.

Ebenso wie in Gehrys Guggenheim Bilbao sind auch hier die ungewöhnlichen äußeren Bauformen ein Teil der Innenraumgestaltung.

Ici, comme pour le Guggenheim Bilbao, les suprenantes formes architecturales extérieures se retrouvent dans les volumes intérieurs.

The powerful sculptural volumes of Frank Gehry take on a life of their own in the interior, just like the music they are intended to celebrate.

Die kraftvollen skulpturalen Bau-körper, die das Innere des Gebäudes beherrschen, entwickeln ein Eigen-leben, so wie die Musik, die sie versinnbildlichen sollen.

Les puissants volumes plastiques de Frank Gehry possèdent une vie intérieure propre, de même que la musique qu'ils célèbrent.

GIGON/GUYER

Annette Gigon/ Mike Guyer Architekten
Carmenstrasse 28
8032 Zurich
Switzerland

Tel: +41 1 257 1111
Fax: +41 1 257 1110
e-mail: info@gigon-guyer.ch
Web: www.gigon-guyer.ch

Born in 1959 in Herisau, Switzerland, **ANNETTE GIGON** received her diploma from the ETH in Zurich in 1984. She worked in the office of Herzog & de Meuron in Basle (1985-88) before setting up her own practice (1987) and creating her present firm with **MIKE GUYER** in 1989. Born in 1958 in Columbus, Ohio, Mike Guyer also graduated from the ETH in 1984. He worked with Rem Koolhaas (OMA, 1984-87) and taught with Hans Kollhoff at the ETH (1987-88). Gigon/Guyer's built work includes the Kirchner Museum (Davos, 1990-92); the Vinikus Restaurant (Davos, 1990-92); a renovation of the Oskar Reinhart Collection am Römerholz (Winterthur, 1997-98), all in Switzerland. They have participated in numerous international competitions: for the Nelson-Atkins Museum extension (Kansas City, Missouri, 1999), or the Santiago de Compostela "City of Culture" project (1999). Current work includes the extension of the Aviation/Space Museum (Lucerne, Switzerland, 2000-03). The office currently employs 18 architects.

ANNETTE GIGON, geboren 1959 im schweizerischen Herisau, erwarb 1984 ihr Diplom an der Eidgenössischen Technischen Hochschule (ETH) in Zürich. Von 1985 bis 1988 arbeitete sie im Büro von Herzog & de Meuron in Basel, bevor sie 1987 ein eigenes Büro und 1989 zusammen mit **MIKE GUYER** ihre jetzige Firma gründete. Auch der 1958 in Columbus, Ohio, geborene Mike Guyer schloss 1984 sein Studium an der ETH ab. Von 1984 bis 1987 arbeitete er im Office for Metropolitan Architecture (OMA) von Rem Koolhaas und lehrte von 1987 bis 1988 zusammen mit Hans Kollhoff an der ETH Zürich. Zu den Schweizer Bauprojekten von Gigon/Guyer gehören das Kirchner-Museum in Davos (1990-92), das Restaurant Vinikus in Davos (1990-92) und die Renovierung der Sammlung Oskar Reinhart am Römerholz in Winterthur (1997-98). Darüber hinaus nahmen sie an zahlreichen internationalen Wettbewerben teil, wie dem für die Erweiterung des Nelson-Atkins Museum in Kansas City, Missouri (1999) oder dem für das »City of Culture«-Projekt in Santiago de Compostela (1999). Derzeit arbeiten sie und ihre 18 Angestellten unter anderem an einem Erweiterungsbau des Museums für Flugwesen und Raumfahrt in Luzern, der 2003 fertiggestellt werden soll.

Né en 1959 à Herisau, Suisse, **ANNETTE GIGON** est diplômée de l'ETH de Zurich (1984). Elle a travaillé dans l'agence d'Herzog & de Meuron à Bâle (1985-88) avant de créer sa propre structure (1987) et de s'associer à **MIKE GUYER** en 1989. Né en 1958 à Columbus, Ohio, celui-ci est également diplômé de l'ETH (1984). Il a travaillé auprès de Rem Koolhaas (OMA) (1984-87), et enseigné avec Hans Kollhoff à l'ETH (1987-88). Parmi leurs réalisations, toutes en Suisse : le Kirchner Museum (Davos, 1990-92) ; le restaurant Vinikus (Davos, 1990-92) ; la rénovation de la Collection Oskar Reinhart am Römerholz (Winterthur, 1997-98). Ils ont participé à de nombreux concours internationaux comme celui de l'extension du Nelson-Atkins Museum (Kansas City, Missouri, 1999), et du projet de « Cité de la culture » de Saint-Jacques de Compostelle (1999). Ils travaillent actuellement sur un projet de musée de l'aviation et de l'espace pour Lucerne (2000-03). Leur agence emploie aujourd'hui 18 architectes.

MUSEUM LINER

Appenzell, Switzerland, 1996-98

*Planning: 6/96-6/97. Construction: 7/97-8/98. Client: Stiftung Carl Liner Vater und Sohn, Appenzell
Floor area: 1 600 m². Exhibition area: 650 m². Costs: SF 6 200 000.*

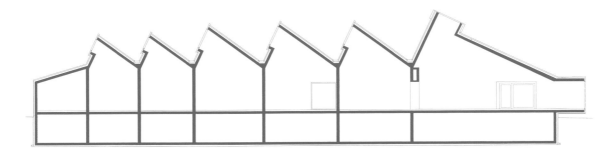

The **MUSEUM LINER** is intended to display the work of two local artists, Carl August Liner and his son Carl Walter Liner. The display areas create a rather sober impression with poured concrete floors and natural overhead lighting, supplemented when necessary by fluorescent tube lighting. There are ten rooms varying in size, forming a total exhibition area of 650 m². The structure also includes a lobby, cloakroom, lounge, screening room, two offices and storage space. Exterior cladding of the roof and walls is in sandblasted chrome steel. The sawtooth roof facilitates natural lighting, but it also echoes local industrial architecture and the surrounding mountainous countryside. Construction cost was 6.2 million Swiss francs excluding the land.

Das **MUSEUM LINER** wurde neben Wechselausstellungen für die Präsentation der Werke der beiden einheimischen Künstler Carl August Liner und seines Sohns Carl Walter Liner konzipiert. Die Ausstellungsräume mit ihren Böden aus Gussbeton und den Oberlichtern, deren natürliche Belichtung bei Bedarf durch fluoreszierende Leuchtstoffröhren ergänzt werden kann, erzeugen eine eher sachliche Atmosphäre. Zehn Räume von unterschiedlicher Größe ergeben zusammen eine Ausstellungsfläche von 650 m². Das Haus enthält außerdem ein Foyer, eine Garderobe, einen Raum für Filmvorführungen, zwei Büros und einen Lagerraum. Dach und Außenwände sind mit sandgestrahltem Chromstahl verkleidet. Das Sheddach sorgt nicht nur für eine natürliche Belichtung, sondern greift darüber hinaus die Formensprache der lokalen Industriearchitektur sowie der umliegenden Berglandschaft auf. Die Baukosten ohne Grundstück beliefen sich auf 6,2 Millionen Schweizer Franken.

Le **MUSEUM LINER** est consacré à l'œuvre de deux artistes locaux, Carl August Liner et son fils, Carl Walter Liner. Les espaces d'exposition aux sols de béton coulé éclairés par des verrières zénithales complétées en cas de nécessité par un éclairage fluorescent, donnent une impression de grande sobriété. Les dix salles offrent une surface totale de 650 m². Le bâtiment comprend par ailleurs un hall d'accueil, un vestiaire, un salon, une salle de projection, deux bureaux et un espace de stockage. Le revêtement extérieur du toit et des murs est en acier chromé sablé. Le toit en dents de scie facilite l'éclairage naturel et rappelle certaines architectures industrielles locales ainsi que l'environnement montagneux. L'ensemble a coûté 6,2 millions de SF, terrain non compris.

In line with a good deal of recent Swiss architecture, Gigon/Guyer adopt the simplest possible approach to the design of the museum, eliminating all superfluous elements.

In Anlehnung an zahlreiche Beispiele der neueren schweizerischen Architektur entschieden sich Gigon/Guyer für eine möglichst schlichte und formal reduzierte Gestaltung des Museums.

Dans l'esprit d'une tendance de l'architecture suisse récente, Gigon/Guyer ont adopté l'approche la plus simple possible et éliminé tous les éléments superflus.

The sandblasted chrome steel panels on the exterior facades are set in an irregular, overlapping pattern, giving a more organic "scaly" impression than might be expected at first. Window openings at ground level are few, but powerful in their brutal simplicity.

Die sandgestrahlten Chromstahlplatten der Außenfassaden sind überlappend in einem unregelmäßigen Muster angeordnet, wodurch der Bau eine unerwartet organische, schuppenartige Gestalt erhält. Die wenigen, durch ihre breiten Rahmungen betonten Fensteröffnungen im Erdgeschoss durchbrechen die Fassaden auf fast brutale Art.

Les panneaux en acier chromé et sablé des façades extérieures se chevauchent pour créer un effet « d'écaille » organique et inattendu. Les ouvertures au niveau du sol sont rares, mais très présentes par leur simplicité brutaliste.

ZAHA HADID

Zaha M Hadid Ltd.
Studio 9
10 Bowling Green Lane
London EC1R 0BQ
England

Tel: +44 20 7253 5147
Fax: +44 20 7251 8322
e-mail: zaha@hadid.u-net.com

Landscape Formation One ▶

ZAHA HADID, born in Baghdad in 1950, studied architecture at the Architectural Association (AA) in London, beginning in 1972, and was awarded the Diploma Prize in 1977. She then became a partner of Rem Koolhaas in the Office for Metropolitan Architecture, and taught at the AA, at Harvard, the University of Chicago, in Hamburg and at Columbia University in New York. Well-known for her paintings and drawings she has had a substantial influence, despite having built relatively few buildings. She has completed the Vitra Fire Station (Weil am Rhein, Germany, 1990-94) and exhibition designs such as that for "The Great Utopia," Solomon R. Guggenheim Museum, New York (1992). Significant competition entries include her design for the Cardiff Bay Opera House (Wales, 1994-96), the Habitable Bridge (London, 1996), and the Luxembourg Philharmonic Hall (1997).

ZAHA HADID, 1950 in Bagdad geboren, studierte ab 1972 an der Architectural Association (AA) in London und erhielt 1977 den Diploma Prize. Danach wurde sie Partnerin von Rem Koolhaas im Office for Metropolitan Architecture (OMA) und lehrte an der AA und in Harvard, der University of Chicago, in Hamburg und an der Columbia University in New York. Hadid ist durch ihre Gemälde und Zeichnungen bekannt geworden. Obwohl nur wenige ihrer Entwürfe realisiert wurden, so das Vitra-Feuerwehrhaus in Weil am Rhein (1990-94), hat sie großen Einfluß ausgeübt. 1992 entwarf sie das Ausstellungsdesign für »The Great Utopia« im New Yorker Guggenheim Museum. Zu ihren bedeutendsten Wettbewerbsbeiträgen gehören Entwürfe für das Cardiff Bay Opera House in Wales (1994-96), für die Habitable Bridge in London (1996) und die Luxemburger Philharmonie (1997).

Née en 1950 à Bagdad, **ZAHA HADID** a étudié l'architecture à l'Architectural Association (AA) de Londres de 1972 à 1977, date à laquelle elle obtient le Prix du diplôme. Elle est ensuite associée dans l'agence de Rem Koolhaas, Office for Metropolitan Architecture, et enseigne à l'AA, Harvard, University of Chicago, Columbia University, New York, et à l'Université de Hambourg. Elle est connue pour ses peintures et ses dessins. Bien que n'ayant pas beaucoup construit, elle exerce une réelle influence. Parmi ses réalisations : le poste d'incendie de Vitra (Weil-am-Rhein, Allemagne, 1990-94) et des projets d'expositions comme « La Grande utopie », Solomon R. Guggenheim Museum, New York, 1992. Elle a participé à des concours dont les plus importants sont le projet de la Cardiff Bay Opera House (Pays-de-Galles, 1994-96), le Pont habitable (Londres, 1996) et la Salle de concerts philharmoniques de Luxembourg (1997).

LANDSCAPE FORMATION ONE

Weil am Rhein, Germany, 1996-99

Planning: 12/96-12/97. Construction: 1/98-1/99. Floor area: 845 m². Costs: DM 3 200 000
Client: Landesgartenschau Weil am Rhein 1999 GmbH by order of the city Weil am Rhein.

Above right: As though emerging from the landscape itself, the structure's dynamic lines correspond very closely to the architectural drawings for which Zaha Hadid has become famous.

Oben rechts: Mit seinen dynamischen Umrisslinien wirkt der Bau, als sei er aus der Landschaft selbst hervorgegangen und erinnert damit stark an die Architekturzeichnungen, für die Zaha Hadid berühmt wurde.

En haut à droite : Semblant émerger du sol, les lignes dynamiques de la construction sont très proches des dessins architecturaux qui ont fait la célébrité de Zaha Hadid.

Built for the 1999 horticulture show hosted by Weil am Rhein, **LANDSCAPE FORMATION ONE** (in colaboration with Schumacher, mayer bährle) was conceived as a series of paths that integrate themselves directly into the surrounding gardens. Located in close proximity to the Vitra factories, which were built by such renowned architects as Frank O. Gehry, Tadao Ando, Álvaro Siza and Zaha Hadid, the 845-m² building includes a restaurant, offices and an exhibition space. Constructed of three distinct concrete strands, the building is inserted with remarkable sensitivity into its site so as to maximize its temperature stability both in winter and in summer. With its terraces and walkways, the building is not such an alien presence as its complex design might have implied, and as Zaha Hadid's reputation might have led some to expect. Rather it blends gently into the landscape and fulfills its assigned role admirably well.

LANDSCAPE FORMATION ONE wurde (in Zusammenarbeit mit Schumacher, mayer bährle) für die 1999 in Weil am Rhein eröffnete Landesgartenschau als eine Serie von Wegen und Räumen entworfen, die sich unmittelbar in die umgebende Gartenanlage eingliedern. In der Nähe der Vitra Fabrikgebäude gelegen, die von Architekten wie Frank O. Gehry, Tadao Ando, Álvaro Siza und Zaha Hadid gestaltet wurden, beherbergt der 845 m² große Komplex ein Restaurant, Büroräume und einen Ausstellungsraum. Er wurde aus drei scharf konturierten Betonelementen konstruiert und so sensibel in seine Umgebung eingepasst, dass sowohl im Winter wie auch im Sommer eine optimale Temperaturstabilität gewahrt bleibt. Mit seinen Terrassen und Gehwegen wirkt der Bau keineswegs so fremdartig, wie man es aufgrund des komplexen Entwurfs und bei Zaha Hadids Ruf für extreme Architektur vielleicht hätte erwarten können. Vielmehr fügt es sich sanft in die umgebende Landschaft ein und erfüllt damit seine Funktion auf bewundernswert gelungene Weise.

Édifiée pour une exposition sur le jardin qui s'est tenue à Weil-am-Rhein en 1999, **LANDSCAPE FORMATION ONE** (en collaboration avec Schumacher, mayer bährle) consiste en une série de cheminements qui viennent s'intégrer aux jardins voisins. Situé non loin du complexe Vitra, édifié par des architectes comme Frank O. Gehry, Tadao Ando, Álvaro Siza et Zaha Hadid, le bâtiment de 845 m² comprend un restaurant, des bureaux et un espace d'exposition. Construit en trois parties distinctes, il s'inscrit de manière remarquablement sensible dans son site au point de réguler la stabilité de sa température en été comme en hiver. Avec ses terrasses et ses allées, il ne semble pas aussi étrange que sa conception complexe pourrait le laisser supposer compté tenu de la réputation de Zaha Hadid. Il se fond délicatement dans le paysage et rempli admirablement le rôle qui lui a été assigné.

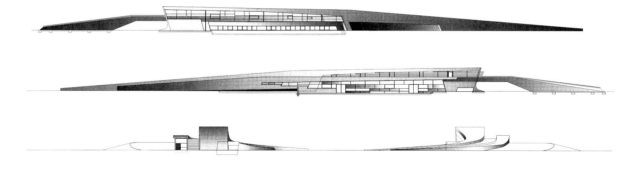

Characterized by an extended horizontality, the structure gives an even stronger impression of movement at night than during the day.

Der durch seine strenge Horizontalität gekennzeichnete Komplex wirkt bei Nacht noch dynamischer als bei Tag.

Caractérisé par son horizontalité dilatée, le bâtiment donne une impression de mouvement encore plus forte la nuit que le jour.

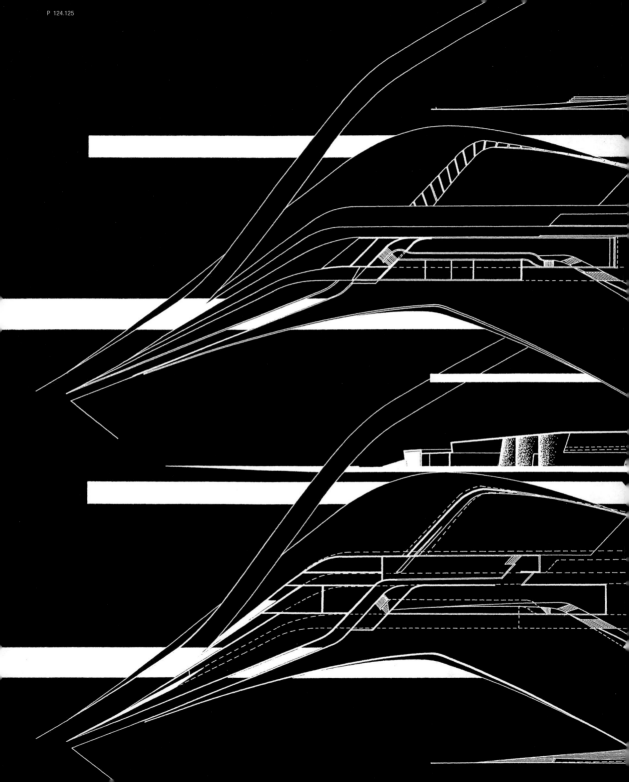

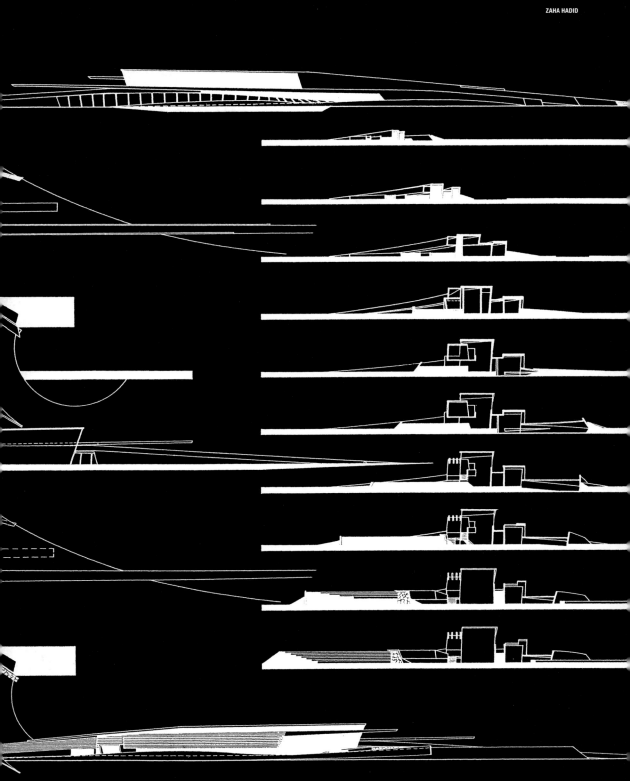

HIROSHI HARA Φ

Hiroshi Hara + Atelier
10-3 Hachiyama-cho
Shibuya-ku, Tokyo 150-0035
Japan

Tel: +81 3 3464 8670
Fax: +81 3 3464 8612
e-mail: atelier-phi@mvg.biglobe.ne.jp

Ito House ▶

Born in Kawasaki, Japan, in 1936, **HIROSHI HARA** received his B.A. from the University of Tokyo (1959), his M.A. in 1961 and his Ph.D. from the same institution in 1964, before becoming an associate professor in the university's Faculty of Architecture. Though his first work dates from the early 1960s, he began his collaboration with Atelier Φ in 1970. Notable structures include numerous private houses, such as his own residence, Hara House (Machida, Tokyo, 1973-74). He participated in the 1982 International Competition for the Parc de la Villette, Paris, and built the Yamato International Building (Ota-ku, Tokyo, 1985-86), the Ida City Museum (Nagano, 1986-88), and the Sotetsu Culture Center (Yokohama, Kanagawa, 1988-90). His recent work includes the Umeda Sky Building (Kita-ku, Osaka, 1988-93), and the JR Kyoto Railway Station (Sakyo-ku, Kyoto, 1991-97).

HIROSHI HARA, geboren 1936 in Kawasaki, erwarb 1959 den Bachelor of Arts, 1961 den Master of Arts und 1964 den Doktorgrad an der Universität Tokio, wo er zum außerordentlichen Professor an der dortigen Architekturfakultät berufen wurde. Obwohl sein erster Bau aus den frühen 60er-Jahren datiert, begann seine Zusammenarbeit mit Atelier Φ erst 1970. Zu Haras Bauten zählen zahlreiche Wohnhäuser, so sein eigenes Haus, Haus Hara in Machida, Tokio (1973-74). 1982 nahm Hara am internationalen Wettbewerb für den Parc de la Villette in Paris teil. Weitere von Hara ausgeführte Bauten sind das Yamato International Building in Ota-ku, Tokio (1985-86), das Ida City Museum in Nagano (1986-88) und das Sotetsu-Kulturzentrum in Yokohama, Kanagawa (1988-90). Zu seinen jüngeren Arbeiten gehören das Umeda Sky Building in Kitaku, Osaka (1988-93) und der Bahnhof der Japan Railway (JR) in Sakyo-ku, Kioto (1991-97).

Né à Kawasaki, Japon, en 1936, **HIROSHI HARA** est Bachelor of Arts de l'Université de Tokyo (1959), Master of Arts (1961) et docteur de cette même université (1964) avant de devenir professeur associé de la faculté d'architecture. Ses premières œuvres datent du début des années 1960, mais il n'entame sa collaboration avec l'atelier Φ qu'en 1970. Parmi ses réalisations notoires : de nombreuses résidences privées, dont la sienne, Hara House (Machida, Tokyo, 1973-74). Il participe en 1982 au concours international pour le Parc de la Villette, construit le Yamamoto International Building (Ota-ku, Tokyo, 1985-86), le musée municipal d'Ida (Nagasaki, 1986-88) et le centre culturel Sotetsu (Yokohama, Kanagawa, 1988-90). Œuvres récentes au Japon : l'Umeda Sky Building (Kita-ku, Osaka, 1988-93) et la gare JR de Kyoto (Sakyo-ku, Kyoto, 1991-97).

ITO HOUSE

Chijiwa, Nagasaki, Japan, 1997-98

Design: 5/97-10/97. Construction: 12/97-8/98.
Floor area: 176 m² (all three buildings).

ITO HOUSE is divided into three sections, and covers a total floor area of 176 m². The "parent's" section measuring 100 m² in floor area, consists of a basement and two stories built of reinforced concrete and steel; the "children's" section, covering a floor area of 41 m², consists of two stories constructed of wood and steel. Both sections have a gray wood cladding on their upper sections. The third section, a one-story "study" covering a floor area of 35 m², is built of wood. Placed in a spectacular wooded setting, these three units stand out from the surrounding pine trees like geometric objects – upright rectangular forms for the two-story houses for parents and children, and a lower triangular shape for the study. The gray wood of the residence spaces rests upon the fully glazed ground floors set on concrete podiums, creating an unexpected visual imbalance.

Das **ITO HOUSE** ist in drei Teile gegliedert, die insgesamt eine Nutzfläche von 176 m² bieten. Der 100 m² umfassende Wohnbereich für die Eltern, der aus einem Souterrain und zwei aus Stahlbeton und Stahl erbauten Etagen besteht, sowie ein 41 m² großer Wohnbereich für die Kinder, dessen zwei Stockwerke aus Holz und Stahl konstruiert sind, haben im oberen Teil eine graue Holzverkleidung. Der dritte Teil, ein eingeschossiges Atelier, nimmt eine Fläche von 35 m² ein und besteht aus Holz. Auf einem besonders schön bewaldeten Grundstück gelegen, heben sich diese drei Gebäudeteile – hochaufgerichtete, rechteckige Formen für die zweistöckigen Gebäude der Eltern und der Kinder und der niedrigere, dreieckige Baukörper des Ateliers – wie geometrische Objekte von den Kiefern der Umgebung ab. Die graue Holzverkleidung der Wohnbereiche ruht auf vollständig verglasten Untergeschossen, die wiederum auf Betonsockeln aufliegen, wodurch ein ungewöhnliches optisches Ungleichgewicht entsteht.

La **MAISON ITO** est divisée en trois zones et totalise une surface de planchers de 176 m². La partie «parents», de 100 m², consiste en un sous-sol et deux niveaux en béton armé. La partie «enfants», de 41 m² se répartit sur deux étages en bois et acier. Leur partie haute est habillée de bois gris. La troisième zone, le «bureau», de 35 m² sur un seul niveau, est en bois. Ces trois volumes se détachent de leur environnement de pins à la manière d'objets géométriques : volumes rectangulaires des parties des parents et des enfants, volume triangulaire, moins haut, pour le bureau. Les volumes d'habitation, en bois gris, reposent sur un rez-de-chaussée entièrement vitré appuyé sur un soubassement en béton, créant ainsi un déséquilibre visuel inattendu.

Despite an extremely simple plan,
the scaling and volumetric distribution
of the Ito House give it an unusual
appearance. The essentially vertical
form echoes the pine trees, and the
mostly horizontal cladding gives the
upper cube a more stable aspect.

Die besondere Formgebung und
Raumaufteilung verleihen dem Ito
House trotz seines äußerst einfa-
chen Grundrisses ein ungewöhnliches Aussehen. Seine im Wesentlichen vertikale Form harmoniert mit
den umstehenden Kiefern, während
die weitgehend horizontal angelegte
Holzverkleidung den oberen Baukörpern Gewicht verleiht.

L'extrême simplicité du plan n'empêche pas une forme originale obte-
nue par un travail sur la distribution
des volumes et les échelles. Essentiellement verticale, la forme de la
maison rappelle celle d'un pin, tandis
que le bardage horizontal confère
poids et stabilité au cube de la partie
supérieure.

A Parents
B Children
C Study
D Planned

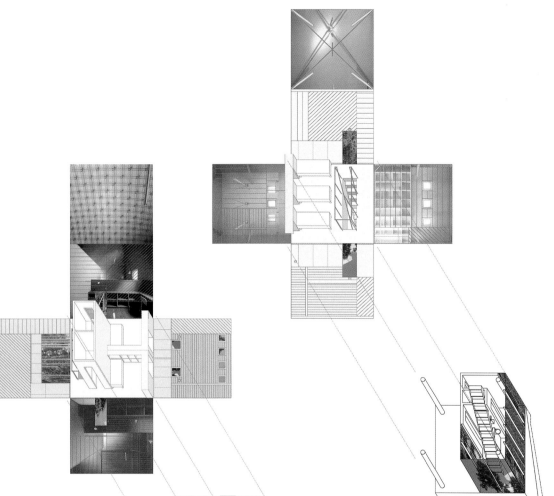

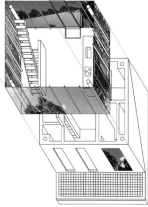

By placing the more opaque, cubic
volume above a light, glass-enclosed
lower level, the architect appears
to reverse the normal hierarchy of
stability (i. e. going upwards from
heavier to lighter materials).

Indem der Architekt den massiveren,
würfelförmigen Baukörper auf ein
rundum verglastes Untergeschoss
setzt, kehrt er die übliche Vorstellung
von Stabilität, die schwere Materialien
für unten und leichte für oben vor-
sieht, um.

En plaçant un cube opaque au-dessus
de l'étage à parois de verre, l'architecte a inversé la hiérarchie habituel-
le de la perception de la stabilité.

ZVI HECKER

Zvi Hecker Architekt
Oranienburger Strasse 41
10117 Berlin
Germany

Tel: +49 30 282 6914
Fax: +49 30 282 7322
e-mail: z.hecker@berlin.snafu.de

Palmach Museum of History ▶

Born in 1931 in Krakow, Poland, **ZVI HECKER** grew up in Samarkand and Krakow before moving to Israel in 1950. He studied architecture at Krakow Polytechnic (1949-50), the Israeli Institute of Technology (Technion), Haifa (1950-54) receiving a degree in engineering and architecture (1955). He studied painting at Avni Academy of Art, Tel Aviv (1955-57). After two years of military service in the Corps of Engineers of Israeli Army, Hecker set up private practice in 1959, working with Eldar Sharon until 1964 and Alfred Neumann until 1966. His buildings include the City Hall, (Bat-Yam, 1960-63), Club Méditerranée (Ahziv, 1961-62), Aeronautic Laboratory, Technion Campus (Haifa, 1963-66), Ramot Housing (Jerusalem, 1973, 1979-82, and 1984-86), and Spiral Apartment House (Ramat Gan, 1981-89), all in Israel. Recent projects include the Heinz Galinski School (1991-95) and the "Berliner Berge" residential neighborhood (1994) in Berlin, and the Palmach Museum of History, Tel Aviv (1992-98), published here.

ZVI HECKER, geboren 1931 im polnischen Krakau, wuchs in Samarkand und Krakau auf, bevor er 1950 nach Israel auswanderte. Von 1949 bis 1950 studierte er Architektur am Krakauer Polytechnikum und von 1950 bis 1954 am Israeli Institute of Technology (Technion) in Haifa, wo er 1955 seinen Abschluß in Ingenieurbau und Architektur machte. Anschließend studierte er bis 1957 Malerei an der Avni Academy of Art in Tel Aviv. Nach seinem zweijährigen Militärdienst im Ingenieurskorps der israelischen Armee eröffnete Hecker 1959 sein eigenes Büro, wo er bis 1964 mit Eldar Sharon und bis 1966 mit Alfred Neumann zusammenarbeitete. Zu seinen Bauten gehören das Rathaus von Bat-Yam (1960-63), der Club Méditerranée in Ahziv (1961-62), die Luftfahrtforschungsanstalt auf dem Technion-Campus in Haifa (1963-66), die Ramot-Wohnanlage in Jerusalem (1973, 1979-82 und 1984-86) sowie das Spiral-Etagenhaus in Ramat Gan (1981-89), alle in Israel. Neuere Projekten sind die Heinz Galinski-Schule (1991-95) und die Wohnhausanlage »Berliner Berge« (1994) in Berlin sowie das hier vorgestellte Palmach Museum of History in Tel Aviv.

Né en 1931 à Cracovie, Pologne, **ZVI HECKER** grandit à Samarkhande et à Cracovie avant d'émigrer en Israël en 1950. Il étudie l'architecture à l'Ecole polytechnique de Cracovie (1949-50), à l'Institut israélien de Technologie (Technion) de Haïfa (1950-54) dont il est diplômé en ingénierie et architecture. Il étudie également la peinture à l'Académie d'art Avni (Tel-Aviv, 1955-57). Après deux ans de service militaire dans le Corps des ingénieurs de l'armée israélienne, il crée son agence en 1959 et collabore avec Eldar Sharon jusqu'en 1964 ainsi qu'avec Alfred Neumann jusqu'en 1966. Parmi ses réalisations : un hôtel de ville (Bat-Yam, 1960-63), le Club Méditerranée (Ahziv, 1961-62), le laboratoire d'aéronautique (campus de Technion, Haïfa, 1963-66), les logements Ramot (Jérusalem 1973, 1979-82 et 1984-86), l'immeuble d'appartements Spiral (Ramat Gan, 1981-89). Il a récemment réalisé l'école Heinz Galinski (1991-95) et les immeubles d'habitation Berliner Berge (1994), ainsi que le Musée d'histoire Palmach (Tel Aviv) publié ici.

PALMACH MUSEUM OF HISTORY

Tel Aviv, Israel, 1992-98

Construction: 1992-98. Client: Palmach Veterans Association.
Floor area: ca. 5 100 m². Costs: ca. DM 13 500 000.

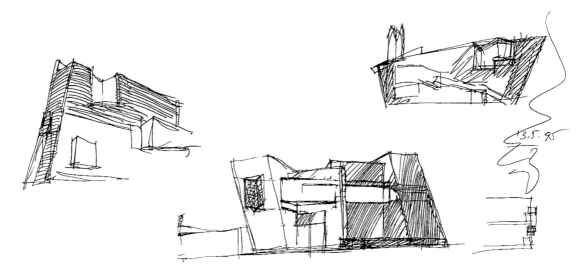

Palmach was a Jewish underground organization fighting British rule in Palestine, before being incorporated into the Israeli Defense Forces. The 5 100-m² **PALMACH MUSEUM OF HISTORY** made of bare concrete, local sandstone, and plaster houses a permanent exhibition as well as a 400-seat auditorium, a youth center, a cafeteria and offices. As the architect says, "The Museum is not a building, but rather a sequence of retaining walls, wrapped around a central courtyard and its existing trees. To preserve the natural character of the site, much of the Museum space has been designed underground. The plan of the building reflects the form of the site, as the elevation mirrors the terraced character of the landscape." Indeed, the high cost of preserving the landscape dictated that many architectural details in this complex were left intentionally rough. Hecker collaborated with the architect Rafi Segal on this project.

Palmach war eine jüdische Untergrundorganisation, die vor ihrer Eingliederung in die israelische Armee gegen die britische Mandatsherrschaft in Palästina kämpfte. Das 5 100 m² große **PALMACH MUSEUM OF HISTORY** aus nacktem Beton, örtlichem Sandstein und Gipsputz beherbergt eine ständige Ausstellung zur Geschichte der Palmach, ein Auditorium mit 400 Sitzen, ein Jugendzentrum, ein Café sowie Büroräume. Der Architekt erklärt dazu: »Das Museum ist weniger ein Gebäude als eine Abfolge von Schutzmauern, die einen zentralen Innenhof und dessen Baumbestand umschließen. Um den natürlichen Charakter des Grundstücks zu erhalten, wurde ein großer Teil der Ausstellungsfläche ins Untergeschoss verlegt. Der Grundriss des Gebäudes nimmt Bezug auf die Form des Geländes, so wie die Schrägen und die unterschiedlichen Ebenen die terrassenförmig angelegte Landschaft spiegeln.« Tatsächlich geboten die hohen Kosten der Landschaftserhaltung, viele architektonische Details dieses Gebäudes bewußt im Rohzustand zu belassen. Bei diesem Projekt arbeitete Hecker mit dem Architekten Rafi Segal zusammen.

Palmach était une organisation clandestine juive qui avait combattu les Britanniques en Palestine avant d'être incorporée aux forces de défense israéliennes. La **PALMACH MUSEUM OF HISTORY** de 5 100 m² en béton brut, grès local et plâtre enduit abrite une exposition permanente ainsi qu'un auditorium de 400 places, un centre de jeunesse, une cafétéria et des bureaux. Pour Hecker, « Le Musée n'est pas un bâtiment, mais plutôt une séquence de murs de soutènement autour d'une cour centrale plantées d'arbres existants. Pour préserver le caractère naturel du site, une grande partie des espaces muséaux est aménagée en sous-sol. Le plan reflète la forme du terrain, en particulier en section, où il suit les contours en terrasses du paysage. » Le coût élevé qu'a entraîné le respect du site explique que de nombreux détails d'exécution aient été volontairement laissés bruts. Hecker a collaboré sur ce projet avec l'architecte Rafi Segal.

Zvi Hecker has shown a capacity to create powerful, unexpected buildings, whose style has an organic relationship to both their sites and to programmatic requirements.

In diesem Entwurf zeigt sich Zvi Heckers Fähigkeit, kraftvolle, ungewöhnliche Bauten zu schaffen, die in Stil und Aufbau genau ihrem Standort und ihren inhaltlichen Anforderungen entsprechen.

Zvi Hecker a souvent montré sa capacité à créer de surprenantes architectures, dont le style plein de force reste en relation organique avec le site et fidèle au programme.

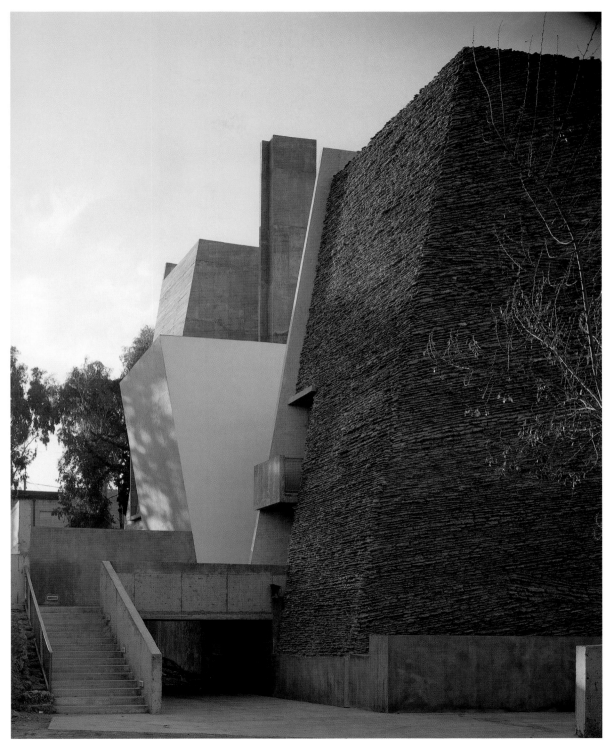

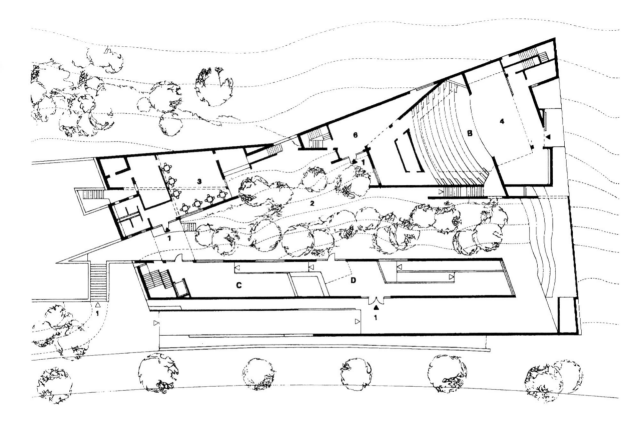

A - Exibition space
B - Auditorium
C - Administration
D - Reception

1 - Entrance
2 - Courtyard
3 - Canten
4 - Memorial space
5 - Stage
6 - Lobby
7 - Gallery

A - Ausstellungsbereich
B - Auditorium
C - Verwaltung
D - Empfang

1 - Eingang
2 - Hof
3 - Cafeteria
4 - Gedenkstätte
5 - Bühne
6 - Lobby
7 - Galerie

A - Espace d'exposition
B - Auditorium
C - Administration
D - Réception

1 - Entrée
2 - Cour intérieure
3 - Rampe
4 - Mémorial
5 - Scène
6 - Vestibule
7 - Galerie

Blending a closed, fortress-like
exterior (above) with the obvious
need for a museum to be open
to the public, Hecker laid out a
plan in the form of overlapping
triangles (left).

Links: Grundlage des Entwurfs sind
einander überschneidende Dreiecke.
Oben: Dadurch wird eine harmonische
Verbindung zwischen der geschlossenen, festungsartigen Außenfassade
und der für ein Museum notwendigen
Offenheit geschaffen.

Combinant une forme fermée de
forteresse aux besoins d'ouverture
d'un musée (ci-dessus), Hecker a
imaginé un plan composé de triangles
imbriqués (à gauche).

HERZOG & DE MEURON

Herzog & de Meuron
Rheinschanze 6
4056 Basel
Switzerland

Tel: +41 61 385 5757
Fax: +41 61 385 5758
e-mail: info@herzogdemeuron.ch

JACQUES HERZOG and **PIERRE DE MEURON** were both born in Basel in 1950. They received degrees in architecture from the ETH Zurich in 1975 and founded their firm Herzog & de Meuron in Basel in 1978. **HARRY GUGGER** was born in Grezenbach, Switzerland in 1956, he studied at ETH Zurich and Columbia University, New York (1984-89) and received his degree in architecture from the ETH Zurich in 1989. He is a partner since 1991. **CHRISTINE BINSWANGER** was born in Kreuzlingen, Switzerland in 1964. She studied at the ETH Zurich (1984-90) and received her degree in 1990. She is a partner since 1994. Their built work includes the Antipoles I Student Housing at the Université de Bourgogne (Dijon, 1991-92) and the Ricola Europe Factory and Storage Building (Mulhouse, 1993), both in France, the Sammlung Goetz building (Munich, 1989-92), the Museum Küppersmühle/Sammlung Grothe (Duisburg, Germany, 1997-99), and the Kramlich Residence and Media Collection (Oakville, Napa Valley, California, 1999-2002). Most notably they were chosen early in 1995 to design the new Tate Modern gallery in London, situated in the Bankside Power Station on the Thames, opposite St. Paul's Cathedral, which opened in May 2000. They were also shortlisted in the competition for the new design of the Museum of Modern Art in New York (1997).

JACQUES HERZOG und **PIERRE DE MEURON** wurden beide 1950 in Basel geboren. Sie studierten an der ETH in Zürich, wo sie 1975 ihr Diplom machten. 1978 gründeten sie ihre Firma Herzog & de Meuron in Basel. **HARRY GUGGER** wurde 1956 in Grezenbach, Schweiz geboren. Er studierte an der ETH, Zürich und an der Columbia University, New York (1984-89) und erhielt sein Diplom von der ETH 1989. Seit 1991 ist er Partner. **CHRISTINE BINSWANGER** wurde 1964 in Kreuzlingen, Schweiz geboren. Sie studierte ebenfalls an der ETH (1984-90), wo sie 1990 ihr Diplom ablegte. Sie ist seit 1994 Partner. Zu ihren Bauten gehören das Studentenwohnheim Antipodes I der Université de Bourgogne in Dijon (1991-92), das Fabrik- und Lagergebäude der Firma Ricola Europe in Mühlhausen (1993), die Galerie der Sammlung Goetz in München (1989-92), das Museum Küppersmühle/Sammlung Grothe in Duisburg (1997-99) und die Kramlich Residenz und Media Sammlung in Oakville, Napa Valley, Kalifornien (1999-2002). 1995 erhielten sie ihren bedeutendsten Auftrag: die Tate Modern Gallery, die im Mai 2000 in der umgebauten Bankside Power Station an der Themse, gegenüber St. Paul's Cathedral, eröffnet wurde. Beim Wettbewerb für die Umgestaltung des Museums of Modern Art in New York (1997) kamen Herzog & de Meuron in die engere Wahl.

JACQUES HERZOG et **PIERRE DE MEURON**, sont tous deux nés à Bâle en 1950. Ils sont diplômés en architecture de l'ETH de Zurich (1975) et fondent leur agence, Herzog & de Meuron, à Bâle en 1978. **HARRY GUGGER**, naît à Grezenbach, Suisse en 1956, étudie à l'ETH Zurich et à la Columbia University, New York (1984-90) et est diplômé de l'ETH (1989). Depuis 1991, il est accocié. **CHRISTINE BINSWANGER** est née en 1964 à Kreuzlingen en Suisse. Elle a aussi étudié à l'ETH (1984-90) dont elle a été diplômée en 1990. Elle est associée depuis 1994. Parmi leurs réalisations: le foyer d'étudiants Antipodes I pour l'Université de Bourgogne à Dijon (1991-92), l'usine-entrepôt Ricola Europe, à Mulhouse (1993), une galerie pour une collection privée d'art contemporain, la Sammlung Goetz, à Munich (1989-92), le Musée Küppersmühle/Sammlung Grothe de Duisburg (1997-99) et la Kramlich Residence and Media Collection en Oakville, Napa Valley, Californie (1999-2002). Ils sont été sélectionnés en 1995 pour l'extension de la Tate Modern gallery de Londres, installée dans l'ancienne centrale électrique de Bankside Power Station, au bord de la Tamise, face à la cathédrale St. Paul. La Tate Modern a été inaugurée en Mai 2000. Ils comptaient parmi les architectes retenus pour le concours de la transformation du Museum of Modern Art de New York (1997).

HOUSE
Leymen, France, 1996-97

Planning: 1996. Construction: 1997. Client: Hanspeter Rudin.
Floor area: 260 m². Costs: FF 3 300 000.

This 260-m² **HOUSE**, made of pale gray exposed concrete, is placed unexpectedly on a platform resting on pilotis that makes it appear to float, despite the weight of its concrete walls. The entrance stairway made of cast concrete is set beneath the house, as if to heighten the distance between the residence and the land on which it is placed, almost precariously. In the interior, a relatively simple plan allows for unexpected spaces like the large, high bathroom. The stairway bisects the house, which consists of a kitchen and bedroom on the first level, bathroom and another bedroom on the second level, and a laundry under the eaves. Far from wanting to protect the rough concrete finish of the house, the architects have arranged for water runoffs to mark the west facade over time.

Weil dieses **HAUS** mit 260 m² Bruttogeschossfläche aus hellgrauem Sichtbeton auf eine Plattform gesetzt wurde, die auf Stützen ruht, wirkt es, als würde es trotz der Schwere seiner Betonmauern schweben. Die aus Gußbeton bestehende Eingangstreppe wurde unter das Haus verlegt, so als sollte die Distanz zwischen Wohnhaus und dem Gelände, auf dem es – beinahe unsicher – steht, noch zusätzlich betont werden. Im Inneren erlaubt ein relativ schlichter Grundriß die Gestaltung ungewöhnlicher Räume, wie etwa eines großen, hohen Badezimmers. Die Treppe teilt das Haus in zwei Hälften, die aus Küche und Schlafzimmer im ersten Obergeschoß, Badezimmer und einem weiteren Schlafzimmer im zweiten Stock und einer Waschküche unterhalb der Plattform bestehen. Die rauhen Betonoberflächen wurden bewußt ungeschützt gelassen, so dass die Westfront mit der Zeit durch die Spuren des Regenwassers markiert wird.

Cette **MAISON** de 260 m² en béton gris pâle est curieusement juchée sur une plate-forme qui repose elle-même sur des pilotis. Elle donne ainsi l'impression de flotter, malgré le poids de ses murs en béton. L'escalier d'entrée en béton brut est placé à l'arrière, comme pour accroître l'espace entre la partie résidentielle et le terrain sur lequel elle s'appuie de manière presque précaire. A l'intérieur, le plan relativement simple ne renonce pas pour autant à des volumes surprenants entre centres, une vaste salle-de-bains toute en hauteur. L'escalier sépare en deux la maison qui se compose d'une cuisine et d'une chambre au premier niveau, d'une salle-de-bains et d'une autre chambre au second et d'une buanderie sous le toit. Au lieu de vouloir protéger la surface de béton brut de la façade, les architectes ont fait en sorte que l'eau de ruissellement du toit ou des murs marque la façade ouest.

Against all expectations, the House sits above the ground, as though it had been dropped in this location by a mysterious force. Aside from this particularity, it retains relatively conventional lines, with large openings on its lower level.

Das Haus erhebt sich auf einer Plattform über dem Erdboden, wodurch es zu schweben scheint. Abgesehen von dieser Besonderheit hat es eine relativ konventionelle Form, mit großen Fensteröffnungen im unteren Stockwerk.

La maison se dresse sur son terrain, comme si elle venait d'y être déposée par quelque mystérieuse force. Elle conserve cependant une apparence conventionnelle. De grandes ouvertures ont été pratiquées au niveau du rez-de-chaussée.

Within, the house is faithful to the
architectural austerity that Herzog &
de Meuron are well known for.

Die Innenraumgestaltung zeigt die
architektonische Strenge, für die
Herzog & de Meuron bekannt sind.

L'intérieur de la maison est caractéristique de l'austérité architecturale
qui a fait la notoriété d'Herzog &
de Meuron.

TATE MODERN

London, England, 1998-2000

*Competition: 1994-95. Planning: 1995-97. Construction: 1998-5/2000. Client: Tate Gallery, London.
Total floor area: 34 000 m². Total project costs: £134 000 000. Total construction costs: £81 000 000.*

Located opposite St. Paul's Cathedral on the Thames, the Bankside Power Station was built in two phases in 1947 and 1963 by Sir Giles Gilbert Scott, who was also the inventor of the famous red English telephone box, and finally shut down in 1981 because it was polluting London too much. The Bankside Power Plant is dominated by a 99-m-high chimney, visible from much of inner London. The Tate Gallery took an option to purchase the building in 1994, and organized a competition the following year that selected Herzog & de Meuron as architects, over competitors like Tadao Ando, Rem Koolhaas, and Renzo Piano. Preserving the spectacular space of the former Turbine Hall as the entrance area, Jacques Herzog, Pierre de Meuron, Harry Gugger and Christine Binswanger have opted for an approach that conserves the rough, industrial qualities of the building, while providing 10 000 m² of state-of-the-art exhibition space, the **TATE MODERN**, on the Thames side of the building. Polished concrete and rough-cut wood alternate on the floor surfaces, and numerous viewpoints permit visitors to orient themselves vis-à-vis the Thames and the Turbine Hall. A rather harsh fluorescent lighting scheme might appear to be the only fault of this ambitious project.

Das gegenüber von St. Paul's Cathedral am Themse-Ufer gelegene Bankside-Kraftwerk wurde in zwei Phasen, 1947 und 1963, von dem Architekten Sir Giles Gilbert Scott erbaut, der auch als Schöpfer der berühmten englischenTelefonzellen bekannt geworden ist. 1981 wurde die Anlage, die von einem weithin sichtbaren, 99 m hohen Schornstein überragt wird, wegen zu hoher Emissionswerte stillgelegt. Die Tate Gallery erwarb 1994 eine Kaufoption auf das Gebäude und beauftragte ein Jahr später, nach einem internationalen Wettbewerb mit Teilnehmern wie Tadao Ando, Rem Koolhaas und Renzo Piano, Herzog & de Meuron mit der Umgestaltung des Kraftwerks zu einem Museum für moderne Kunst, der **TATE MODERN**. Jacques Herzog, Pierre de Meuron, Harry Gugger und Christine Binswanger entschieden sich für die Erhaltung des rauhen, industriellen Charakters des Bauwerks: Der spektakuläre Raum der früheren Turbinenhalle wurde als Eingangsbereich genutzt, während man den 10 000 m² umfassenden Ausstellungsbereich auf die Uferseite des Gebäudes verlegte. Für die Böden wurde abwechselnd geschliffener Beton und grob bearbeitetes Holz verwendet; zahlreiche Aussichtspunkte ermöglichen den Besuchern die Orientierung. Das eher kalt wirkende, fluoreszierende Lichtdesign könnte sich als einziger Makel dieses ehrgeizigen Projekts herausstellen.

Face à la cathédrale St. Paul de l'autre côté de la Tamise, la centrale électrique de Bankside fut édifiée en deux phases, 1947 et 1963, par Sir Giles Gilbert Scott – par ailleurs designer de la célèbre cabine téléphonique rouge britannique – puis fermée en 1981 pour pollution excessive. Elle est dominée par une cheminée de 99 m de haut, visible d'une grande partie de la capitale. La Tate Gallery prit une option d'achat en 1994, organisa un concours l'année suivante et choisit l'agence Herzog & de Meuron parmi des concurrents comme Tadao Ando, Rem Koolhaas ou Renzo Piano. En décidant de conserver le magnifique espace de l'ancien hall des turbines pour en faire le hall d'entrée, Jacques Herzog, Pierre de Meuron, Harry Gugger et Christine Binswanger ont opté pour une approche qui préserve les qualités industrielles et « brutes » du bâtiment tout en dégageant 10 000 m² d'espaces d'exposition de la **TATE MODERN** derrière la façade donnant sur la Tamise. Le béton poli et le bois brut alternent au sol et de nombreux points de vue permettent aux visiteurs de s'orienter. Un éclairage fluorescent assez brutal semble être le seul défaut de cet ambitieux projet.

Rather than the monumental Thames-side entrance that one might expect for such an institution, the architects have opted for a low, recessed entrance on the western side of the building.

Statt eines monumentalen Haupteingangs auf der Uferseite haben die Architekten einen niedrigen, in die Westwand des Gebäudes eingelassenen Zugang gewählt.

Les architectes ont préféré une entrée basse et en retrait sur la façade ouest à une entrée monumentale donnant sur la Tamise.

TATE MODERN L

Altering the austere facade of the
original structure only at some points,
such as for the glazed ground level
cafeteria (above), Herzog & de Meuron
have carried the austerity of the
exterior over into the galleries, with
their untreated wood floors (right).

Oben: Herzog & de Meuron haben die
nüchterne Fassadengestaltung des
ehemaligen Kraftwerks nur an wenigen Stellen verändert – so für die
verglaste Cafeteria im Erdgeschoss.
Rechts: In den Ausstellungsräumen
wird der schlichte und nüchterne
Eindruck in den Böden aus unbehan-
deltem Holz fortgeführt.

Ne modifiant l'austère façade originale qu'à certains endroits, comme pour
la cafétéria vitrée du rez-de-chaussée
(ci-dessus), Herzog & de Meuron ont
maintenu cette austérité dans les
salles d'exposition aux sols en bois
brut (à droite).

The most spectacular internal feature of the Tate Modern is indisputably the Turbine Hall, whose volume has been left essentially intact. The large neon-filled light boxes on the sides of the space correspond to openings where visitors can look down on the Turbine Hall from the galleries.

Das spektakulärste Element der Innenraumgestaltung der Tate Modern ist zweifellos die ehemalige Turbinenhalle, deren Ausmaße im Wesentlichen unverändert blieben. Von den großen Neon-Leuchtkästen an den Seitenwänden können die Besucher in die Halle blicken.

L'élément intérieur le plus impressionnant est le hall des turbines, dont le volume a été pratiquement laissé intact. Les vastes boîtes latérales éclairées au néon sont des balcons d'ou les visiteurs peuvent regarder le hall à partir des galeries.

STEVEN HOLL

Steven Holl Architects
435 Hudson Street, Suite 402
New York, NY 10014
United States

Tel: +1 212 989 0918
Fax: +1 212 463 9718
e-mail: mail@stevenholl.com
Web: www.stevenholl.com

STEVEN HOLL, born in 1947 in Bremerton, Washington, gained his B.Arch. at the University of Washington, Seattle (1970), and then studied in Rome and at the Architectural Association (AA) in London (1976). He began his career in California and opened his own office in New York in 1976. He taught at the University of Washington, Syracuse University, and, since 1981, at Columbia University in New York. Notable buildings: Hybrid Building (Seaside, Florida, 1984-88); Berlin AGB Library (Berlin, competition entry, 1988); Void Space/Hinged Space, Housing, Nexus World (Fukuoka, Japan, 1989-91); Stretto House (Dallas, Texas, 1989-92); Makuhari Housing (Chiba, Japan, 1992-97); Chapel of St. Ignatius, Seattle University (Seattle, Washington, 1994-97); and the Kiasma Museum of Contemporary Art (Helsinki, Finland, 1993-98). Recent work also includes the renovation and extension of the Cranbrook Institute of Science (Bloomfield Hills, Michigan) published here. Winner of the 1998 Alvar Aalto Medal, Holl is presently working on the Bellevue Art Museum, Bellevue, Washington, and the Knut Hamsun Museum, Hamarøy, Norway.

STEVEN HOLL, geboren 1947 in Bremerton, Washington, erwarb 1970 den Bachelor of Architecture der University of Washington in Seattle und studierte anschließend in Rom sowie bis 1976 an der Londoner Architectural Association. Er begann seine Karriere als Architekt in Kalifornien und eröffnete 1976 ein eigenes Büro in New York. Holl lehrte zunächst an der University of Washington und der Syracuse University und seit 1981 an der Columbia University in New York. Zu seinen Projekten gehören: das Hybrid Building in Seaside, Florida (1984-88), der Wettbewerbsbeitrag für die Amerika-Gedenkbibliothek in Berlin (1988), das Wohnungsprojekt Void Space/Hinged Space Nexus World in Fukuoka, Japan (1989-91), das Haus Stretto in Dallas, Texas (1989-92), die Wohnsiedlung Makuhari in Chiba, Japan (1992-97), die St. Ignatius-Kapelle der Seattle University in Seattle, Washington (1994-97) und das Kiasma Museum für Zeitgenössische Kunst in Helsinki, Finnland (1993-98). Zu seinen jüngsten Arbeiten gehören der hier vorgestellte Umbau und die Erweiterung des Cranbrook Institute of Science in Bloomfield Hills, Michigan. Gegenwärtig arbeitet Steven Holl, der 1998 mit der Alvar-Aalto-Medaille ausgezeichnet wurde, am Art Museum in Bellevue, Washington und am Knut-Hamsun-Museum in Hamarøy, Norwegen.

STEVEN HOLL, né en 1947 à Bremerton (Washington), Bachelor of Architecture de l'University of Washington (1970), études à Rome et à l'Architectural Association, Londres (1976). Il débute sa carrière en Californie et ouvre sa propre agence à New York, en 1976. Enseignant à l'University of Washington, à la Syracuse University, et, depuis 1981, à la Columbia University, New York. Principales réalisations : Hybrid Building (Seaside, Floride, 1984-88) ; participation au concours de la Bibliothèque AGB, Berlin (1988) ; immeuble d'habitatious Void Space/Hinged Space, Nexus World (Fukuoka, Japon,1989-91), Stretto House (Dallas, Texas, 1989-92) ; immeuble d'habitatious Makuhari (Chiba, Japon, 1992-97) ; Kiasma Musée d'art contemporain (Helsinki, Finlande, 1993-98). Parmi ses travaux récents : rénovation et extension du Cranbrook Institute of Science (Bloomfield Hills, Michigan), publié ici. Médaille Alvar Aalto en 1998, Holl travaille actuellement sur le Bellevue Art Museum (Bellevue, Washington) et sur le Knut Hamsun Museum (Hamarøy, Norvège).

CRANBROOK INSTITUTE
OF SCIENCE

Bloomfield Hills, Michigan, USA, 1996-99

Construction: 9/96-6/98 (addition), 1/98-8/99 (renovation). Client: Cranbrook Educational Community.
Floor area: 2 778 m² (addition), 5 946 m² (renovation).

Winner of the 1995 New York AIA Design Award, the **CRANBROOK INSTITUTE OF SCIENCE** includes approximately 2 800 m² of new addition and 6 000 m² renovation of the existing science museum, originally built by Eliel Saarinen. "Our aim," says the architect, "is to make the least intrusion on the architecture of the original Saarinen building while maximizing the potential for circulation and visiting experiences with the addition." The addition is intended to be free and open-ended – easily adaptable to change. Shaped roughly like a "U", the structure is composed of a steel truss frame spanned in precast concrete planks, clad in yellow Kasota stone near the entrance and concrete block to the north. The inner part of the "U" faces the similarly shaped existing museum, forming a new plaza space between the two buildings.

Mit dem **CRANBOOK INSTITUTE OF SCIENCE** gewann Steven Holl 1995 den Design Award des American Institute of Architects in New York. Das Projekt umfasst die Renovierung einer 6 000 m² großen Fläche des ursprünglich von Eliel Saarinen erbauten Wissenschaftsmuseums sowie einen neuen Anbau von ca. 2 800 m². »Unser Ziel war es«, sagt der Architekt, »so wenig wie möglich in die Architektur des Originalgebäudes von Saarinen einzugreifen und zugleich den Besucherverkehr und das Besuchserlebnis zu maximieren.« Der Anbau soll offen, erweiterbar und leicht zu verändern sein. Der fast U-förmig gestaltete Bau besteht aus einem Stahlhängewerk, das in großflächige Betonfertigteile eingespannt wurde, welche in der Nähe des Eingangs mit gelbem Kasota-Stein und auf der Nordseite mit Betonformstein verkleidet sind. Die offene Seite des »U« liegt der des ähnlich geformten Museums gegenüber, wodurch zwischen den beiden Gebäuden ein neuer Platz entsteht.

Le **CRANBROOK INSTITUTE OF SCIENCE** qui a remporté le Design Award 1995 de l'American Institute of Architecture de New York comprend la rénovation des 6 000 m² du musée des sciences existant, édifié par Eliel Saarinen, et une extension de 2 800 m². « Notre but », précise Steven Holl, « est d'intervenir le moins possible sur l'architecture originale de Saarinen tout en maximisant le potentiel de circulation et d'intérêt de la visite au moyen de l'extension. » Celle-ci, de plan libre, ne se « termine » pas, ce qui la rend facilement adaptable à une future évolution. Sa structure, qui reprend en gros le contour d'un U, se compose d'une ossature de portiques d'acier recouverte de plaques de béton préfabriquées, habillées de pierre de Kasota jaune près de l'entrée et de parpaings en béton au Nord. La partie interne de l'U fait face au musée existant, de forme similaire, ce qui crée une sorte de place publique entre les deux bâtiments.

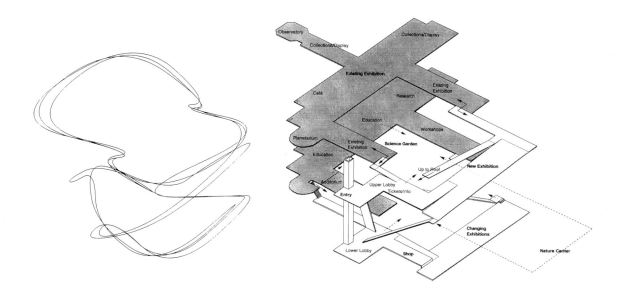

The complex articulated volumes of the Cranbrook Institute are typical of the architectural designs of Steven Holl.

Komplex gegliederte Baukörper, wie die des Cranbrook Institute of Science, sind charakteristisch für die Architekturentwürfe von Steven Holl.

La complexité de l'articulation des volumes du Cranbrook Institute est typique du style de Steven Holl.

These two views of the same stairway give an idea of Holl's handling of volumes, but also of light. Despite being relatively simple in appearance, the stairway design is quite distant from Modernist purity.

Die beiden Ansichten des Treppenaufgangs vermitteln einen Eindruck von Holls Umgang mit räumlichen Formen und Licht. Obwohl die Gestaltung relativ schlicht wirkt, ist sie weit entfernt von modernistischem Purismus.

Ces deux vues du même escalier illustrent le traitement des volumes cher Holl et son approche de la lumière. Bien que d'apparence relativement simple, son dessin est assez éloigné de la pureté moderniste.

DAVID HOVEY

Optima, Inc.
630 Vernon Avenue
Glencoe, Illinois 60022
United States

Tel: +1 847 835 8400
Fax: +1 847 835 3073

Modular Steel House ▶

Born in Wellington, New Zealand, in 1944, **DAVID HOVEY** attended the Illinois Institute of Technology (1967-70) and worked as an assistant architect in the 20th Century Art Department at The Art Institute of Chicago (1967-70), before working in the offices of A. S. Takeuchi (1971-74) and C. F. Murphy (1974-78). He created his present firm, Optima, Inc., in 1978. His work includes a number of multi-family residential developments in Evanston, Wilmette, Deerfield, and Chicago, Illinois, mixed-use developments in Glenview, Wilmette, and Highland Park, as well as single family prototype residences like the one published here. David Hovey has been Associate Professor of Architectural Design at the Illinois Institute of Technology since 1978.

DAVID HOVEY, 1944 in Wellington, Neuseeland geboren, studierte von 1967 bis 1970 am Illinois Institute of Technology und hatte während dieser Zeit eine Assistentenstelle als Architekt in der Abteilung Kunst des 20. Jahrhunderts am Art Institute of Chicago inne. Von 1971 bis 1974 war er Mitarbeiter im Büro von A. S. Takeuchi und von 1974 bis 1978 bei C. F. Murphy. 1978 gründete er sein eigenes Büro, Optima Inc. Zu seinen Bauten gehören mehrere Wohnhausanlagen in Evanston, Wilmette, Deerfield und Chicago, Illinois, Mehrzweckgebäude in Glenview, Wilmette und Highland Park sowie verschiedene Prototypen für Einfamilienhäuser wie das hier vorgestellte Modular Steel House. David Hovey ist seit 1978 als außerordentlicher Professor für Architekturdesign am Illinois Institute of Technology tätig.

Né à Wellington, Nouvelle-Zélande, en 1944, **DAVID HOVEY** suit l'enseignement de l'Illinois Institute of Technology (1967-70) et fait ses débuts comme architecte assistant au département d'art du XXe siècle de l'Art Institute de Chicago (1967-70) avant d'entrer dans l'agence de A. Soane. Takeuchi (1971-74), puis dans celle de C. F. Murphy (1974-78). Il crée son agence actuelle, Optima Inc. en 1978. Parmi ses réalisations : plusieurs programmes immobiliers à Evanston, Wilmette, Deerfield et Chicago, immeubles mixtes à Glenview, Wilmette et Highland Park ainsi que des prototypes de maisons individuelles comme celle publiée dans ces pages. David Hovey est Professeur associé de conception architecturale à l'Illinois Institute of Technology depuis 1978.

MODULAR STEEL HOUSE

Glencoe, Illinois, USA, 1998

Design and construction period: 6 months. Floor area: 790 m².

Set on a lot above Lake Michigan, the 830-m² **MODULAR STEEL HOUSE** was designed and built in a remarkably short six-month period. The architect explains that "The design integrates existing materials and systems from every industry rather than developing customized components to perform the same function. Off-site pre-fabrication of all components ensured an efficient, fast-track construction schedule and simplified the assembly of the building on this steeply sloped site." Hovey used press-formed aluminum panels made for buses as the exterior cladding, for example. Intended to evolve over time, with different elements being added or removed, this residence, the architect's own, is conceived as a laboratory for the design of modernist industrially inspired houses.

Das auf einem Grundstück oberhalb des Michigans-Sees gelegene 820 m² große **MODULAR STEEL HOUSE** wurde in der erstaunlich kurzen Zeit von sechs Monaten geplant und ausgeführt. Der Architekt erklärt, dass »die Gestaltung auf bereits bestehende Baumaterialien und -systeme aus verschiedenen Industriezweigen zurückgreift, statt für die gleiche Funktion maßgeschneiderte Teile anzufertigen. Durch die Vorfabrikation sämtlicher Bauteile wurde ein zügiger Bauzeitplan gewährleistet und die Errichtung auf diesem steil abfallenden Hanggrundstück erleichtert.« So setzte Hovey z. B. als Außenverkleidung pressgeformte Aluminiumtafeln ein, wie sie für die Karosserie von Bussen verwendet werden. Dieses für den Architekten selbst erbaute Wohnhaus soll sich durch Hinzufügen oder Entfernen verschiedener Bauteile mit der Zeit entwickeln und damit als Prototyp für die Gestaltung neuartiger, von der modernen Industriebauweise inspirierter Häuser dienen.

Sur un terrain qui domine le Lac Michigan, la **MODULAR STEEL HOUSE** de 830 m² conçue et construite dans le délai remarquablement court de six mois est la résidence personnelle de D. Hovey. Il explique que dès le départ « Le projet a pris en compte des matériaux et des procédés existants plutôt que d'avoir à imaginer des éléments spéciaux pour remplir la même fonction. La préfabrication en atelier de tous les composants a permis de respecter un calendrier de construction ultra rapide tout en simplifiant l'assemblage sur un terrain en pente raide. » Pour l'extérieur, Hovey s'est servi de panneaux d'aluminium emboutis d'habitude utilisés pour les carrosseries de bus. Prévue pour évoluer dans le temps, par l'adjonction ou la suppression d'éléments, cette résidence est en fait un laboratoire de recherche pour des maisons modernistes d'inspiration industrielle.

Although it does share a rectangular purity of outline with early Modernist houses, the Modular Steel House also has a close connection to efficient industrial architecture.

Mit seinen klaren rechteckigen Konturen erinnert das Gebäude sowohl an Häuser der frühen Moderne als auch an funktionale Industriearchitektur.

Proche de certaines compositions modernistes par la pureté des lignes, la Modular Steel House cultive un rapport étroit avec l'architecture industrielle.

0   25'

The use of pilotis combined with its
industrial vocabulary gives the house
an ephemeral or movable feeling,
and certainly does not emphasize
its residential character.

Die Verwendung von Stahlstützen und
einer industriellen Formensprache
erweckt den Eindruck von Veränderbarkeit und Mobilität, der eher
untypisch für ein Wohnhaus ist.

Le recours aux pilotis et à un vocabulaire industriel crée une impression
d'éphémère et de mobilité qui atténue
le caractère résidentiel.

ARATA ISOZAKI

Arata Isozaki & Associates
9-6-17 Akasaka, Minato-ku
Tokyo 107-0052
Japan

Tel: +81 3 3405 1526
Fax: +81 3 3475 5265

COSI ▶

Born in Oita City on the Island of Kyushu in 1931, **ARATA ISOZAKI** graduated from the Architectural Faculty of the University of Tokyo in 1954 and established Arata Isozaki & Associates in 1963, having worked in the office of Kenzo Tange before. Winner of the 1986 Royal Institute of British Architects Gold Medal, he has been a juror of major competitions such as the 1988 competition for the new Kansai International Airport. Notable buildings include: The Museum of Modern Art, Gunma (Takasaki, Japan, 1971-74), the Tsukuba Center Building (Japan, 1978-83), the Museum of Contemporary Art (Los Angeles, 1981-86), Art Tower Mito (Japan, 1986-90), Team Disney Building (near Orlando, Florida, 1990), Center of Japanese Art and Technology (Krakow, Poland, 1991-94), and B-con Plaza (Oita, Japan, 1991-95). Recent projects include the Higashi Shizuoka Plaza Cultural Complex and the Convention and Arts Center "Granship" (1993-98), both in Shizuoka, Japan, the Nara Centennial Hall (Nara, Japan, 1992-98), and the Center of Science and Industry (COSI), Columbus, Ohio, published here.

ARATA ISOZAKI, geboren 1931 in Oita auf der Insel Kyushu, beendete 1954 sein Architekturstudium an der Universität Tokio. Danach arbeitete er im Büro von Kenzo Tange und gründete 1963 Arata Isozaki & Associates. 1986 wurde er mit der Gold Medal des Royal Institute of British Architects ausgezeichnet. Er war Preisrichter in bedeutenden Wettbewerben, so 1988 bei der Ausschreibung für den Internationalen Flughafen Kansai. Zu Isozakis Bauten zählen das Gunma Prefectural Museum of Fine Arts in Takasaki (1971-74) und das Tsukuba Center Building (1978-83), beide in Japan, das Museum of Contemporary Art in Los Angeles (1981-86), der Art Tower Mito, Japan (1986-90), das Team Disney Building bei Orlando, Florida (1990), das Zentrum für japanische Kunst und Technologie in Krakau, Polen (1991-94) und die B-con Plaza in Oita, Japan (1991-95). Seine neuesten Projekte sind der Kulturkomplex Higashi Shizuoka und das Konferenz- und Kunstzentrum »Granship« (1993-98), beide im japanischen Shizuoka, die Nara Centennial Hall in Nara, Japan (1992-98) sowie das hier vorgestellte Center of Science and Industry (COSI) in Columbus, Ohio.

Né à Oita, (île de Kyushu) en 1931, **ARATA ISOZAKI** est diplômé de la faculté d'architecture de l'Université de Tokyo en 1954. Il fonde Arata Isozaki & Associates en 1963 après avoir travaillé dans l'agence de Kenzo Tange. Titulaire de la médaille d'or du Royal Institute of British Architects en 1986, il est juré dans de nombreux concours internationaux dont celui de l'aéroport international de Kansai (1988). Parmi ses réalisations les plus connues : Le Musée d'art moderne, Gunma (Takasaki, Japon, 1971-74), le Centre Tsukuba (Tsukuba, Japon, 1978-83), le Museum of Contemporary Art (Los Angeles, 1981-86), la Tour d'art Mito (Japon, 1986-90), l'immeuble Team Disney (près d'Orlando, Floride, 1990-94), B-con Plaza (Oita, Japon, 1991-95). Projets récents : le complexe culturel Higashi Shizuoka Plaza, et le Centre des Arts « Granship » (1993-98) tous deux à Shizuoka, Japon, le Hall du Siècle de Nara (Nara, Japon, 1992-98) et le Center of Science and Industry (COSI) à Columbus, Ohio, publié ici.

COSI

Columbus, Ohio, USA, 1994-99

*Planning: 4/94-1/97. Construction: 4/97-11/99. Client: State of Ohio and COSI Building
Development & Financial Resource Corporation. Floor area: 29 796 m²*

Located on a 6.87-hectares site on the west bank of the Scioto River across from the downtown area of Columbus, Ohio's 21st Century Center of Science & Industry is made up of a new westward-facing structure of 21 367 m² and a renovated eastward-facing former high school containing a further 8 361 m². The new building, very much in the spirit of Arata Isozaki's recent work, is a partial ellipse 20 m high and 293 m long. It is made of white-gray, precast concrete panels articulated by stainless steel joints. A sky-lit cubic atrium measuring 23 m on each side and a 230-seat dome theater for interactive digital presentations on astronomy, oceanography and life sciences are among the prominent features of the building, which also offers 10 219 m² of exhibition space. A "civic gathering place," the new **COSI** complex is part of a broader urban development plan for Columbus.

Ohio's 21st Century Center for Science & Industry befindet sich auf einem 6,87 ha großen Gelände am Westufer des Scioto Flusses gegenüber dem Stadtzentrum von Columbus. Es besteht aus einem neuen, nach Westen ausgerichteten Trakt mit 21 367 m² und einem renovierten, nach Osten ausgerichteten Teil mit 8 361m², der früher eine High School beherbergte. Der im Geist von Isozakis jüngsten Arbeiten gestaltete Neubau hat die Form einer Halb-Ellipse mit einer Länge von 293 m und einer Höhe von 20 m. Er besteht aus großflächigen weiß-grauen Betonfertigteilen, die durch Verfugungen aus Edelstahl gegliedert sind. Ein von oben natürlich belichtetes, auf jeder Seite 23 m messendes kubisches Atrium und ein Kuppelsaal mit 230 Sitzen für interaktive digitale Vorführungen über Astronomie, Ozeanographie und Life Sciences (Gen- und Arzneimitteltechnologie) gehören zu den hervorstechenden Merkmalen des Gebäudes, das außerdem über eine Ausstellungsfläche von 10 219 m² verfügt. Ein im neuen **COSI** eingerichteter »Versammlungsraum für die Bürger« ist Teil eines größeren Stadtentwicklungsplans für Columbus.

Situé sur une terrain de 6,87 ha sur la rive ouest de la Scioto River face au centre de Columbus, Ohio's 21st Century Center of Science & Industry se compose d'un bâtiment neuf de 21 367 m² orienté ouest, et d'un ancien collège de 8 361 m² orienté est. Le nouveau bâtiment, bien dans l'esprit des plus récentes réalisations d'Isozaki, est un segment d'ellipse de 20 m de haut et 293 de long. Il est construit en panneaux de béton moulé gris-blanc entre lesquels courent des joints d'acier inox. Un atrium cubique à éclairage zénithal de 23 m de côté et un théâtre sous coupole de 230 places, prévu pour des présentations numérisées interactives d'astronomie, d'océanographie et de sciences de la vie, font partie des points forts de ce bâtiment qui offre par ailleurs 10 219 m² d'espaces d'exposition. « Lieu de réunions publiques » le nouveau complexe **COSI** fait partie d'un vaste programme de développement urbanistique de la ville de Columbus.

Isozaki's first large-scale US commission since he designed the Los Angeles Museum of Contemporary Art (MoCA, 1981-86), COSI's shape shares the broad sweeping curves of works like the Shizuoka Convention and Arts Center "Granship" (Shizuoka, Japan, 1995-98).

COSI ist Isozakis erstes Großprojekt in den USA seit dem Los Angeles Museum of Contemporary Art (MoCA, 1981-86). Die weit geschwungenen Bogenlinien (oben rechts) lassen sich mit dem Konferenz- und Kunstzentrum »Granship« in Shizuoka Japan, 1995-98) vergleichen.

Première commande américaine importante d'Isozaki depuis le Museum of Contemporary Art de Los Angeles (1981-86), COSI (en haut à droite) rappelle les amples courbes de réalisations comme le Centre d'arts et de congrès de Shizuoka « Granship » (Japon, 1995-98).

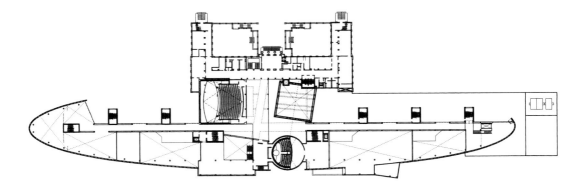

Far from his Post-Modern days, Isozaki has evolved towards the type of mega-form that is popular in many contemporary architectural circles, using computer-aided design to solve construction problems.

Im Gegensatz zu seiner postmodernen Phase neigt Isozaki inzwischen zu Mega-Formen, die heute bei vielen Architekten beliebt sind; dabei verwendet er CAD-Programme zur Lösung von Konstruktionsproblemen.

En s'éloignant de sa phase postmoderne, Isozaki a évolué vers un type de « méga-formes » apprécié de nombreux cercles architecturaux contemporains et pour lesquelles la CAO joue un rôle important.

JAKOB + MACFARLANE

Jakob + MacFarlane SARL d'Architecture
13-15, rue des Petites Écuries
75010 Paris
France

Tel: +33 1 4479 0572
Fax: +33 1 4800 9793
e-mail: jakmak@club-internet.fr

DOMINIQUE JAKOB, born in Paris in 1966, received her degree in art history at the Université de Paris 1 (1990) before obtaining her degree in architecture at the École d'Architecture Paris-Villemin (1991). She has taught at the École Spéciale d'Architecture (1998-99) and the École d'Architecture Paris-Villemin (1994-2000). Born in Christ Church, New Zealand in 1961, **BRENDAN MACFARLANE** received his B.Arch. degree at the Southern California Institute of Architecture (1984), and his M.Arch. degree at the Harvard Graduate School of Design (1990). He has taught at the Berlage Institute, Amsterdam (1996), the Bartlett School of Architecture in London (1996-98), and the École Spéciale d'Architecture in Paris (1998-99). Both Jakob and MacFarlane have worked in the office of Morphosis in Santa Monica. Their main projects include the T House, La-Garenne-Colombes, France (1994,1998), the restaurant of the Centre Georges Pompidou, Paris, published here, and the reconstruction of the Maxime Gorki Theater, Le-Petit-Quévilly, France (1999-2000).

DOMINIQUE JAKOB, 1966 in Paris geboren, schloss 1990 ihr Studium der Kunstgeschichte an der Université de Paris 1 ab und machte 1991 ihren Abschluss in Architektur an der École d'Architecture Paris-Villemin. Von 1998 bis 1999 lehrte sie an der École Spéciale d'Architecture und von 1994 bis 2000 an der École d'Architecture Paris Villemin. Der 1961 in Christ Church, Neuseeland geborene **BRENDAN MACFARLANE** erwarb 1984 seinen Bachelor of Architecture an Southern California Institute of Architecture (SCI-Arc) und 1990 seinen Master of Architecture an der Harvard Graduate School of Design (GSD). Er lehrte am Berlage-Institut in Amsterdam (1976), der Bartlett School of Architecture in London (1996-98) und an der École Spéciale d'Architecture in Paris (1998-99). Sowohl Jakob als auch MacFarlane haben im Architekturbüro Morphosis in Santa Monica gearbeitet. Zu ihren wichtigsten Projekten gehören das T-Haus im französischen La-Garenne-Colombes (1994, 1998), das hier vorgestellte Restaurant im Pariser Centre Georges Pompidou und die Neugestaltung des Maxime Gorki-Theaters in Le-Petit-Quévilly in Frankreich (1999-2000).

DOMINIQUE JAKOB, née à Paris en 1966, est diplômée d'histoire de l'art de l'Université de Paris 1 (1990) puis diplômée d'architecture de l'Ecole d'architecture de Paris-Villemin (1991). Elle a enseigné à l'Ecole Spéciale d'Architecture (1988-99) puis à l'Ecole d'architecture de Paris-Villemin (1994-2000). Né en Christ Church, Nouvelle-Zélande en 1961, **BRENDAN MACFARLANE** est Bachelor of Architecture du Southern California Institute of Architecture (1994) et Master of Architecture de l'Harvard Graduate School of Design (1990). Il a enseigné à l'Institut Berlage, Amsterdam (1996), à la Bartlett School of Architecture, Londres (1996-98) et à l'Ecole Spéciale d'Architecture de Paris (1998-99). Tous deux ont travaillé dans l'agence de Morphosis à Santa Monica. Parmi leurs principaux projets : la Maison T (La Garenne-Colombes, France, 1994-98), le restaurant du Centre Georges Pompidou (1999-2000), publiée ici, et la restructuration du Théâtre Maxime Gorki (Le Petit Quevilly, France, 1999-2000).

CENTRE GEORGES POMPIDOU RESTAURANT

Paris, France, 1998-2000

Competition: 1998. Construction: 3/99-1/2000. Client: Costes.
Floor area: 900 m² (restaurant), 450 m² (terrace). Costs: 16 000 000 FF.

Designed in conjunction with the overall renovation of the Centre by Renzo Piano and Jean-François Baudin, the **CENTRE GEORGES POMPIDOU RESTAURANT** occupies a corner with a spectacular view of Paris. The aluminum floor rises up to form four "sky grottoes" that house the kitchen, toilets, a bar and a VIP guestroom. The overall silver color scheme is broken in the interior rooms with bright red, yellow, green and orange rubber coating applied to the aluminum walls. Steel-frame tables, with battery-operated lights that make them appear to glow from within, were designed by the architects to fit into the overall grid, as were the steel and polyurethane chairs. Although the design competition was organized by the Centre before the operators of the restaurant, the well-known Costes brothers, had been selected, they were able to participate in the decision regarding the final details of the concept.

Das **CENTRE GEORGES POMPIDOU RESTAURANT**, das einen phantastischen Ausblick auf Paris bietet, wurde im Rahmen der von Renzo Piano und Jean-François Baudin durchgeführten umfassenden Renovierung des Gebäudes entworfen. Der Aluminiumboden erhebt sich zu vier Volumen, den »Himmelshöhlen«, in denen die Küche, Toiletten, eine Bar und ein VIP-Raum untergebracht sind. Die insgesamt vorherrschende silberne Farbgebung wird in den Innenräumen von hellroten, gelben, grünen und orangen Gummibelägen auf den Aluminiumwänden durchbrochen. Stahlrahmentische, die mit batteriebetriebenen Lampen von innen beleuchtet werden, und die Stühle aus Stahl und Polyurethan wurden von den Architekten entworfen. Obwohl der Designwettbewerb vom Centre Pompidou durchgeführt wurde, bevor die bekannten Costes-Brüder als Restaurantbetreiber ausgewählt waren, konnten sie sich an der Entscheidung über das endgültige Baukonzept beteiligen.

Créé dans le cadre de la rénovation d'ensemble du Centre par Renzo Piano et Jean-François Bodin, le **CENTRE GEORGES POMPIDOU RESTAURANT** occupe un angle du bâtiment, au 6ème étage, et bénéficie donc d'une vue spectaculaire sur Paris. Le sol d'aluminium semble se soulever pour former quatre « grottes » qui abritent la cuisine, les toilettes, un bar et un salon VIP. Leur intérieur revêtu de caoutchouc rouge vif, jaune, vert et orange, rompt avec la coloration générale argentée. Des tables à piétement d'acier, dotées d'un éclairage sur batterie qui leur donne l'impression de luire de l'intérieur, ont été dessinées par les architectes pour s'intégrer dans la trame générale, de même que les sièges en acier et polyuréthane. Si le concours a été organisé avant que le concessionnaire – les Frères Costes – n'ait été choisi, celui-ci a pu participer à la mise au point des détails.

P 174.175

The aluminum volumes added to the Pompidou Center's top floor house bathrooms, kitchens and a bar.

Im Restaurant im obersten Stock des Centre Pompidou sind in von Aluminium-Wänden begrenzten Volumen, die Küche, Toiletten, eine Bar und ein VIP-Raum untergebracht.

Les volumes d'aluminium du dernier étage abritent la cuisine, un bar et les toilettes.

FRANÇOISE-HÉLÈNE JOURDA

JOURDA Architectes
9-11 Passage Bullourde
75011 Paris
France

Tel: +33 1 5528 8220
Fax: +33 1 5528 8518

Mont-Cenis Academy and Municipal District Center ▶

Born in 1955, **FRANÇOISE-HÉLÈNE JOURDA** received her diploma as an architect in 1979. She has taught at the École d'architecture in Lyons, at University of Architecture in Oslo, at the University of Minnesota, and at the Technical University of Kassel, Germany. She has worked most notably on the Law Courts of Melun, France (1994), Futuroscope and Entertainment Center (Krefeld, Germany, 1996), a park and housing area with a 13 000-m² greenhouse (Potsdam, Germany, 1997), the Clinique de l'Europe (Lyons, France, 1998), and the Decathlon Store in Hanover, Germany (1999), which is serving as the French Pavilion for Expo 2000. Current work includes glass houses for the Botanical Garden Bordeaux, and the National Technical Rugby Center in Le Creusot, both in France.

FRANÇOISE-HÉLÈNE JOURDA, 1955 geboren, machte 1979 ihr Diplom in Architektur. Sie lehrte an der École d'architecture in Lyon, in Oslo, an der University of Minnesota und an der Technischen Hochschule in Kassel. Zu ihren wichtigsten Projekten gehören der Gerichtshof von Melun, Frankreich (1994), das Futuroscope and Entertainment Center in Krefeld (1996), eine Park- und Wohnhausanlage mit einem 13 000 m² großen Gewächshaus in Potsdam (1997), das Hôpital de l'Europe in Lyon (1998) und die Decathlon-Niederlassung in Hannover, die auch als Französischer Pavillon für die Expo 2000 dient. Gegenwärtig arbeitet sie am Centre Hospitalier Jean Mermoz in Lyon, am botanischen Garten in Bordeaux und am National Technical Rugby Center in Le Creusot, alle in Frankreich.

Née en 1955, **FRANÇOISE-HÉLÈNE JOURDA** est diplômée d'architecture en 1979. Elle a enseigné à l'Ecole d'architecture de Lyon, à Oslo, à l'Université du Minnesota et à l'Université Technique de Kassel, Allemagne. Elle a principalement travaillé sur les projets du Palais de Justice de Melun (1995), du Futuroscope (Poitiers), d'un Centre de loisirs (Krefeld, Allemagne, 1997), d'un parc et ensemble de logements avec une serre de 13 000 m² (Potsdam, Allemagne, 1998), sur l'Hôpital de l'Europe (Lyon, France, 1998) et le Magasin Decathlon (Hanovre, Allemagne) qui a servi de Pavillon français pour Expo 2000. Parmi ses chantiers actuels : le Centre hospitalier Jean Mermoz à Lyon, un jardin botanique à Bordeaux, et le Centre Technique National du Rugby au Creusot.

MONT-CENIS ACADEMY
AND MUNICIPAL DISTRICT CENTER

Herne, Germany, 1992-99

Competition: 1992. Planning: 1996. Completion: 8/99. Landscape: Latz, Riehl und Schulz, Kassel.
Client: EMC Mont-Cenis. Floor area: 7 100 m² (total interior: 11 700 m²).
Costs: DM 100 000 000

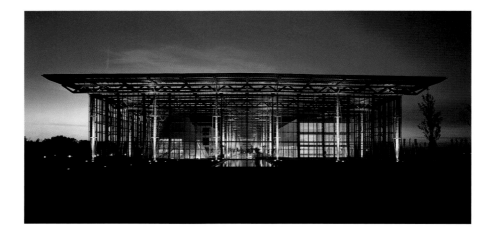

The IBA Emscher Park International Building Exhibition in Herne-Sodingen consists of roughly 100 renovation, architectural, and landscaping projects spread over an area of approximately 800 km² in the Ruhr Valley. Set in a former coal-mining area, the **MONT-CENIS ACADEMY**, originally intended as a training center for government employees, consists of a library, a social welfare center and a community center. The 168-m long building, essentially a timber "shed" with a glass skin, was designed with ecological concerns in mind by Jourda & Perraudin Architectes, Jourda Architectes, HHS Planer + Architekten BDA. The roof of the structure includes a 10 000-m² array of photovoltaic cells intended to amply cover the building's electrical needs. Methane gas released from the former mining zones is recycled to generate electricity, which can be stored in an on-site battery plant. The architect designed the wooden furniture.

Die Internationale Bauausstellung (IBA) Emscher Park in Herne-Sodingen besteht aus fast 100 über eine Fläche von ca. 800 km² im Ruhrtal verteilten Projekten der Renovierung, Architektur und Landschaftsgestaltung. Im ehemaligen Zentrum des Kohlebergbaus gelegen, umfasst der Bau die **AKADEMIE MONT-CENIS** (eine Fortbildungsakademie des Landes Nordrhein-Westfalen) und außerdem eine Bibliothek, einen Bürgersaal und ein Stadtteilbüro. Das 168 m lange Gebäude, das aussieht wie ein »Holzschuppen« mit einer Glashaut, wurde nach ökologischen Gesichtspunkten von der Architektengemeinschaft Jourda & Perraudin Architectes, Jourda Architectes, HHS Planer + Architekten BDA geplant. Das Dach des Gebäudes enthält auf einer Fläche von insgesamt 10 000 m² Photovoltaik-Zellen, die den Energiebedarf des Komplexes decken sollen. Aus den ehemaligen Bergwerksbetrieben gewonnenes Grubengas wird für die Elektrizitätsgewinnung recycelt und in einer vor Ort installierten Batteriespeicheranlage gespeichert. Die Inneneinrichtung aus Holz wurde von der Architektin entworfen.

L'Exposition internationale de la construction (IBA) de Emscher Park à Herne-Sodingen, regroupe environ 100 projets de rénovation, d'architecture et d'aménagements paysagers répartis sur un secteur de 800 km² dans la vallée de la Ruhr. Implantée dans une ancienne région minière, l'**ACADÉMIE MONT-CENIS** qui était au départ un centre de formation pour les fonctionnaires fédéraux, comprend une bibliothèque, un centre social et un centre communautaire. Le bâtiment de 168 m de long – un shed en bois à peau de verre – a été conçu par Jourda & Perraudin Architectes, Jourda Architectes, HHS Planer + Architekten BDA dans un esprit écologique. Le toit est équipé d'un réseau de 10 000 m² de cellules photovoltaïques qui devraient amplement couvrir les besoins énergétiques. Le gaz de méthane récupéré dans les anciennes mines est recyclé pour produire de l'électricité qui peut être accumulée dans une installation in situ. L'architecte a conçu le mobilier en bois.

Various architectural metaphors are used here including references to the industrial shed, or to large greenhouses. Rough wood columns, green plants and water within the confines of the building symbolize the ecological concerns of the architects.

Form und Konstruktion der Akademie erinnern an einen Industriebau oder ein Gewächshaus. Unten rechts: Im Innern symbolisieren Säulen aus roh bearbeitetem Holz, Grünpflanzen und Wasserbecken das ökologische Anliegen der Architekten.

Diverses métaphores architecturales rappellent des entrepôts industriels et des serres. En bas à droite : colonnes de bois brut, plantes vertes et présence de l'eau à l'intérieur du bâtiment reflètent les préoccupations écologiques des architectes.

*Within the shelter of the simple
outside shed, pavilions house a
hotel, the activities of the Academy,
a casino, and a municipal center.*

*Die schlichte Außenhülle umgibt
eine Reihe von Pavillons, in denen ein
Hotel, die Arbeitsräume der Akademie,
ein Casino, ein Bürgersaal und ein
Stadtteilzentrum untergebracht sind.*

*A l'abri de cette vaste serre, des
pavillons abritent un hôtel, les acti-
vités de l'académie et un centre
municipal.*

REI KAWAKUBO

Comme des Garçons Co., Ltd.
5-11-5 Minamiaoyama
Minato-ku
Tokyo
Japan

Tel.: +81 3 3407 2480
Fax.: +81 3 5485 2439

REI KAWAKUBO created the Comme des Garçons label in 1969 and established Comme des Garçons Co. Ltd. in Tokyo in 1973. She opened her Paris boutique in 1982, and one in New York one year later. Although she is best known as a fashion designer, she has long had an interest in furniture and architecture. Rei Kawakubo introduced the Comme des Garçons furniture line in 1983. The Flagship Store in Aoyama, Tokyo, which she recently redesigned with the assistance of Takao Kawasaki (interior design), Future Systems (architect/facade), Christian Astuguevieille (art director/interior) and Sophie Smallhorn (artist/interior), was first opened in 1989. Rei Kawakubo received an Honorary Doctorate from the Royal College of Art, London, in 1997. The New York boutique, published here, was designed by Rei Kawakubo with Takao Kawasaki and Future Systems.

REI KAWAKUBO schuf 1969 das Modelabel Comme des Garçons und gründete 1973 die Firma Comme des Garçons Co. Ltd. in Tokio. 1982 eröffnete sie ihre Boutique in Paris und zwei Jahre später eine in New York. Obwohl sie vor allem als Modedesignerin bekannt ist, hat sie seit langem ein großes Interesse an Inneneinrichtung und Architektur. 1983 brachte sie ihre erste Kollektion von Comme des Garçons-Möbeln heraus, 1997 wurde ihr vom Royal College of Art in London der Titel eines Ehrendoktors verliehen. Rei Kawakubo hat ihr 1989 eröffnetes Hauptgeschäft in Aoyama, Tokio, vor einem Jahr in Zusammenarbeit mit Takao Kawasaki (Inneneinrichtung), Future Systems (Fassade), Christian Astuguevieille (Artdirector/Interieur) und Sophie Smallhorn (Künstlerin/Interieur) neu gestaltet. Die ebenfalls hier vorgestellte New Yorker Boutique wurde von Rei Kawakubo zusammen mit Takao Kawasaki und Future Systems entworfen.

REI KAWAKUBO a créé la marque Comme des Garçons en 1969 et fondé Comme des Garçons Co. Ltd à Tokyo en 1973. Elle a ouvert sa boutique parisienne en 1982, puis celle de New York en 1984. Bien qu'elle soit surtout connue comme styliste de mode, elle s'intéresse depuis longtemps au design de mobilier et à l'architecture. Elle a lancé une ligne de meubles Comme des Garçons en 1983. Son magasin principal à Aoyama, Tokyo, qu'elle a récemment rénové en collaboration avec Takao Kawasaki (architecte d'intérieur), Future Systems (architecture, façade), Christian Astuguevieille (directeur artistique, aménagements intérieurs) et Sophie Smallhorn (artiste, aménagements intérieurs) avait été ouverte en 1989. Elle est docteur honoraire du Royal College of Arts de Londres (1997). La boutique new-yorkaise, également publiée ici, a été conçue par Rei Kawabuko avec Takao Kawasaki et Future Systems.

COMME DES GARÇONS
FLAGSHIP STORE

Tokyo, Japan, 1999

Planning: 1998. Construction: 1999 (one month)
Client: Comme des Garçons. Floor area: 698 m².

Set on Aoyama Street as are several other exclusive fashion boutiques, the **COMME DES GARÇONS FLAGSHIP STORE** was built under the direction of Rei Kawakubo by Takao Kawasaki (interior design), Future Systems (architect/facade), Christian Astuguevieille (art director/interior), and Sophie Smallhorn (artist/interior). The undulating glass facade, overlaid with blue circular dots, allows passersby to look in, but not enough to really capture the interior of the space. The large enameled forms of the interior partitions, designed by Kawakubo, divide the space, at the same time making it appear rather complex. Visitors discover clothes or shoes, displayed in small quantities, as they stroll through and around Kawakubo's units. Here architecture and fashion converge, and the design further contributes to setting out the intention Comme des Garçons wishes to project – an image that goes beyond clothing.

Der in der Aoyama-Straße neben mehreren anderen exklusiven Modeboutiquen gelegene Tokioter **COMME DES GARÇONS FLAGSHIP STORE** wurde unter der Leitung von Rei Kawakubo von Takao Kawasaki (Innenarchitekt), Future Systems (Architekt/Fassade), Christian Astuguevieille (Artdirector/Interieur) und Sophie Smallhorn (Künstlerin/Interieur) ausgeführt. Die wellenförmige, mit blauen, kreisrunden Tupfen bedeckte Glasfront erlaubt den Vorübergehenden, hineinzusehen, ohne dass sie jedoch das Innere konkret erkennen könnten. Die vuluminösen Formen der von Kawakubo entworfenen emaillierten Trennwände gliedern den Raum einerseits und lassen ihn gleichzeitig sehr komplex erscheinen. Während man in und zwischen diesen Einheiten umhergeht, entdeckt man die sparsam dekorierten Kleidungsstücke und Schuhe. Hier ergänzen sich Architektur und Mode, und das Design trägt zusätzlich zu dem Image bei, das Comme des Garçons vermitteln möchte: ein Image, das über den Verkauf von Bekleidung hinausgeht.

Situé rue Aoyama, comme de nombreuses boutiques de mode de luxe, le **COMME DES GARÇONS FLAGSHIP STORE** a été aménagé sous la direction de Rei Kawakubo par Takao Kawasaki (architecture intérieure), Future Systems (Architecte/façade), Christian Astuguevieille (directeur artistique/aménagements intérieurs) et Sophie Smallhorn (artiste/aménagements intérieurs). La façade en verre ondulé, plaquée de disques bleus, permet aux passants de voir l'intérieur, sans qu'il puisse en capter le volume. Les grands cocons émaillés, dessinés par Kawabuko, divisent l'espace tout en lui conférant une plus grande complexité. Les visiteurs découvrent les vêtements ou les chaussures présentés en très petit nombre, en se promenant autour d'eux. Cette convergence de la mode et de l'architecture contribue à l'image de Comme des Garçons qui va bien au delà de l'univers vestimentaire.

The undulating glass facade of Comme des Garçons' Aoyama Flagship Store was designed by the architects Future Systems, transforming a relatively innocuous modern space into a remarkable boutique.

Die wellenförmige Glasfront des Tokioter Hauptgeschäfts von Comme des Garçons wurde vom Architekturbüro Future Systems entworfen, das damit ein konventionelles Ladenlokal in eine auffallende Boutique verwandelte.

La façade ondulée en verre du magasin mère de Comme des garçons d'Aoyama a été conçue par Future Systems. Elle fait d'un volume moderne relativement anodin un lieu remarquable.

Rei Kawakubo designed the interior volumes of the shop with the assistance of architect Takao Kawasaki. Their unusual shapes give an almost labyrinthine aspect to the space.

Die Innenräume wurden von Rei Kawakubo in Zusammenarbeit mit dem Architekten Takao Kawasaki ausgeführt. Die ungewöhnlichen Formen geben dem Raum fast labyrinthischen Charakter.

Rei Kawabuko a conçu les volumes intérieurs de son magasin avec l'assistance de l'architecte Takao Kawasaki. Leur forme inhabituelle donne l'impression d'être dans un labyrinthe.

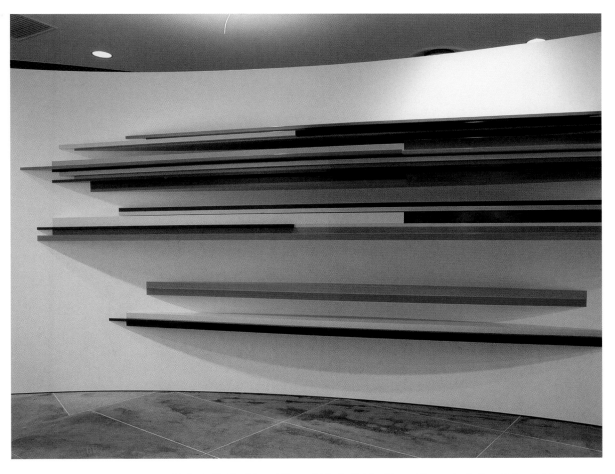

Art director Christian Astuguevieille and artist Sophie Smallhorn collaborated with Rei Kawakubo on the artistic elements of the interior.

Artdirector Christian Astuguevieille und die Künstlerin Sophie Smallhorn schufen gemeinsam mit Rei Kawakubo die Kunstwerke im Verkaufsraum.

Le directeur artistique Christian Astuguevieille et l'artiste Sophie Smallhorn ont collaboré avec Rei Kawabuko pour créer le décor intérieur du magasin.

KHRAS

KHRAS arkitekter
Teknikerbyen 7
2830 Virum
Denmark

Tel: +45 4585 4444
Fax: +45 4585 3615

e-mail: khr@khras.dk
Web: www.khras.dk

Bang & Olufsen Headquarters ▶

JAN SØNDERGAARD was born in 1947. He attended the Copenhagen Advanced College of Building Technology (1972), and the School of Architecture, Royal Academy of Fine Arts, Copenhagen (1979), and is a certified carpenter. He has been a partner of KHRAS architects since 1988. Nominated for the European Mies van der Rohe Award in both 1992 and 1994, he has designed the Danish Pavilion for Expo '92, Seville, Spain, the headquarters of Pihl & Son, Lyngby, near Copenhagen (1993-94), Denmark, an extension of the Royal Danish Embassy in Moscow (1995-97) and the headquarters for Bayer Denmark (1995-97) and Unicon Beton (1986-88), both in Copenhagen.

JAN SØNDERGAARD wurde 1947 geboren. Er ist ausgebildeter Zimmermann, studierte in Kopenhagen bis 1972 an der höheren Lehranstalt für angewandte Bautechnik und bis 1979 an der Architekturschule der Königlichen Akademie der Künste. Seit 1988 ist er Partner von KHRAS arkitekter. Zu seinen Projekten gehören der Dänische Pavillon für die Expo '92 in Sevilla, die Zentrale von Pihl & Son in Lyngby bei Kopenhagen, Dänemark (1993-94), die Erweiterung der Königlich Dänischen Botschaft in Moskau (1995-97) und die Hauptsitze von Bayer Dänemark (1995-97) und Unicon Beton (1986-88), beide in Kopenhagen. 1992 und 1994 wurde er für den Mies-van-der-Rohe-Preis der Europäischen Gemeinschaft nominiert.

Né en 1947, **JAN SØNDERGAARD** est diplômé de l'Ecole d'architecture de l'Académie Royale des Beaux-Arts de Copenhague (1979), du Collège Supérieur de Technologie de la Construction de Copenhague (1972). Il est par ailleurs charpentier diplômé. Associé de KHRAS architects depuis 1988. Cité pour le Prix européen Mies van der Rohe en 1992 et 1994, il a conçu le Pavillon danois pour Expo '92 à Séville, le siège de Pihl & Son, Lyngby, près de Copenhague Danemark (1993-94), une extension de l'Ambassade royale du Danemark à Moscou (1995-97), et le siège de Bayer Danemark (1995-97) et d'Unicon Beton (1986-88) à Copenhague.

BANG & OLUFSEN HEADQUARTERS

Struer, West Jutland, Denmark, 1996-99

*Planning and construction: 7/96-8/99. Client: Bang & Olufsen A/S.
Floor area: 5 150 m². Costs: ca. 70 000 000 DKR.*

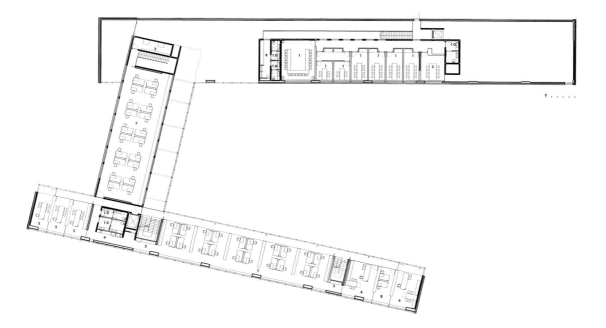

As the architect of the **BANG & OLUFSEN HEADQUARTERS** Jan Søndergaard says, "The design of the building borrows its inspiration from the typical solitary farmhouses of the area. The farm building with its courtyard forms an introverted space with the possibility of visual contact between all functions of the production." Using a simple geometric vocabulary, he nonetheless succeeds in creating a complex spatial experience. Icelandic basalt, brick, sandblasted glass, and poured-in-place concrete contrast with the light wood floors. The clients, well known for their high-quality audio equipment, wanted "a building which in its essence expressed the identity of B&O." They also demanded that the building be "unpretentious" and held within "average or normal" Danish construction cost schedules. The architects were also responsible for the furniture, lamp and sanitation designs. Natural ventilation systems improve the energy consumption of the building.

Der Architekt Jan Søndergaard beschreibt seine **BANG & OLUFSEN HEADQUARTERS** so: »Der Entwurf des Gebäudes geht auf die für diese Gegend charakteristischen Bauernhöfe zurück. Zusammen mit seinem Hof bildet ein solches Gebäude einen nach außen abgeschlossenen Raum, der den Blickkontakt zwischen allen Produktionsbereichen ermöglicht.« Trotz seiner schlichten Formensprache ist es dem Architekten gelungen, ein komplexes Raumerlebnis zu erzeugen. Isländischer Basalt, Backstein, sandgestrahltes Glas und vor Ort gegossener Beton kontrastieren mit den hellen Holzböden. Die für ihre hochwertigen Audiogeräte bekannten Auftraggeber wollten »ein Gebäude, das die Identität von B&O zum Ausdruck bringt«. Sie verlangten außerdem, das Gebäude solle »unprätentiös« sein und seine Baukosten sollten sich innerhalb eines für Dänemark »durchschnittlichen oder normalen« Rahmens bewegen. Die Architekten waren auch verantwortlich für die Entwürfe von Möbeln, Lampen und sanitären Einrichtungen. Ein natürliches Belüftungssystem sorgt für einen reduzierten Energieverbrauch des Gebäudes.

Comme l'explique l'architecte Jan Søndergaard : « Les **BANG & OLUFSEN HEADQUARTERS** s'inspire des fermes isolées typiques de la région. Le corps de bâtiment de la ferme et sa cour forment un espace introverti qui permet un contact visuel entre toutes les fonctions de production. » S'appuyant sur un vocabulaire géométrique simple, il réussit néanmoins à créer un jeu spatial complexe. Le basalte d'Islande, la brique, le verre sablé et le béton coulé sur place contrastent avec les sols en bois clair. Le client, connu pour la qualité exceptionnelle de sa production audio et vidéo, souhaitait « un bâtiment dont essence exprime l'identité de B&O, » tout en restant « sans prétention », dans le cadre des budgets « moyens ou normaux », que l'on consacre à l'architecture au Danemark. Les architectes ont également dessiné le mobilier, les luminaires et les sanitaires. Des systèmes de ventilation naturelle réduisent la consommation d'énergie.

Depending on the angles from which they are seen, the rectangular volumes of the Bang & Olufsen building take on a more or less solid (right), or weighty (left) appearance.

Je nach Blickwinkel wirken die rechteckigen Bauteile des Bang & Olufsen-Gebäudes massiv und gewichtig (rechts) oder transparent und leicht (unten).

Selon l'angle de vision, les volumes du siège de Bang & Olufsen semblent massifs (à droite) ou transparents (ci-dessous).

The placement of an office block on thin pilotis permits it to hover above the landscape, at once both solid and immaterial.

Der auf dünne Pilotis gesetzte Gebäudetrakt scheint über der Landschaft zu schweben – gleichzeitig schwerelos und erdverbunden.

L'implantation d'une aile de bureaux sur pilotis la fait flotter au-dessus du terrain, objet à la fois massif et immatériel.

Left: The spectacular overhang of the suspended office block emphasizes its incongruity in the relatively untouched landscape. Above: Within, light and views to the exterior soften the corporate atmosphere.

Links: Fast fremd wirkt dieser weit vorkragende Bauteil in der nahezu unberührten Landschaft. Oben: Einfallendes Tageslicht und Ausblicke in die Umgebung sollen die korporative Atmosphäre im Inneren mildern.

A gauche : Le spectaculaire porte-à-faux de l'aile des bureaux souligne son incongruité dans un paysage resté relativement intact. Ci-dessus : A l'intérieur, la lumière et les cadrages des vues sur l'extérieur atténuent l'atmosphère austère de ce siège social.

House in Suzaku ►

WARO KISHI

Waro Kishi + K. Associates
3F Yamashita Bldg.
10 Nishimotomachi
Koyama, Kita-ku
Kyoto 603 8113
Japan

Tel.: +81 75 492 5175
Fax: +81 75 492 5185
e-mail: warox@ja2.so-net.ne.jp

Born in Yokohama in 1950, **WARO KISHI** graduated from the Department of Electronics of Kyoto University in 1973, and from the Department of Architecture of the same institution two years later. He completed his postgraduate studies in Kyoto in 1978, and worked in the office of Masayuki Kurokawa in Tokyo from 1978 to 1981. He established Waro Kishi + K. Associates in Kyoto in 1993. In Japan he completed the Autolab Automobile Showroom (Kyoto, 1989), Kyoto-Kagaku Research Institute (Kizu-cho, Kyoto, 1990), Yunokabashi Bridge (Ashikita-cho, Kumamoto, 1991), Sonobe SD Office (Sonobe-cho, Funai-gun, Kyoto, 1993), and numerous private houses. Recent work includes his Memorial Hall (Ube, Yamaguchi, 1997), and houses in Higashi-nada (Kobe, 1997) in Suzaku (Nara, 1998) and in Bunkyo (Bunkyo-ku, Tokyo, 2000).

WARO KISHI, geboren 1950 in Yokohama, studierte an der Universität Tokio bis 1973 Elektrotechnik und bis 1975 Architektur. 1978 schloss er sein Graduierten-studium an der Universität Kioto ab und arbeitete danach bis 1981 im Büro von Masayuki Kurokawa in Tokio. 1993 gründete Kishi dort seine eigene Firma, Waro Kishi + K. Associates. In Japan hat er den Automobilsalon Autolab in Kioto (1989), das Forschungsinstitut Kioto-Kagaku in Kizu-cho (1990), die Yunokabashi-Brücke in Ashikita-cho, Kumamoto (1991), das Bürogebäude Sonobe SD in Sonobe-cho, Funai-gun, Kioto (1993) sowie zahlreiche Wohnhäuser gebaut. Zu seinen jüngsten Werken gehören die Memorial Hall in Ube, Yamaguchi (1997) und Häuser in Higashi-nada (Kobe, 1997) in Suzaka (Nara, 1998) und in Bunkyo (Bunkyo-ku, Tokio, 2000).

Né à Yokohama en 1950, **WARO KISHI** est diplômé du département d'électronique de l'Université de Kyoto en 1973, et du département d'architecture de la même institution en 1975. Il poursuit des études de spécialisation à Kyoto de 1978 à 1981. Il fonde Waro Kishi + K. Associates à Kyoto en 1993. Au Japon, il a réalisé, entre autres, le hall d'exposition automobile Autolab (Kyoto, 1989), l'Institut de Recherches Kyoto-Kagaku (Kizu-cho, Kyoto, 1990), le pont Yunokabashi (Ashikita-cho, Kumamo-to, 1991), les bureaux de Sonobe SD (Sonobe-cho, Funai-gun, Kyoto, 1993) ainsi que de nombreuses résidences privées. Parmi ses récents chantiers : le mémorial de Ube (Yamaguchi, 1997) et des maisons à Higashi-nada (Kobe, 1997) à Suzaka (Nara, 1998) et à Bunkyo (Bunkyo-ku, Tokyo, 2000).

HOUSE IN SUZAKU

Nara, Japan, 1997-98

*Completion: April 1998. Client: withheld. Floor area: 178 m². Construction: 10/97-10/98
Costs: withheld.*

Situated in a new residential area on the outskirts of Nara, the **HOUSE IN SUZAKU** is made up of two separate 9 x 5.4-m units, the one on the east containing the living room, dining room and roof garden, the one on the west housing the bedrooms and a tea ceremony room. A courtyard connects the two areas, and the whole building has a floor space of 178 m², set on a 304-m² lot. Built of reinforced concrete, the House in Suzaku displays the minimalist purity for which Waro Kishi is known, combining a modernist vocabulary with a respect for a Japanese sensibility of space and light.

Das **HAUS IN SUZAKU** Haus liegt in einem Neubaugebiet an der Peripherie von Nara und besteht aus zwei getrennten, jeweils 9 x 5,4 m großen Einheiten. Der östliche Teil enthält das Wohnzimmer, das Esszimmer und einen Dachgarten, während im westlichen die Schlafzimmer und ein Raum für die Teezeremonie untergebracht sind. Ein Hof verbindet die beiden auf einem 304 m² großen Grundstück errichteten Bereiche, die insgesamt eine Nutzfläche von 178 m² haben. In seiner Gestaltung aus Stahlbeton und der Kombination einer modernen Formensprache mit der japanischen Sensibilität im Umgang mit Raum und Licht verkörpert das Haus in Suzaku einen minimalistischen Purismus, der für Waro Kishi charakteristisch ist.

Située dans une banlieue résidentielle de Nara, la **MAISON DE SUZAKU** se compose de deux éléments de 9 x 5,4 m, celui de l'est abrite la salle-de-séjour, la salle-à-manger et le toit-terrasse aménagé en jardin, l'autre à l'ouest est consacré aux chambres et à un salon pour la cérémonie du thé. Une cour les relie. L'ensemble représente une surface de 178 m² sur une parcelle de 304 m². Construite en béton armé, cette maison illustre la pureté minimaliste à laquelle Kishi doit sa réputation : vocabulaire moderniste et respect de la sensibilité japonaise pour l'espace et la lumière.

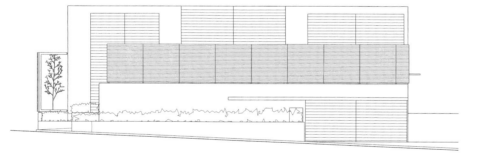

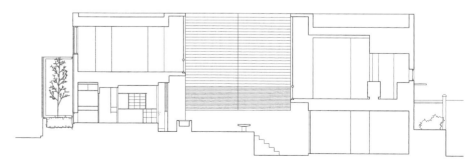

The internal courtyard is a typical feature of traditional Japanese houses, emphasizing the connection to nature that is recalled in Japanese architecture, even in dense urban areas.

Der Innenhof ist ein charakteristisches Merkmal der traditionellen japanischen Wohnhausarchitektur und schafft selbst in dicht besiedelten Stadtgebieten eine Verbindung zur Natur.

La cour intérieure est caractéristique des maisons japonaises traditionnelles. Elle illustre un lien avec la nature qu'aime maintenir l'architecture japonaise, même en zone urbaine dense.

Right: Space for the tea ceremony is laid out along essentially traditional lines, but this is in no way contradictory with the very modern design of the house itself.

Rechts: Die Gestaltung des Raums für die Teezeremonie folgt im Wesentlichen traditionellen Prinzipien, steht jedoch nicht in Widerspruch zu dem äußerst modernen Entwurf des Hauses selbst.

A droite : L'espace prévu pour la cérémonie du thé est conçu de façon traditionnelle, sans contredire pour autant la conception très actuelle de la maison.

LAMOTT ARCHITEKTEN

Lamott Architekten BDA
Silberburgstraße 129 a
70176 Stuttgart
Germany

Tel.: +49 711 481 061
Fax: +49 711 4870 291
e-mail: mail@lamott.de
web: www.lamott.de

Public Library ▶

ANSGAR LAMOTT was born in 1958 in Landau/Pfalz. He studied architecture at the University of Stuttgart (1978-85) and began to practice as an architect in 1985. A member of the architecture group Ostend 106 until 1996, he has taught at the Univeristy of Stuttgart (1994-96) and at the University College Biberach. He established his office with Caterina Lamott in 1996. **CATERINA LAMOTT** (née Karakitsou) was born in 1956 in Athens, Greece. She studied at the University of Stuttgart, obtaining her diploma as an architect in 1981. She was also a member of the Ostend 106 group until 1996. The firm's projects include an elementary school in Hardthausen-Gochsen (1997); a public library in Landau (1996-98); a sports hall in Herxheim (1999); a Catholic Church center in Völklingen/Saarland (2000); and a music school in Fellbach (2000), all in Germany.

ANSGAR LAMOTT, 1958 in Landau/Pfalz geboren, studierte von 1978 bis 1985 Architektur an der Universität Stuttgart. Bis 1996 war er Mitglied der Architekten-gruppe Ostend 106 und lehrte von 1989 bis 1992 und 1994 bis 1996 an der Universität Stuttgart und von 1994 bis 1996 am Universitätskolleg Biberach. 1996 gründete er zusammen mit seiner Frau Caterina Lamott das Architekturbüro Lamott Architekten. **CATERINA LAMOTT** (geborene Karakitsou) wurde 1956 in Athen geboren und stu-dierte wie ihr Mann an der Universität Stuttgart, wo sie 1981 ihr Architekturdiplom erwarb. Auch sie war bis 1996 Mitglied der Gruppe Ostend 106. Zu ihren gemeinsam ausgeführten Projekten gehören eine Grundschule in Hardthausen-Gochsen (1997), die Stadtbibliothek von Landau (1998), eine Sporthalle in Herxheim (1999), ein katho-lisches Gemeindezentrum in Völklingen/Saarland (2000) und eine Musikschule in Fellbach (2000).

ANSGAR LAMOTT est né en 1958 à Landau, Palatinat. Il étudie l'architecture à l'Université de Stuttgart (1978-85) et pratique dès 1985. Membre du groupe Ostend 106 jusqu'en 1996, il enseigne à l'Université de Stuttgart (1994-96) et au collège universitaire de Biberach. Il crée son agence en association avec Caterina Lamott en 1996. **CATERINA LAMOTT** (née Karakitsou) a vu le jour en 1956 à Athènes. Elle étudie à l'Université de Stuttgart dont elles est architecte diplômée en 1981. Elle est également membre du groupe Ostend 106 jusqu'en 1996. L'agence a réalisé une école primaire à Hardthausen-Gochsen (1997) ; une bibliothèque publique à Landau (1996-98) ; une salle de sport à Herxheim (1999) ; un centre paroissial catholique à Völklingen/Sarre, 2000, et une école de musique à Fellbach (2000), toutes en Allemagne.

PUBLIC LIBRARY

Landau, Germany, 1996-98

Competition: 7/92. Planning: 11/94-7/96. Construction: 8/96-2/98. Client: Karl + Edith Fix-Stiftung, Landau.
Total floor area: 1 780 m². Costs: ca. 8 000 000 DM

Built at a cost of 8 million DM, this 1 780-m² **PUBLIC LIBRARY** is housed in the former Landau slaughterhouse, originally built in 1895. Planned to accommodate a collection of some 75 000 books, CDs and periodicals, the original building was enlarged with a glass-enclosed annex, creating an obvious transition between the old and the new building. As the architects say, "The points at which the former outer wall has been perforated are rendered as wounds." The ground floor contains the entry, foyer, exhibition area and a café, the children's library and the main reading room with open stacks, connecting bridges that link the old and new spaces, the offices and meeting rooms are located above. Concerned that they were dealing with a heavy, antiquated structure originally used for a very different purpose the architects have created a thoroughly modern and convivial library.

Die 1 780 m² große, für 8 Millionen DM errichtete **STADTBIBLIOTHEK** befindet sich im ehemaligen Landauer Schlachthaus von 1895. Konzipiert für die Unterbringung eines Bestands von fast 75 000 Büchern, CD's und Zeitschriften, wurde das ursprüngliche Gebäude mit einem verglasten Anbau versehen, der alte und neue Gebäudeteile verbindet. Die Architekten erklären dazu: »Die Stellen, an denen die früheren Außenwände durchbrochen wurden, sind als Wunden kenntlich gemacht.« Im Erdgeschoss befinden sich der Eingang, ein Foyer, ein Ausstellungsbereich mit Café, die Kinderbücherei und der Hauptlesesaal mit dem Freihandmagazin sowie Laufstege, welche die alten und neuen Bereiche, die Büros und die darüberliegenden Konferenzräume miteinander verbinden. Angesichts der Tatsache, dass sie es mit einem massiven alten Baukörper zu tun hatten, der ursprünglich für einen völlig anderen Zweck konzipiert wurde, haben die Architekten eine durch und durch moderne und einladende Bibliothek geschaffen.

Construite pour un budget de DM 8 millions, cette **BIBLIOTHÈQUE PUBLIQUE** de 1 780 m² est installée dans les anciens abattoirs de Landau datant de 1895. Programmé pour 75 000 livres, CD et périodiques, le bâtiment original a été agrandi par une annexe de verre, qui différencie ainsi nettement les parties anciennes et nouvelles de l'ensemble. « Les endroits où l'ancien mur périphérique a été percé sont traités comme des blessures », explique l'architecte. Le rez-de-chaussée contient l'entrée, un hall d'accueil, une zone d'exposition et un café, l'étage abrite la bibliothèque des enfants, la salle de lecture principale à rayonnages ouverts, des passerelles qui relient les deux espaces, des bureaux et des salles de réunion. Conscient d'intervenir dans un édifice à la fois massif et ancien, conçu pour des fonctions très différents, les architectes ont réussi à créer une bibliothèque à la fois moderne et réellement conviviale.

The juxtaposition and interpenetration of old and new architectural forms is a theme in this design where industrial architecture intended for another purpose is augmented and transformed to meet new needs.

Das Nebeneinander und gegenseitige Durchdringen von alten und neuen Architekturformen bestimmt diesen Entwurf, auf dessen Grundlage ein ursprünglich als Schlachthaus genutzter Baukörper erweitert und den neuen Bedürfnissen angepasst wurde.

La juxtaposition et l'interpénétration de formes architecturales anciennes et nouvelles est un des thèmes de ce projet dans lequel l'architecture industrielle est détournée, enrichie et transformée pour répondre à de nouveaux besoins.

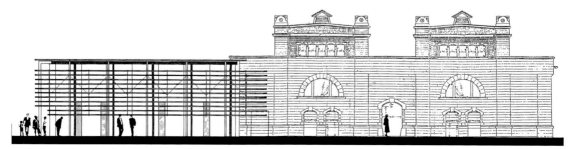

FUMIHIKO MAKI

Maki and Associates
Hillside West Building C
13-4 Hachiyama-cho
Shibuya-ku, Tokyo 150-0035
Japan

Tel: +81 3 3780 3880
Fax: +81 3 3780 3881

Born in Tokyo in 1928, **FUMIHIKO MAKI** received his B.Arch. degree from the University of Tokyo in 1952, and M.Arch. degrees from the Cranbrook Academy of Art (1953) and the Harvard Graduate School of Design (1954). He worked for Skidmore, Owings and Merrill in New York (1954-55) and Sert Jackson and Associates in Cambridge, Massachusetts (1955-58) before creating his own firm, Maki and Associates, in Tokyo in 1965. Notable buildings include Fujisawa Municipal Gymnasium (Fujisawa, Kanagawa, 1984), Spiral (Minato-ku, Tokyo, 1985), National Museum of Modern Art (Sakyo-ku, Kyoto, 1986), Tepia (Minato-ku, Tokyo, 1989), Nippon Convention Center Makuhari Messe (Chiba, 1989), Tokyo Metropolitan Gymnasium (Shibuya, Tokyo, 1990), and Center for the Arts Yerba Buena Gardens (San Francisco, California, 1993). Recent and current projects include Nippon Convention Center Makuhari Messe Phase II (Chiba, 1997) and the Hillside West buildings, part of his ongoing Hillside Terrace project, both completed in 1998, as well as the Asahi Television Headquarters & Studios (Tokyo, to be completed in 2003), and the MIT Media Laboratory (Cambridge, Massachusetts, to be completed in 2004).

FUMIHIKO MAKI, geboren 1928 in Tokio, erwarb 1952 den Bachelor of Architecture an der Universität Tokio, den Master of Architecture 1953 an der Cranbrook Academy of Art und 1954 an der Harvard Graduate School of Design (GSD). Er arbeitete in den Büros Skidmore, Owings and Merrill in New York (1954-55) und Sert Jackson and Associates in Cambridge, Massachusetts (1955-58), bevor er 1965 seine eigene Firma, Maki and Associates in Tokio gründete. Zu seinen herausragenden Bauten gehören die Städtische Sporthalle in Fujisawa, Kanagawa (1984), das Medienzentrum Spiral, Minato-ku, Tokio (1985), das Staatliche Museum für Moderne Kunst in Sakyo-ku, Kioto (1986), das Tepia-Gebäude in Minato-ku, Tokio (1989), das Nippon Convention Center Makuhari Messe in Chiba (1989), die Städtische Sporthalle in Shibuya, Tokio (1990) und das Center for the Arts Yerba Buena Gardens in San Francisco (1993). Zu seinen jüngsten Projekten gehören das Nippon Convention Center, Makuhari Messe Phase II in Chiba und die Hillside West-Gebäude als Teil seines laufenden Hillside Terrace-Projekts, beide 1998 fertiggestellt, außerdem die Asahi Television Headquarters & Studios (Tokio, geplante Fertigstellung 2003) und das Medienlabor des Massachusetts Institute of Technology (Cambridge, Massachusetts, geplante Fertigstellung 2004).

Né à Tokyo en 1928, **FUMIHIKO MAKI** est Bachelor of Architecture de l'Université de Tokyo en 1952, et Master of Architecture de la Cranbrook Academy of Art (1953) et de la Harvard Graduate School of Design (1954). Il travaille pour Skidmore, Owings and Merrill à New York (1954-55), et Sert Jackson and Associates à Cambridge, Massachusetts (1955-58), avant de créer sa propre agence, Maki and Associates, à Tokyo (1965). Parmi ses réalisations les plus connues : le gymnase municipal de Fujisawa (Fujisawa, Kanagawa, Japon,1984), Spiral (Minato-ku, Tokyo, 1985), Musée national d'art moderne (Sakyo-ku, Kyoto, 1986), Tepia (Minato-ku, Tokyo, 1989), le Centre de Congrès Nippon de Makuhari (Chiba, Japon, 1989), le gymnase métropolitain de Tokyo (Shibuya, Tokyo, 1990), le Center for the Arts Yerba Buena Gardens (San Francisco, Californie, 1993). En 1998, il achève la phase II (extension) du Centre de Congrès Nippon de Makuhari (Chiba) et les immeubles de Hillside West qui font partie de Hillside Terrace, son projet en cours ainsi que les quartiers généraux et les studios de Asahi (date prévue des travaux 2003) et le laboratoire de développement pour les médias du Massachusetts Institute of Technology (Cambridge, Massachusetts, date prévue des travaux 2004).

HILLSIDE WEST

Tokyo, Japan, 1996-98

Planning: 3/96-6/97. Completion: 11/98. Client: Asakura Real Estate.
Floor area: 2 958 m². Costs: withheld at owner's request.

A tripartite design, Hillside West includes a visible street-side element (right), a housing block and Maki's own offices, seen at the upper right of the drawing above.

Das Hillside West-Gebäude besteht aus drei Elementen: ein straßenseitig gelegener Baukörper, ein Wohnblock und rechts dahinter, in dem flachen Komplex, Makis eigenes Büro.

Projet en trois parties, Hillside West comprend un élément donnant sur la rue, un bloc d'appartements et les bureaux de l'agence de Maki (dans la partie supérieure droite du dessin).

Fumihiko Maki has been building along Old Yamate Street in the Shibuya district of Tokyo since 1967. This building complex, known as Hillside Terrace, is exemplary in its constancy, and contributes to the district's pleasant, urban atmosphere. In 1993, Maki was awarded the Third Prince of Wales Prize in Urban Design for the Hillside Terrace Complex. His most recent addition to the area, **HILLSIDE WEST,** has a total floor area of 2 958 m² and is situated down the street from the other buildings on an odd-shaped sloping lot that Maki has transformed into housing, office space (including his own) and an exhibition area. From its most visible facade on Old Yamate Street, shielded with a subtle, perforated aluminum screen, to the interior walkway leading toward his offices, this building is a testimony not only to Maki's talent as an architect, but also to his ability to evoke a civilized understanding of urban life in the midst of Tokyo's sprawling complexity.

Fumihiko Maki arbeitet schon seit 1967 an der Old Yamate Street im Tokioter Shibuya Distrikt. Der Hillside Terrace genannte Gebäudekomplex, für den Maki 1993 mit dem Third Prince of Wales Prize in Urban Design ausgezeichnet wurde, ist exemplarisch in seiner Konsistenz und trägt zu der urbanen Atmosphäre des Stadtviertels bei. Sein zuletzt hinzugefügter Teil, das **HILLSIDE WEST**-Gebäude, hat eine Gesamtnutzfläche von 2 958 m². Es wurde ein Stück entfernt von den anderen Gebäuden auf einem unregelmäßig geformten Hanggrundstück errichtet und enthält Wohnungen, Büros (darunter das des Architekten) sowie einen Ausstellungsbereich. Von der mit einem zarten Aluminiumgitter abgeschirmten sichtbaren Front an der Old Yamate Street bis zu dem Gehweg, der zu Makis Büros führt, zeugt dieses Bauwerk nicht nur von Makis Talent als Architekt, sondern ebenso von seiner Fähigkeit, inmitten des ausufernden Stadtgebietes von Tokio den Geist einer kultivierten Urbanität aufleben zu lassen.

Depuis 1967, Fumihiko Maki est responsable d'un long chantier en bordure de la vieille rue Yamate dans le quartier Shibuya de Tokyo. Cet ensemble de bâtiments, appelé Hillside Terrace, est exemplaire pour sa continuité et contribue à l'agrément urbain du quartier. En 1993, Maki a obtenu le Third Prince of Wales Prize in Urban Design pour ce projet. **HILLSIDE WEST,** sa plus récente réalisation, a une surface brute de 2 958 m². Construite dans la même rue, en contrebas des immeubles déjà achevés, elle se situe sur une parcelle en pente et de forme complexe. Maki a édifié là des logements, des bureaux (dont celui de son agence) et un espace d'exposition. Que ce soit par sa façade sur la rue protégée par un subtil écran d'aluminium perforé, ou ses allées intérieures qui conduisent aux bureaux de l'architecte, cet immeuble témoigne du talent de Maki et de sa capacité de concrétiser une demarche personelle et une certaine idee de l'urbanisme au cœur de l'envahissant désordre de Tokyo.

Right: The passageway, neither fully interior nor fully exterior, leading to Maki's offices.

Rechts: Der überdachte Durchgang zu Makis Büro changiert zwischen Innen- und Außenraum.

Le passage couvert (à droite) qui conduit aux bureaux de Maki n'est ni intérieur ni vraiment extérieur.

MARMOL RADZINER

Marmol Radziner + Associates AIA
architecture + construction
2902 Nebraska Avenue
Santa Monica, California 90404
United States

Tel.: + 1 310 264 1814
Fax: + 1 310 264 1817
Web: www.marmol-radziner.com

Restored Kaufmann House ▶

LEONARDO MARMOL, the Managing Principal of Marmol Radziner received his B.Arch. degree from Cal Poly San Luis Obispo in 1987. He has worked as the head of consulting teams on projects for the Los Angeles Unified School District and the LA Department of Airports. Aside from the restoration of the Kaufmann House, he oversaw the restoration of the Raymond Loewy House by Albert Frey, also located in Palm Springs. **RONALD RADZINER** received his M.Arch degree from the University of Colorado in 1986. He is the Design Principal of the firm, created in 1989. He is currently working on the design of the San Francisco Offices of TBWA/Chiat/Day, and the Accelerated School in South Central Los Angeles. Marmol Radziner has approximately 50 employees. Their work on the Kaufmann House earned them two AIA California Council awards for historic preservation, a National AIA Honor Award, and an Honor Award from the California Preservation Foundation.

LEONARDO MARMOL, Geschäftsführer von Marmol Radziner, erwarb 1987 seinen Bachelor of Architecture an der Cal Poly San Luis Obispo. Er war als leitender Berater für Bauprojekte der Schul- und der Flughafenverwaltung von Los Angeles tätig und beaufsichtigte die Renovierungsarbeiten am Haus Kaufmann und am Haus Raymond Loewy von Albert Frey, beide in Palm Springs. **RONALD RADZINER** machte 1986 seinen Master of Architecture an der University of Colorado und ist heute Planungschef der 1989 gegründeten Firma. Derzeit arbeitet er an der Gestaltung einer Niederlassung von TBWA/Chiat/Day in San Francisco und der Schule für Hochbegabte in South Central Los Angeles. Das Büro Marmol Radziner hat ungefähr 50 Angestellte. Für ihre Arbeit am Haus Kaufmann erhielten sie zwei Preise für die Erhaltung historisch wertvoller Bauwerke des AIA California Council, den National AIA Honor Award und den Ehrenpreis der California Preservation Foundation.

LEONARDO MARMOL, directeur de l'agence Marmol Radziner est Bachelor of Architecture de Cal Poly San Luis Obispo (1987). Il a été responsable d'équipes de consultants pour des projets du Los Angeles Unified School District et pour le département des aéroports de Los Angeles. Hormis la restauration de Kaufmann House, il a supervisé la restauration par Albert Frey de la maison de Raymond Loewy, également à Palm Springs. **RONALD RADZINER,** Master of Architecture de l'Université du Colorado (1986), dirige l'agence créée en 1989. Il travaille actuellement au projet des bureaux de San Francisco de l'agence de publicité TBWA/Chiat/Day et de l'Accelerated School de South Central Los Angeles. Marmol Radziner emploient environ 50 personnes. Leur intervention sur la Kaufmann House leur a valu deux prix du Conseil de Californie de l'AIA pour la préservation de monuments historiques, un prix d'honneur national de l'AIA et un prix d'honneur de la California Preservation Foundation.

KAUFMANN HOUSE RESTORATION

Palm Springs, California, USA, 1994-98

Planning: 1993-94. Construction: 1994-98. Client: Brent and Beth Harris.
Floor area: 474m² before restoration, 297m² after restoration.

Originally designed in 1946 by the architect Richard Neutra, the **KAUFMANN HOUSE** was built for the same client who commissioned Frank Lloyd Wright to design Falling Water. Because successive owners since its original construction had significantly modified the house, the owners decided to return it to its original state. Originally 297 m² in size, the house had been expanded to almost 474 m². The architects removed the later additions, basing the restoration on Julius Shulman's famous photographs of the house, taken in 1947. The architects decided to return the garden to the indigenous desert landscape that existed in Neutra's time. A discreet heating, ventilation and air conditioning system was added, as was a new pool house, named the Harris Pool House.

Das 1946 von dem Architekten Richard Neutra entworfene **KAUFMANN HOUSE** wurde ursprünglich für denselben Bauherrn gebaut, der Frank Lloyd Wright mit dem Bau von Falling Water beauftragt hatte. Da das Haus von den nachfolgenden Eigentümern stark verändert worden war, beschlossen die Eigentümer, es in seinen Originalzustand zurückzuversetzen. Ursprünglich 297 m² groß, war das Gebäude auf fast 474 m² erweitert worden. Bei ihrer Restauration entfernten die Architekten diese späteren Anbauten, wobei sie sich an Julius Shulmans berühmten Photographien des Hauses von 1947 orientierten. Außerdem entschieden sie sich, den Garten in jene Wüstenlandschaft zurückzuverwandeln, die das Haus zu Neutras Zeiten umgeben hatte. Neu hinzugefügt wurden eine unauffällige Heizungs-, Belüftungs- und Klimaanlage sowie ein neues Schwimmbad, Harris Pool House genannt.

Œuvre de Richard Neutra (1946), la **KAUFMANN HOUSE** avait été édifiée pour le même client éclairé qui avait commandé Falling Water à Frank Lloyd Wright. Depuis sa construction, les propriétaires successifs avaient fortement modifié la maison. Ils ont décidé de revenir à son état premier, même si la surface d'origine de 297 m² a gagné 177 m². Marmol Radziner ont supprimé certaines extensions tardives en s'appuyant sur des photos prises en 1947 par Julius Shulman. De plus, ils ont entrepris de rendre au jardin l'aspect désertique qu'il avait du temps de Neutra. Un système discret de chauffage, de ventilation et de conditionnement de l'air a été ajouté, ainsi qu'un nouveau pavillon de piscine, appelé la Harris Pool House.

As Julius Shulman's well-known 1947 photograph (below) of the house shows, the restoration (right) of the Kaufmann House has been faithful to the spirit of Neutra.

Wie Julius Shulmans bekannte Photographie des Hauses von 1947 (unten) zeigt, haben die Architekten bei ihrer Restauration (rechts) den Geist von Richard Neutras Werk bewahrt.

Comme le montre la célèbre photographie de Julius Shulman (ci-dessous) prise en 1947, la restauration de la Kaufmann House (à droite) a été fidèle a l'esprit de Neutra.

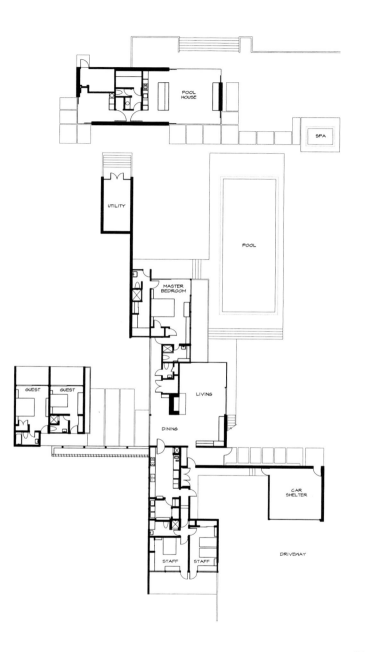

POOL
HOUSE

SPA

UTILITY

POOL

MASTER
BEDROOM

GUEST   GUEST

LIVING

DINING

CAR
SHELTER

STAFF   STAFF

DRIVEWAY

0'   10'   20'

RICHARD MEIER

Richard Meier & Partners
475 Tenth Avenue
New York, NY 10018
United States

Tel: +1 212 967 6060
Fax: +1 212 967 3207
e-mail: rmp@richardmeier.com
Web: www.richardmeier.com

Neugebauer House ▶

Born in Newark, New Jersey, in 1934, **RICHARD MEIER** received his architectural training at Cornell University, Ithaca, New York and worked in the office of Marcel Breuer (1960-63) before establishing his own practice in 1963. He won the Pritzker Prize, 1984, and the Royal Gold Medal, 1988. Notable buildings include The Atheneum (New Harmony, Indiana, 1975-79), Museum for the Decorative Arts (Frankfurt, Germany, 1979-85), High Museum of Art (Atlanta, Georgia, 1980-83), Canal+ Headquarters (Paris, France, 1988-92), City Hall and Library (The Hague, 1990-95), Barcelona Museum of Contemporary Art (1988-95), and the Getty Center (Los Angeles, California, 1984-97). Current work includes a US Courthouse and Federal Building, Phoenix, Arizona (1995-2000).

RICHARD MEIER, geboren 1934 in Newark, New Jersey, studierte Architektur an der Cornell University und arbeitete bei Marcel Breuer (1960-63), bevor er 1963 sein eigenes Büro eröffnete. Er wurde 1984 mit dem Pritzker Prize und 1988 mit der Royal Gold Medal ausgezeichnet. Zu seinen bedeutendsten Bauten gehören das Athenäum in New Harmony, Indiana (1975-79), das Museum für Kunsthandwerk in Frankfurt am Main (1979-85), das High Museum of Art, Atlanta (1980-83), die Hauptverwaltung von Canal+ in Paris (1988-92), Rathaus und Bibliothek, Den Haag (1990-95), das Museum für Zeitgenössische Kunst, Barcelona (1988-95) und das Getty Center in Los Angeles (1984-97). Zu seinen jüngsten Projekten gehört das U. S. Courthouse and Federal Building in Phoenix, Arizona (1995-2000).

Né à Newark (New Jersey), en 1934, **RICHARD MEIER** étudie à Cornell University et travaille dans l'agence de Marcel Breuer (1960-63) avant de se mettre à son compte en 1963. Prix Pritzker 1984, Royal Gold Medal, 1988. Principales réalisations : The Athenaeum, New Harmony (Indiana, 1975-79), Musée des Arts Décoratifs de Francfort-sur-le-Main (1979-1984), High Museum of Art (Atlanta, Géorgie, 1980-83), siège de Canal+ (Paris, 1988-91), hôtel de ville et bibliothèque (La Haye, 1990-95), Musée d'Art Contemporain de Barcelone (1988-95), Getty Center (Los Angeles, Californie, 1984-96). Il achève actuellement un tribunal fédéral et un immeuble de l'administration fédérale à Phoenix (Arizona, 1995-2000).

NEUGEBAUER HOUSE

Naples, Florida, USA, 1995-98

Planning: 1995-96. Construction: 1996-98.
Client: Klaus and Ursula Neugebauer. Floor area: 697 m².

Richard Meier's most recent house, the **NEUGEBAUER HOUSE**, is also one of his finest. Located on the Bay of Doubloon, the house has an unusual V-shaped roof. Meier explains that local building regulations required a slanted roof, but did not indicate the direction of the slant. Using 3cm-thick glass for heat insulation, he devised a complex system of brise-soleils. The house's horizontal, shed-like design represents a change in the architect's design options, which are usually more complex, articulated geometric forms, as is the case in another waterfront home, the Ackerberg House in California, but he certainly retains his preference for a white, light-filled architecture.

Richard Meiers jüngstes Haus, das **NEUGEBAUER HOUSE**, ist gleichzeitig eines seiner besten. Es ist an der Bucht von Doubloon gelegen und hat ein ungewöhnliches, V-förmiges Dach. Meier erklärt dazu, dass in den örtlichen Bauvorschriften ein schräges Dach vorgeschrieben, aber nicht die Richtung der Schräge angegeben war. Unter Verwendung einer Wärmedämmung aus 3 cm dickem Glas entwarf er ein komplexes System aus »Brisesoleils« (Sonnenschutz an der Außenseite der Fenster). Die langgestreckte, schuppenartige Form des Hauses ist eine Erweiterung der Gestaltungsmöglichkeiten des Architekten, der bislang meist mit komplex gegliederten geometrischen Formen gearbeitet hat. Dies war auch bei einem anderen Strandhaus, dem Ackerberg House in Kalifornien, der Fall. Seine Vorliebe für eine weiße, lichterfüllte Architektur behielt Meier jedoch auch in der Gestaltung dieses Hauses bei.

En bordure de la baie de Doubloon, la dernière maison de Richard Meier, la **MAISON NEUGEBAUER**, est l'une de ses créations les plus raffinées. Elle se caractérise par un étonnant toit en V. Meier explique que la réglementation locale exigeait un toit en pente, sans en indiquer l'orientation. Il a mis au point un système complexe de brise-soleil en verre de 3 cm d'épaisseur qui isole de la chaleur. L'horizontalité et la simplicité du plan représentent un changement pour l'architecte qui, jusqu'alors, mettait plutôt en œuvre des formes géométriques complexes, comme pour Ackerberg House, une villa construite au bord de l'océan, en Californie. Il conserve néanmoins son goût pour une architecture lumineuse et un blanc immaculé.

Richard Meier quite simply turned the slanted roof required by local zoning restrictions upside down, to allow the house to open out onto the water in a spectacular way.

Durch das »auf den Kopf stellen« des von den örtlichen Bauvorschriften geforderten Satteldachs öffnet sich das Haus auf ganz ungewöhnliche Weise zum Meer.

Richard Meier a tout simplement inversé le toit à deux pentes exigé par la réglementation d'urbanisme locale, permettant ainsi à la maison de s'ouvrir sur l'océan.

In typical fashion, Richard Meier uses the white luminosity of his spaces to their best advantage, particularly in this near tropical climate.

In charakteristischer Weise setzt Richard Meier in seiner Innenraum-gestaltung Licht und weiße Farbe ein, was die Räume, besonders in dieser fast tropischen Umgebung, optimal zur Geltung bringt.

L'une des caractéristiques de Richard Meier est de savoir tirer le meilleur parti de la lumineuse blancheur d'espaces situés à proximité des tropiques.

JOSÉ RAFAEL MONEO

José Rafael Moneo
Cinca 5
28002 Madrid
Spain

Tel: +34 91 564 2257
Fax: +34 91 563 5217

JOSÉ RAFAEL MONEO was born in Tudela, Navarra (Spain), in 1937. He graduated from the Escuela Técnica Superior de Arquitectura (ETSA) in Madrid in 1961. The following year, he went to work with Jørn Utzon in Denmark. Rafael Moneo has taught extensively, including at the ETSA in Madrid and Barcelona. He was chairman of the Department of Architecture at the Graduate School of Design at Harvard from 1985 to 1990. Moneo received the Pritzker Prize in 1996. His recent work includes the National Museum of Roman Art (Mérida, Spain, 1980-86); San Pablo Airport (Seville, 1987-92), built for Expo '92; Atocha Railway Station (Madrid, 1985-92); Pilar and Joan Miró Foundation (Palma de Mallorca, 1987-92); transformation of the Villahermosa Palace in Madrid into a museum for the Thyssen-Bornemisza Collection (1989-92); the Davis Art Museum at Wellesley College (Wellesley, Massachusetts, 1990-93); Hyatt Hotel; and an office building (Berlin, 1993-98); the Auditorium (Barcelona, 1989-99); and an Auditorium and Cultural Center in San Sebastián (1991-99).

JOSÉ RAFAEL MONEO, 1937 in Tudela, Navarra (Spanien) geboren, schloß 1961 sein Studium an der Escuela Técnica Superior de Arquitectura (ETSA) in Madrid ab. Im darauffolgenden Jahr ging er nach Dänemark, um dort mit Jørn Utzon zu arbeiten. Rafael Moneo hat an zahlreichen Architekturschulen gelehrt, so an der ETSA in Madrid und in Barcelona. Von 1985 bis 1990 war er Leiter des Department of Architecture der Graduate School of Design (GSD) in Harvard. 1996 erhielt er den Pritzker Prize. Zu Moneos neueren Bauten gehören das Nationalmuseum für Römische Kunst in Mérida, Spanien (1980-86), der für die Expo '92 gebaute Flughafen San Pablo in Sevilla (1989-91), der Bahnhof Atocha in Madrid (1991), die Stiftung Pilar und Joan Miró in Palma de Mallorca (1987-92), die Umgestaltung des Villahermosa-Palasts in Madrid für die Sammlung Thyssen-Bornemisza (1992), das Davis Art Museum am Wellesley College in Wellesley, Massachusetts (1990-93), das Hyatt Hotel und ein Bürogebäude am Potsdamer Platz in Berlin (1993-98) sowie ein Auditorium in Barcelona (1999) und das hier vorgestellte Kursaal/Kulturzentrum im baskischen San Sebastián (1991-99).

JOSÉ RAFAEL MONEO naît à Tuleda, province de Navarre, Espagne, en 1937. Il est diplômé de l'Escuela Tecnica de Arquitectura de Madrid en 1961. En 1962, il part au Danemark pour travailler avec Jørn Utzon. Il enseigne beaucoup, y compris aux ETSA de Madrid et de Barcelone. Président du département d'architecture de la Graduate School of Design de Harvard de 1985 à 1990. Il obtient le Prix Pritzker en 1996. Parmi ses réalisations récentes : le Musée national d'art romain (Merida, Espagne, 1980-86), le terminal de l'aéroport de San Pablo (Séville, 1989-91) édifié pour Expo '92, la gare d'Atocha (Madrid, 1991), la Fondation Pilar et Joan Miró (Palma de Mallorca, 1987-1992), la transformation du Palais Villahermosa à Madrid pour la Collection Thyssen-Bornemisza (1992), le Davis Art Museum du Wellesley College (Wellesley, Massachusetts, 1993), l'hôtel Hyatt et un immeuble de bureaux, Potsdamer Platz (Berlin, 1993-98), un auditorium à Barcelone (1999) et l' auditorium du Kursaal et centre culturel de San Sebastián, Pays basque, Espagne (1991-99).

MURCIA TOWN HALL ANNEX

Murcia, Spain, 1991-98

*Planning: 1991-95. Construction: 1995-98. Client: Municipal Government of Murcia.
Floor area: 3 000 m². Costs: Ptas 500 million.*

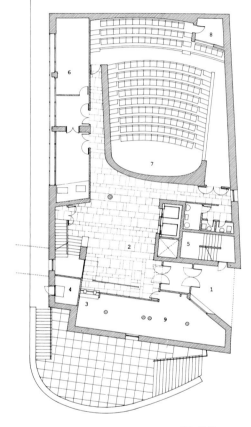

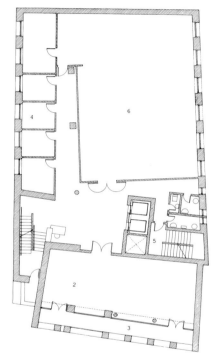

Ground floor	Erdgeschoss	Rez-de-chaussée
1 - Entrance hall	1 - Eingangshalle	1 - Entrée
2 - Vestibule/Information	2 - Vorhalle/Information	2 - Accueil, information
3 - Cashier	3 - Kasse	3 - Caisse
4 - Garbage room	4 - Abstellraum	4 - Local pour les poubelles
5 - Emergency stair	5 - Feuertreppe	5 - Escalier de secours
6 - Office	6 - Büro	6 - Bureau
7 - Lecture hall	7 - Vorlesungssaal	7 - Salle de lecture
8 - Projection room	8 - Projektionsraum	8 - Salle de projections
9 - General office	9 - Verwaltung	9 - Administration centrale

First floor	1. Etage	Premier étage
1 - Vestibule/Information	1 - Vorhalle/Information	1 - Accueil, information
2 - Reception room	2 - Empfang	2 - Accueil
3 - Gallery	3 - Galerie	3 - Galerie
4 - Office	4 - Büro	4 - Bureau
5 - Emergency stair	5 - Feuertreppe	5 - Escalier de secours
6 - General offices	6 - Verwaltung	6 - Administration centrale

Situated on Plaza Cardenal Belluga, near the cathedral and the Cardinal's Palace, the **MURCIA TOWN HALL ANNEX** presented Rafael Moneo with the difficult task of designing a building that neither challenged the architectural power of the older structures nor timidly denied contemporary municipal power. The reinforced concrete town hall is clad in local sandstone and brick. The interior finishes are plaster and wood paneling, with stone and wood floors. The building specifications required space for the municipal offices, a tourist and information center, a lecture hall, a reception room and a cafeteria. As Rafael Moneo says, "The facade/retable is organized like a musical score, numerically accepting the horizontal levels of the floor slabs. It resists symmetries, and offers, as the key element, the balcony of the gallery that rests on exactly the same horizontal plane as the central balcony of the piano nobile of the Palace, both at the same height."

Der 3 000 m² umfassende, an der Plaza del Cardenal Belluga nahe der Kathedrale und dem Kardinalspalast gelegene **MURCIA RATHAUS ANNEX** stellte Rafael Moneo vor die schwierige Aufgabe, ein Gebäude zu entwerfen, das weder die architektonische Kraft der alten Bauwerke schmälert, noch schüchtern die Vitalität der modernen Provinzhauptstadt leugnet. Das neue Rathaus ist aus Stahlbeton erbaut und mit örtlichem Sandstein verkleidet. Die Innenraumausstattung besteht aus Gipsputz und Holztäfelung sowie Stein- und Holzfußböden. Der Bauplan verlangte Büros für die Stadtverwaltung, ein Fremdenverkehrsamt, einen Hörsaal, einen Empfangsraum und ein Café. Rafael Moneo erläutert seinen Entwurf: »Die vorgelegte Fassade ist wie eine Partitur angelegt, wobei sich die Anzahl der Geschosse zahlenmäßig an der Fassade widerspiegelt. Entgegen jeder Symmetrie gestaltet, bietet sie als beherrschendes Bauelement den Balkon der Galerie, der auf derselben horizontalen Ebene ruht wie der zentrale Balkon im Hauptgeschoß (piano nobile) des Kardinalspalasts.«

Situé Plaza del Cardenal Belluga près de la cathédrale et du palais du Cardinal, le nouveau l'**ANNEX D'HÔTEL DE VILLE DE MURCIE** de 3 000 m² représentait pour l'architecte un défi délicat : comment respecter la forte présence des bâtiments anciens sans nuire, par timidité, à l'autorité que représente la municipalité moderne. Construit en béton armé, l'hôtel de ville est paré de grès local. Les murs intérieurs sont en plâtre ou en lambris, les sols en bois ou pierre. Le programme comprenait des bureaux administratifs, un centre d'information pour les touristes, une salle de conférence, un salon de réception et une cafétéria. Comme Rafael Moneo le précise : « la façade-retable est organisée à la manière d'une partition musicale, et laisse s'affirmer la présence horizontale des dalles de niveau. Contrairement aux principes de symétrie, l'élément majeur, le balcon de la galerie, est aligné sur le même plan que le balcon central (piano nobile) du palais. »

Rafael Moneo has met the challenge
of integrating a decidedly modern
structure into a tight, traditional
urban environment. A view from the
inside of a balcony shows the proximity to the older buildings of the city.

José Rafael Moneo ist es gelungen,
ein sehr modernes Gebäude in eine
dichtbebaute, traditionelle Umgebung
zu integrieren. Oben: Der Ausblick
vom Balkon macht die Nähe der alten
Bauwerke deutlich.

Rafael Moneo relève ici le défi d'intégrer une construction résolument
moderne dans un tissu urbain traditionnel et serré. Une vue de l'intérieur
d'un balcon montre la proximité des
bâtiments anciens.

ERIC OWEN MOSS

Eric Owen Moss Architects
8557 Higuera Street
Culver City, California 90232
United States

Tel: +1 310 839 1199
Fax: +1 310 839 7922
e-mail: ericmoss@ix.netcom.com
Web: www.ericowenmoss.com

The Umbrella ▶

Born in Los Angeles, California, in 1943, **ERIC OWEN MOSS** received his B.A. degree from the University of California, Los Angeles in 1965, and his M.Arch. from the University of California at Berkeley in 1968. He also received a M.Arch. degree from Harvard in 1972. He founded Eric Owen Moss Architects in 1973. He has been a Professor of Design at the Southern California Institute of Architecture (SCI-Arc) since 1974. His built work includes the Central Housing Office, University of California at Irvine (1986-89), Lindblade Tower (1987-89), Paramount Laundry (1987-89), Gary Group (1988-90), The Box (1990-94), I. R. S. Building (1993-94), and Samitaur (1994-96), all in Culver City. Current work includes high-rise towers in Los Angeles and a residential project in Hollywood, as well as ongoing designs in Culver City.

ERIC OWEN MOSS, geboren 1943 in Kalifornien, erwarb 1965 den Bachelor of Arts an der University of California, Los Angeles (UCLA) und 1968 den Master of Architecture an der University of California at Berkeley. 1972 erwarb er einen weiteren Master of Architecture in Harvard und gründete ein Jahr später das Büro Eric Owen Moss Architecture. Seit 1974 hat er eine Professur für Design am Southern California Institute of Architecture (SCI-Arc) inne. Zu seinen Bauten zählen das Central Housing Office an der University of California in Irvine (1986-89), der Lindblade Tower (1987-89), die Paramount Laundry (1987-89), Gary Group (1988-90), The Box (1990-94), das I. R. S-Gebäude (1993-94) und Samitaur (1994-96), alle in Culver City. Zu seinen jüngsten Projekten gehören Hochhaustürme in Los Angeles und ein Wohnhaus in Hollywood, sowie seine laufenden Planungsarbeiten in Culver City.

Né en 1943 à Los Angeles, **ERIC OWEN MOSS** est diplômé en architecture de University of California, Los Angeles (Bachelor of Arts, 1965) et titulaire de deux masters : University of California at Berkeley (1968) et de Harvard (1972). Il crée Eric Owen Moss Architects en 1973 et enseigne la conception architecturale au Southern California Institute of Architecture (SCI-Arc) depuis 1974. Il fonde sa propre agence à Culver City, Californie, en 1976. Parmi ses réalisations aux Etats-Unis : Central Housing Office, University of California at Irvine (Irvine, 1986-89), à Culver City : Lindblade Tower (1987-89), Paramount Laundry (1987-89), Gary Group (1988-90), The Box (1990-94), l'I. R. S. Building (1993-94) et Samitaur (1994-96). Il travaille actuellement sur un projet de tours de grande hauteur à Los Angeles, sur une résidence à Hollywood ainsi qu'à de nouvelles réalisations à Culver City.

THE UMBRELLA

Culver City, California, USA, 1998-99

Completion: 12/99. Client: Samitaur Constructs.
Floor area: 1 468 m2.

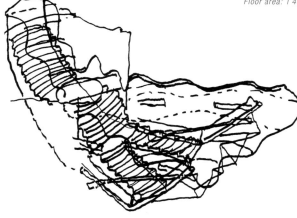

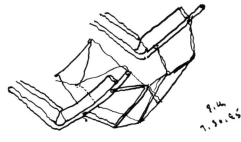

As he has done in other buildings in Culver City, Eric Owen Moss here adds a spectacular sculptural element to the outside of the corner of this structure.

Wie schon bei seinen anderen Bauprojekten in Culver City fügte Moss auch der Fassade dieses Gebäudes ein spektakulär gestaltetes plastisches Element hinzu.

Comme il l'a fait précédemment pour d'autres projets à Culver City, Eric Owen Moss greffe un élément sculptural spectaculaire à l'angle extérieur d'un bâtiment.

Part of the architect's ongoing effort to renovate industrial buildings in Culver City, sponsored by a promoter who owns the Hayden Tract in this district in Los Angeles, **THE UMBRELLA** is a 1 468-m² project undertaken at a cost of $ 1 185 000. It consists of two contiguous warehouses built in the 1940s and renovated to provide 20 private office spaces, two conference areas and large open workspaces. According to Moss, the name "Umbrella" derives from "an experimental piece of construction." "It is a conceptual bowl," says the architect, "an arena the slope of which is determined by the curving top chord of two inverted wood trusses salvaged from the demolition of an adjacent project and inserted here." Like most of his Culver City projects, this renovation does not fundamentally alter the exterior forms of the existing structures but rather adds a sculptural element whose origin is linked to the spaces. It is this added piece that gives an unusual identity to the completed building.

Als Teil der laufenden Renovierungsarbeiten des Architekten an den Industriebauten in Culver City und gesponsert von einem Veranstalter, dem der Hayden Tract in diesem Distrikt von Los Angeles gehört, ist **THE UMBRELLA** (der Regenschirm) ein 1 468 m² umfassendes Projekt, das für 1 850 000 $ realisiert wurde. Es besteht aus zwei aneinander grenzenden Lagerhäusern aus den 1940er-Jahren, die nun zur Unterbringung von 20 Privatbüros, zwei Konferenzsälen und einigen großflächigen, offenen Arbeitsräumen umgebaut wurden. Laut Moss bezieht sich der Name »Umbrella« auf ein experimentelles Bauteil, das der Architekt so beschreibt: »Es beruht auf der Grundidee einer Schüssel und stellt eine Arena dar. Deren Schräge wird von der oberen gekrümmten Spannweite zweier nach innen gekehrter Balken vorgegeben, die beim Abriss eines benachbarten Gebäudes geborgen und hier eingesetzt wurden.« Wie bei den meisten seiner Bauprojekte in Culver City verändert Moss bei dieser Renovierung die äußeren Formen der bestehenden Gebäude nicht grundlegend, sondern fügt lediglich ein plastisch gestaltetes Element hinzu, das sich auf die ursprünglichen Gebäude bezieht. Auch bei The Umbrella ist es dieses zusätzliche Element, das dem fertigen Gebäude seine Individualität verleiht.

Dans le cadre d'un programme permanent de rénovation de bâtiments industriels à Culver City financé par le promoteur propriétaire du Hayden Tract, **THE UMBRELLA** (le parapluie) est un projet de $1 485 000 pour une surface de 1 468 m². Il se compose de deux entrepôts contigus édifiés dans les années 1940 puis transformés par Moss en 20 bureaux indépendants, deux salles de conférence et de vastes plateaux ouverts. Selon l'architecte, le nom de « Umbrella » désigne « une construction expérimentale. Un ‹ bol › conceptuel, une arène, dont la pente est déterminée par la courbe supérieure de deux fermes de bois récupérées dans la démolition d'un projet voisin… » Comme pour la plupart de ses réalisations à Culver City, cette rénovation ne modifie pas fondamentalement les formes extérieures des constructions existantes, mais leur ajoute un élément sculptural lié à la nature de chaque espace. C'est cet ajout qui confère à chaque bâtiment son identité originale.

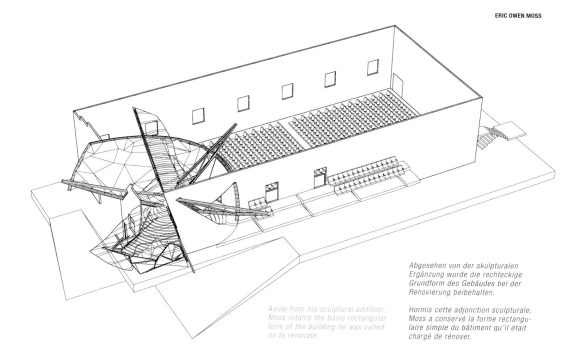

Abgesehen von der skulpturalen
Ergänzung wurde die rechteckige
Grundform des Gebäudes bei der
Renovierung beibehalten.

*Aside from his sculptural addition,
Moss retains the basic rectangular
form of the building he was called
on to renovate.*

Hormis cette adjonction sculpturale,
Moss a conservé la forme rectangulaire simple du bâtiment qu'il était
chargé de rénover.

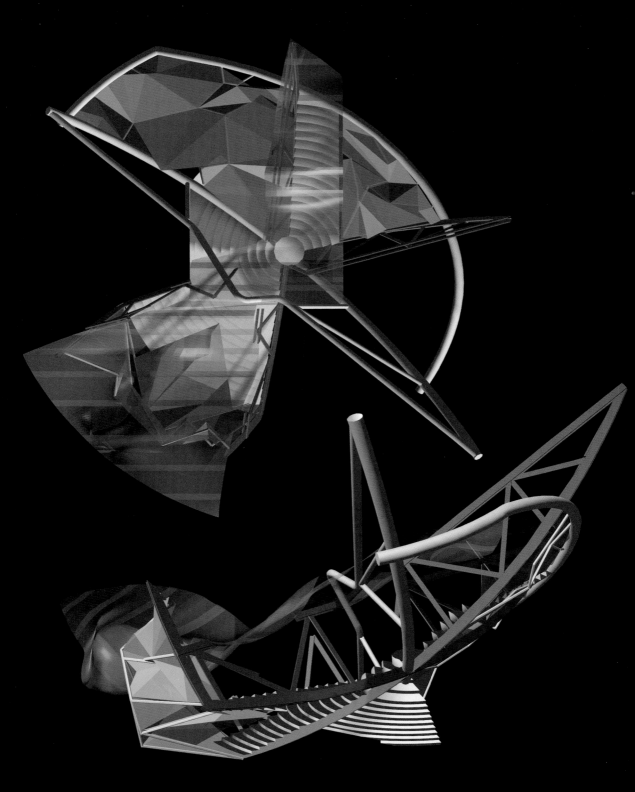

Inside the building, Moss uses his sense of materials and complex spaces to enliven the visitor's experience. Thus a run-down warehouse is transformed into a up-to-date office.

Im Inneren steigert Moss das Raumgefühl mit dem ihm eigenen Gespür für Materialien und komplexe Räume und verwandelt ein baufälliges Lagerhaus in ein modernes Büro.

Moss use de son sens des matériaux et des espaces complexes pour créer un univers stimulant. Un entrepôt abandonné se transforme en bureaux d'avant-garde.

MVRDV

MVRDV
Postbus 63136
3002 JC Rotterdam
Netherlands

Tel: +31 10 477 2860
Fax: +31 10 477 3627
e-mail: office@mvrdv.nl
Web: www.mvrdv.nl

MetaCITY/DATATOWN ►

Winy Maas, Jacob van Rijs and Nathalie de Vries created **MVRDV** in 1991. The name of the firm is made up of the initials of the surnames of the partners. Born in 1959, Maas, like his two partners (van Rijs born in 1964, de Vries born in 1965), studied at the Technical University in Delft. Both Maas and van Rijs worked for the Office for Metropolitan Architecture (OMA). De Vries worked in the office of Mecanoo and van Rijs in the office of Ben van Berkel before founding MVRDV. Aside from the Villa VPRO (Hilversum, 1993-97), their work includes the RVU Building (Hilversum, 1994-97), a Double House (Utrecht, 1995-97), WoZoCo, 100 apartments for elderly people (Amsterdam-Osdorp, 1997), all in the Netherlands, and the Dutch Pavilion for Expo 2000 (Hanover, Germany). They have also worked on urban development schemes such as their Ypenburg project (1998), or the Masterplan for Parklane Airport, Eindhoven, Netherlands.

Winy Maas, Jacob van Rijs und Nathalie de Vries gründeten **MVRDV** im Jahre 1991; der Name des Büros ist aus den Initialen ihrer Nachnamen gebildet. Maas (geboren 1959), van Rijs (geboren 1964) und de Vries (1965 geboren) studierten an der Technischen Universität Delft. Vor der Gründung von MVRDV arbeiteten Maas und van Rijs für das Office for Metropolitan Architecture (OMA), de Vries bei Mecanoo und van Rijs bei Ben van Berkel. Zu ihren Werken gehören die Villa VPRO in Hilversum (1993-97), das RVU-Gebäude in Hilversum (1994-97), ein Doppelhaus in Utrecht (1995-97) sowie WoZoCo, ein Komplex mit 100 Seniorenwohnungen in Amsterdam-Osdorp (1997) und der Niederländische Pavillon für die Expo 2000 in Hannover. Darüber hinaus haben sie Stadtentwicklungsplanungen wie das Projekt Ypenburg (1998) oder den Masterplan für den Flughafen Parklane in Eindhoven erarbeitet.

Winy Maas, Jacob van Rijs et Nathalie de Vries fondent en 1991 l'agence **MVRDV** dont le sigle se compose des initiales de leurs prénoms. Né en 1959, Maas, comme ses deux autres associés (van Rijs né en 1964, de Vries née en 1965) étudie à l'Université Polytechnique de Delft. Maas et van Rijs ont travaillé pour l'Office for Metropolitan Architecture (OMA), de Vries a travaillé pour Mecanoo et van Rijs dans l'agence de Ben van Berkel avant de créer MVRDV. Outre la Villa VPRO (Hilversum, 1993-97), ils ont réalisé l'immeuble RVU (Hilversum, 1994-97), une maison double (Amsterdam-Osdorp, 1997), WoZoCo, 100 logements pour personnes âgées (Amsterdam-Osdorp, 1997) et le Pavillon Néerlandais à Expo 2000, Hanovre. Ils ont également travaillé sur des projets de rénovation urbaine comme « Ypenburg » (1998) ou le plan directeur de l'aéroport Parklane à Eindhoven, Pays-Bas.

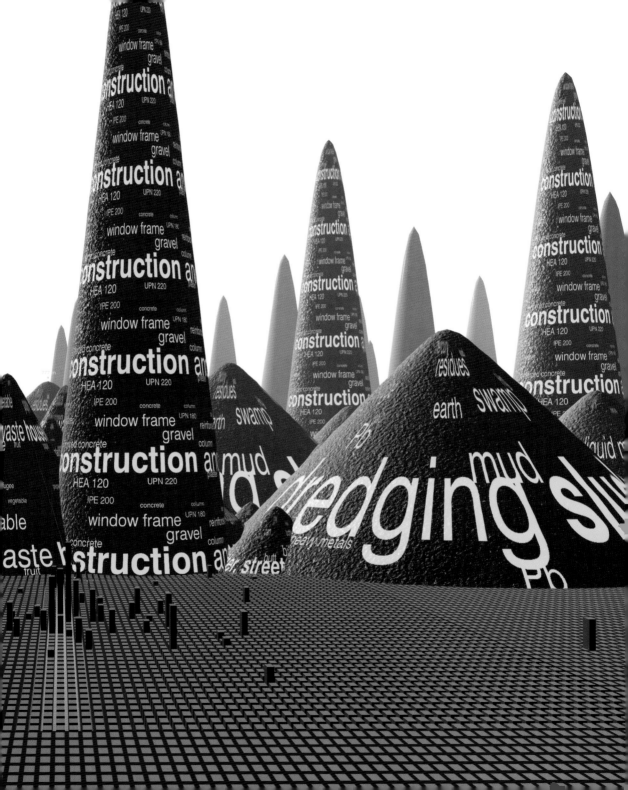

METACITY/DATATOWN

1998-

Research project conceived by Winy Maas which resulted in a video installation
developed by Winy Maas, Jan van Grunsven and Arno van der Mark
in collaboration with Stroom and a book produced by MVRDV.

Based on a video installation produced by MVRDV for the Stroom Center for the Visual Arts in The Hague at the end of 1998, **METACITY/DATATOWN** is essentially an exhibition that has been shown in such locations as Galerie Aedes (Berlin) and Venice Biennale. "Datatown," say the architects, "is based only upon data. It is a city that wants to be described by information; a city that knows no given topography, no prescribed ideology, no representation, no context." Extrapolating from the rapid expansion of urban centers, based on methods of transportation and communication, MVRDV concludes that the Datatown of the future will measure some 400 x 400 km (roughly the distance from Tokyo to Osaka), and that it will have an extremely high population density (1 477 inhabitants per km^2), which would imply a city population of 241 million people. A cross between computer games such as SimCity and genuine urban development ideas, MetaCITY/Datatown is also an aesthetic environment that reflects the design concepts of this influential Dutch firm, even if the world may not be quite ready for the 376 Datatowns they project (i.e. a world urban population of more than 88 billion people).

METACITY/DATATOWN basiert auf einer 1998 von MVRDV für das Stroom Center for the Visual Arts in Den Haag produzierten Video-Installation. Es ist im Wesentlichen als Ausstellung konzipiert, die unter anderem in der Galerie Aedes (Berlin) und auf der Biennale in Venedig gezeigt wurde. Die Architekten beschreiben ihr Projekt so: »Datatown beruht nur auf Daten. Es ist eine Stadt, die allein durch Information beschrieben wird. Sie kennt keine festgelegte Topographie, keine vorgeschriebene Ideologie, keine Repräsentation und keinen Kontext.« Ausgehend von der rasanten Ausdehnung urbaner Zentren und den neuen Transport- und Kommunikationsmethoden, stellt MVRDV folgende Hochrechnung an: Die Datatown der Zukunft wird circa 400 km^2 (in etwa die Entfernung von Tokio nach Osaka) messen und über eine extrem hohe Bevölkerungsdichte verfügen, nämlich 1 477 Einwohner pro km^2, was einer Einwohnerzahl von knapp 241 Millionen Menschen entspricht. MetaCITY/Datatown stellt eine Mischung aus Computerspielen wie SimCity und ernstzunehmenden Ideen für zukünftige Möglichkeiten der Stadtentwicklung dar. Darüber hinaus bildet das Projekt einen ästhetischen Rahmen für die Präsentation der Designkonzepte dieser einflussreichen holländischen Architektengruppe, auch wenn die Welt noch nicht reif sein mag für ihre projektierten 376 Datatowns (d. h. eine Weltbevölkerungszahl von annähernd 88 Milliarden Menschen).

Inspirée d'une installation vidéo produite par MVRDV pour le Centre Stroom d'arts plastiques de la Haye fin 1998, **METACITY/DATATOWN** est essentiellement une exposition présentée dans des lieux comme la Galerie Aedes (Berlin) et la Biennale de Venise. « Datatown », expliquent les architectes « repose uniquement sur les données informatiques. C'est une ville qui se décrit par l'information, une ville sans topographie, sans idéologie prescrite, sans représentation, sans contexte. » Partant de la rapide expansion des centres urbains et de méthodes de transport et de communication, MVRDV conclut que la Datatown du futur mesurera quelques 400 km^2 (sur à peu près la distance de Tokyo à Osaka) et connaîtra une densité de population extrêmement élevée (1 477 habitants au km^2) soit 241 millions de personnes. Au croisement de jeux d'ordinateur comme SimCity et de concepts urbanistiques, MetaCITY/Datatown possède par ailleurs une qualité esthétique qui reflète la pensée de cette influente agence néerlandaise, même si le monde n'est peut-être pas encore prêt pour les 376 « datatowns » qu'elle imagine (soit une population de plus de 88 milliards d'habitants).

Each part of the MVRDV plan is divided by function. Here, the Living Sector, assuming a given population density, as it would appear if it were to
be spread evenly over the entire zone.

Der Entwurf von MVRDV ist in einzelne
Funktionsbereiche aufgeteilt. Der hier
abgebildete »Sector Living« (Lebens-
sektor) geht von einer gleichmäßig
über das gesamte Gebiet verteilten
Bevölkerungsdichte aus.

Le plan est divisé en fonctions. Ici, le
Secteur de vie, conçu pour une densité démographique précise, tel qu'il
apparaîtrait s'il devait couvrir toute la
zone.

The Agricultural Sector consists of millions of individual farming plots. Above: Assuming that there would be no meat consumption, it would be possible to subtract 81 876 km^2 for the production of animal fodder crops.

Der Agrarsektor besteht aus Millionen einzelner Ackerflächen. Oben: Sollte kein Fleisch mehr verzehrt werden, könnten die für den Anbau von Viehfutter vorgesehenen 81 876 km^2 abgezogen werden.

Le Secteur agricole consiste en plusieurs millions de parcelles individuelles cultivables.
Ci-dessus : si la ville était végétarienne, il serait possible d'économiser les 81 876 km^2 prévus pour la production d'aliments pour le bétail.

Above: The total area required for agriculture is 814 215 km², i.e. five times the total area of Datatown. Below: "Lamb consumption per capita." The sector is divided according to its functions into different zones. lamb consumption being one of them.

Oben: Die für die landwirtschaftliche Nutzung erforderliche Gesamtfläche (814 215 km²)entspricht der fünffachen Größe von Datatown. Unten: Lammkonsum pro Kopf – eine der verschiedenen Zonen im Sektor.

Ci-dessus : comme le montre cette image, la surface agricole prévue est de 814 215 km² soit cinq fois celle de Datatown. Ci-dessous : « Consommation d'agneau par tête. » Le secteur est divisé en différentes zones, la production d'agneau étant l'une d'entre elles.

Data Town's CO$_2$-Sector or Forest Sector. Above left: The Industry Sector is compared to a "stacked Ruhr Valley." A series of forests, 3 834 stories high, reaching a height of more than 100 km, are located within the boundaries of the Industry Sector. As the architects claim, this massive CO$_2$-machine of forest-towers "monumentalizes economy and ecology."

Der CO$_2$-Sektor (Wald) von Datatown. Oben links: Der Industriesektor als »aufgestapeltes Ruhrgebiet«, inner-halb dessen sich ein 3 834-geschos-siger Wald befindet, der eine Höhe von mehr als 100 km erreicht (unten links). Diese gewaltige CO$_2$-Maschine (oben rechts) setzt den Waldtürmen der Ökonomie und Ökologie (unten rechts) ein Denkmal.

Le secteur forestier de Datatown. Les architectes comparent le secteur industriel à une « vallée de la Ruhr empilée. » Une série de forêts de 3 834 étages, hautes de plus de 100 km sont implantées dans les limites de ce secteur. Cette énorme machinerie d'absorption de CO_2 « monumentalise l'économie d'énergie et l'écologie. »

The Energy Sector: Assuming that
all of Datatown's energy would be
produced by windmills, the city
would need a windmill park totalling 77 860 km², or half the size
of Datatown.

Der Energiesektor: Davon ausgehend,
die gesamte Energieversorgung von
Datatown erfolge durch Windmühlen,
wäre ein Gebiet von insgesamt
77 860 km² nötig, das entspricht der
Hälfte der Fläche von Datatown.

Le secteur de l'énergie : si toute
l'énergie de Datatown était fournie
par des moulins à vent, la ville
aurait besoin d'un parc éolien de
77 860 km², soit la moitié de sa
surface.

MVRDV

Below: The Water Sector: Assuming
that Datatown's drinking water is
stored in a water-storage-sector
totalling 23.1 km³ the water column
would reach a height of 500 m.

Unten: Der Wassersektor: Das für
Datatown benötigte Trinkwasser würde, in einem Wasser-Speicher-Sektor
von 23,1 km³ aufbewahrt, eine 500 m
hohe Wassersäule ergeben.

Ci-dessous: Le secteur de l'eau: si
l'eau potable de Datatown était réservé dans un réservoir de 23,1 km³, la
colonne de l'eau aurait une hauteur
du 500 m.

The Waste Sector: Each day Datatown produces 315 864 t of waste, yielding a hill with a volume of 1 525 906 m^3 and a height of 73 m.

Above left and right: Anticipating future developments of waste disposal areas, MVRDV writes, "If we stay within the current boundaries of the sector, after 150 years the Waste Sector will become a dolomitic landscape."

Below right: According to the architects, "After a million years, Datatown becomes an alpine mountain range."

Der Abfallsektor: Die von Datatown täglich produzierte Müllmenge von 315 864 t ergibt einen Berg mit einem Volumen von 1 525 906 m^3 und einer Höhe von 73 m.

Oben links und rechts: Die zukünftige Entwicklung der Abfallbeseitigung vorwegnehmend schreibt MVRDV: »Wenn wir innerhalb der jetzigen Grenzen des Sektors bleiben, entwickelt sich der Abfallsektor nach 150 Jahren zu einer Gebirgslandschaft.«

Unten rechts: Nach einer Million Jahren wird ganz Datatown zu einer Gebirgskette.

Le secteur des déchets : chaque jour, Datatown produit 315 864 t de déchets, soit l'équivalent d'une volume de 1 526 000 m^3 pour une hauteur de 73 m.

En haut à gauche et à droite : anticipant le développements des zones de déchets, MVRDV précise : « Si nous nous contentons de ce secteur, en 150 ans, il aura pris l'aspect d'un paysage dolomitique. »

Ci-dessous à droite : selon les architectes : « Au bout d'un million d'années, Datatown ressemblera à une chaîne de montagnes. »

NEUTELINGS RIEDIJK

Neutelings Riedijk Architecten BV
Scheepmakersstraat 13
3011 VH Rotterdam
Netherlands

Tel: +31 10 404 6677
Fax: +31 10 414 2712

Minnaert Building ▶

WILLEM JAN NEUTELINGS was born in 1959 in Bergen op Zoom, Netherlands. He studied at the Technical University in Delft (1977-86) before working in the Office for Metropolitan Architecture with Rem Koolhaas (1981-86). He has taught at the Academy of Architecture in Rotterdam and at the Berlage Institute in Amsterdam (1990-99). **MICHIEL RIEDIJK** was born in Geldrop, Netherlands in 1964. He attended the Technical University in Delft (1983-89) before working with Juliette Bekkering in Amsterdam. He has taught at the Technical University in Delft and Eindhoven and at the Academies of Architecture in Amsterdam, Rotterdam and Maastricht. Neutelings and Riedijk started collaborating in 1991. Their built work includes the Prinsenhoek Residential Complex (Sittard, 1992-95), Tilburg Housing (1993-96), Borneo Sporenburg Housing (Amsterdam, 1994-97), Lakeshore Housing, first phase (Hulzen, 1994-96), and the Building for Veenman Printers (Ede, 1995-97), all in the Netherlands, as well as Hollainhof Social Housing (Ghent, Belgium, 1993-98).

WILLEM JAN NEUTELINGS wurde 1959 in Bergen op Zoom, Niederlande, geboren. Er studierte von 1977 bis 1986 an der Technischen Universität in Delft und arbeitete anschließend im Office for Metropolitan Architecture bei Rem Koolhaas. Von 1990 bis 1999 lehrte er an der Akademie für Architektur in Rotterdam und am Berlage-Institut in Amsterdam. **MICHIEL RIEDIJK**, geboren 1964 im niederländischen Geldrop, studierte an der Technischen Universität in Delft (1983-1989), bevor er bei J. D. Bekkering in Amsterdam arbeitete. Er lehrte an den Technischen Universitäten in Delft und Eindhoven sowie an den Akademien für Architektur in Amsterdam, Rotterdam und Maastricht. Zu den Bauten von Neutelings Riedijk gehören der Wohnkomplex Prinsenhoek in Sittard (1992-95), die Wohnanlagen Tilburg (1993-96) und Borneo Sporenburg in Amsterdam (1994-97), Lakeshore, Phase I in Hulzen (1994-96) und das Veenman Drukkers-Gebäude in Ede (1995-97), alle in den Niederlanden, sowie die Sozialwohnanlage Hollainhof in Gent, Belgien (1993-98).

WILLEM JAN NEUTELINGS, né en 1959 à Bergen op Zoom, Pays-Bas, étudie à l'Université Technique de Delft (1977-86) avant de travailler pour l'Office for Metropolitan Architecture auprès de Rem Koolhaas. Il a enseigné à l'Académie d'architecture de Rotterdam et au Berlage Institute d'Amsterdam (1990-99). **MICHIEL RIEDIJK**, né à Geldrop, Pays-Bas, en 1964, étudie à l'Université Technique de Delft (1983-89) avant de travailler pour J. D. Bekkering à Amsterdam. Il a enseigné à l'Université Technique de Delft, d'Eindhoven et aux Académies d'architecture d'Amsterdam, Rotterdam et Maastricht. Parmi leurs réalisations : le complexe résidentiel de Prinsenhoek (Sittard, 1992-95), un immeuble d'appartement à Tilburg (1993-96), l'immeuble résidentiel Borneo Sporenburg (Amsterdam, 1994-97), les logements de Lakeshore (Hulzen, 1994-96) et l'immeuble de Veenman Drukkers (Ede, 1995-97), toutes aux Pays-Bas, ainsi que les logements sociaux de Hollainhof (Gand, Belgique, 1993-98).

MINNAERT BUILDING

Utrecht, Netherlands, 1994-97

Planning: 1994-96. Construction: 1996-97.
Client: University Utrecht. Floor area: ca. 9 000 m².

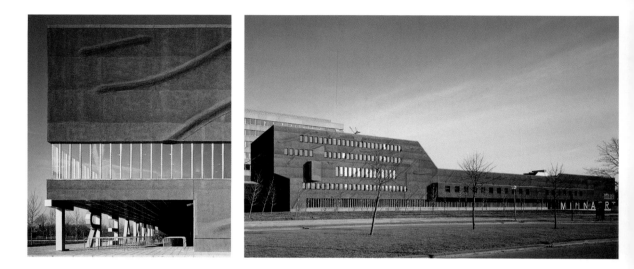

Located on the campus of Uithof University, the **MINNAERT BUILDING** includes three main components – a restaurant, classrooms and laboratories, and work-space. Characterized by its sienna pigmented undulating skin of sprayed concrete, the building includes a 50 x 10-m pond that collects rainwater and is situated in a main hall. The water is pumped in and out of the building by the roof for cooling purposes. Water falls into the basin during rainy periods, adding the element of sound to a composition that intends to evoke the five senses. Large-scale letters spelling the name Minnaert replace columns on part of the south elevation, making the building immediately recognizable to passersby.

Das **MINNAERT-GEBÄUDE** liegt auf dem Uithof-Campus der Universität Utrecht und besteht aus drei Bauteilen, in denen ein Restaurant, Klassen- und Arbeitsräume sowie Laboratorien untergebracht sind. Das durch seine ockerfarben pigmentierte und gewellte Haut aus gespritztem Beton gekennzeichnete Gebäude besitzt in der Haupthalle einen 50 x 10 m großen Brunnen, in dem Regenwasser aufgefangen wird. Zum Zweck der Kühlung wird das Wasser vom Dach aus in das Gebäude hinein und wieder heraus gepumpt. Wenn es regnet, fällt Wasser in das Becken, was der Komposition, die alle Sinne ansprechen will, das akustische Element hinzufügt. Auf der Süd-seite ruht der Bau auf Stützen in Form von großformatigen Buchstaben. Diese ergeben den Namen Minnaert, wodurch das Gebäude für Passanten sofort kenntlich ge-macht wird.

Situé sur le campus de l'Université Uithof, ce bâtiment se compose de trois parties principales : un restaurant, des salles de cours et des laboratoires. Caractérisé par sa peau externe ondulée en béton projeté de couleur terre de Sienne, il possède un bassin de 50 x 10 m dans le hall principal qui récupère les eaux de pluie ; cet élé-ment sonore enrichit une composition qui évoque les cinq sens. L'eau est pompée ou rejetée sur le toit en fonction de la température. Les énormes lettres qui composent le nom de **MINNAERT** remplacent les colonnes sur la façade sud et rendent le bâtiment facilement identifiable.

As the drawing (below right) shows, the architects share a typical Dutch concern for the environmental effi-ciency of their building, this in spite of the rather massive appearance of the structure.

Das Minnaert-Gebäude ist nach umweltfreundlichen Gesichtspunkten konzipiert (unten rechts). Diese ener-giesparende Bauweise, die in den Niederlanden mittlerweile Tradition hat, ist an den eher massiv und geschlossen wirkenden Oberflächen nicht ablesbar.

Le dessin de droite montre que les architectes ont conçu le bâtiment dans un souci de respect de l'envi-ronnement traditionnel aux Pays-Bas, préoccupation qui ne transparaît pas dans l'aspect massif de sa strucutre.

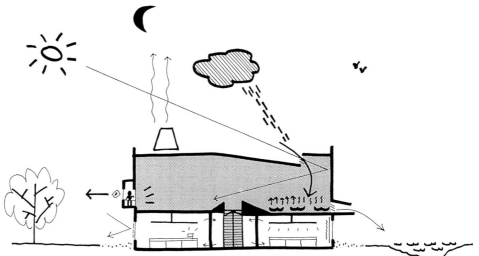

The rather heavy feeling of the interi-
or spaces is somewhat alleviated by
the use of some bright colors. The
angled ceilings and walls are typical
of the architects.

*Die eher schweren Innenräume wer-
den durch einige helle Farbtöne auf-
gelockert. Charakteristisch für den
Stil des Büros sind die schrägen
Decken und Wände.*

*Une certaine lourdeur perçue dans
les espaces intérieurs est allégée par
le recours à des couleurs vives. Les
plafonds et les murs inclinés sont
typiques du style des architectes.*

FIRE STATION

Maastricht, Netherlands, 1996-99

Planning: 1996-98. Construction: 1998-99. Landscape: West-8 Landscape Architects, Rotterdam.
Client: Gemeente Maastricht. Floor area: ca. 4 000 m².

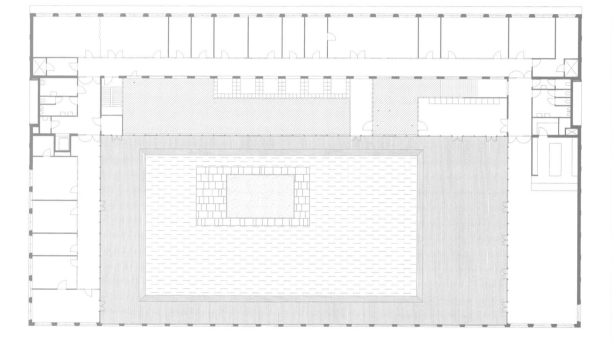

Situated at the northern, industrial periphery of the southern Dutch city of Maastricht, this **FIRE STATION** includes a garage with a workshop and storage area, living and sleeping quarters for the firemen, and offices. A double-height hall with ample natural light gives a different impression than the relatively harsh, gray concrete paneling of the exterior might lead one to believe. The patterning seems to have been inspired by truck tires. The unit cantilevered over the garage entrances gives the entire structure a sense of movement not unlike that obtained by the architects in their Minnaert Building. In the interior, large areas near the central hall painted in red brighten the rather severe gray tonality of the whole. A roof garden with a pond, designed to catch rainwater, also adds a more natural element to the composition.

Dieses **FEUERWEHRHAUS** liegt in einem Gewerbegebiet am Nordrand der niederländischen Stadt Maastricht. Es beherbergt eine Garage mit Werkstatt und Lagerhalle, Wohn- und Schlafräume für die Feuerwehrmänner sowie Büros. Die von natürlichem Licht durchflutete doppelgeschossige Halle vermittelt einen anderen Eindruck als die relativ abweisende graue Betonverkleidung der Außenwände erwarten lässt. Ihre Gestaltung scheint von Lastwagenreifen inspiriert zu sein. Der über den Garageneinfahrten auskragende Bauteil gibt dem gesamten Bau eine Ausstrahlung von Lebendigkeit und Bewegung, die an das Minnaert-Gebäude erinnert. Im Inneren hellen große rot gestrichene Bereiche die etwas streng wirkende graue Farbgebung des Ganzen auf, und auch der Dachgarten mit einem Teich, der zum Auffangen von Regenwasser dient, verleiht dem Bauwerk eine natürliche und aufgelockerte Note.

En pleine banlieue industrielle au nord de Maastricht (Sud des Pays-Bas), ce **CASERNE DE POMPIERS** comprend un garage, un atelier, un entrepôt et des bureaux. Un hall double-hauteur baigné de lumière donne une impression différente de ce que l'austère revêtement extérieur en panneaux de béton gris laisse supposer. Le motif semble avoir été inspiré par des pneus de camions. La partie en porte-à-faux au-dessus des entrées du garage donne à l'ensemble un mouvement assez proche de celui créé par les architectes pour l'immeuble Minnaert. A l'intérieur, à proximité du hall central, de vastes plans peints en rouge animent la tonalité grise assez sévère de l'ensemble. Un toit-terrasse traité en jardin, conçu pour récupérer l'eau de pluie, ajoute un élément naturel à la composition.

There is a kind of solid efficiency in the interior volumes of this fire station. As in the Minnaert Building, the design approach seems to be based on a quest for durability.

Die Innenräume des Feuerwehrhauses sind von wuchtiger Funktionalität gekennzeichnet. Wie im Minnaert-Gebäude drückt der Entwurf das Streben nach Dauerhaftigkeit aus.

Efficacité lourdement soulignée dans les volumes de cette caserne de pompiers. Comme dans l'immeuble Minnaert, l'approche semble axée sur une recherche de durabilité.

A rainwater-collecting pond serves both to make the building more environmentally friendly, and to play on the fire/water opposition that is inscribed in the function of the station.

Ein Auffangbecken für Regenwasser auf dem Dach basiert auf umweltfreundlichen Aspekten und ist gleichzeitig ein spielerischer Hinweis auf den Gegensatz zwischen Feuer und Wasser, der in der Funktion eines Feuerwehrhauses angelegt ist.

Le bassin de collecte des eaux pluviales sert à des fins écologiques tout en jouant sur l'opposition feu-eau inscrite dans la raison d'être de la caserne.

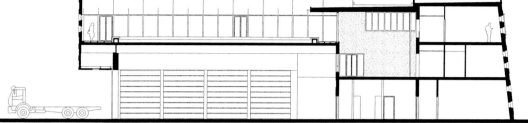

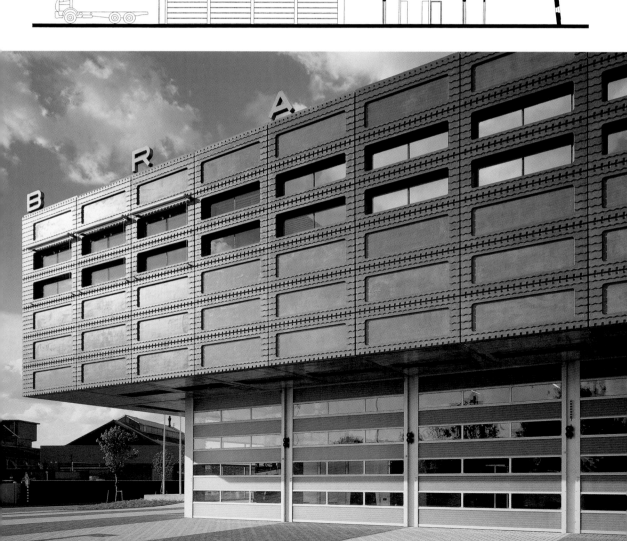

JEAN NOUVEL

Architectures Jean Nouvel
10, Cité d'Angoulême
75011 Paris
France

Tel: +33 1 4923 8383
Fax: +33 1 4314 8110

Born in 1945 in Fumel, France, **JEAN NOUVEL** was admitted to the École des Beaux-Arts in Bordeaux in 1964. In 1970, he created his first office with François Seigneur. His first widely noticed project was the Institut du Monde Arabe (Paris, 1981-87, with Architecture Studio). Other works include his Nemausus housing (Nîmes, 1985-87), offices for the CLM/BBDO advertising firm (Issy-les-Moulineaux, 1988-92), Lyon's Opera House (1986-93), Vinci International Conference Center (Tours, 1989-93), Euralille Shopping Center (Lille, 1991-94), Fondation Cartier (Paris, 1991-95), and Galeries Lafayette (Berlin, 1992-96). Among his unbuilt projects are the "Tours sans fins" (La Défense, Paris, 1989), Grand Stade for the 1998 World Cup (Paris, 1994), and Tenaga National Tower (Kuala Lumpur, Malaysia, 1995). His largest recent project is the Music and Conference Center in Lucerne, Switzerland (1992-99). He won both the competition for the Musée du Quai Branly, Paris (1999-2004) and the competition for the refurbishment of the Reina Sofia Art Center, Madrid, in 1999.

JEAN NOUVEL, geboren 1945 in Fumel, Frankreich, studierte ab 1964 an der École des Beaux-Arts in Bordeaux. 1970 gründete er zusammen mit François Seigneur sein erstes Büro. Weithin bekannt wurde Nouvel mit seinem Institut du Monde Arabe in Paris (1981-87), bei dem er mit Architecture Studio zusammenarbeitete. Weitere herausragende Werke sind die Wohnanlage Nemausus in Nîmes (1985-87), die Büros der Werbeagentur CLM/BBDO in Issy-les-Moulineaux (1988-92), das Opernhaus in Lyon (1986-93), das internationale Kongresszentrum Vinci in Tours (1989-93), das Einkaufszentrum Euralille in Lille (1991-94) und die Fondation Cartier in Paris (1991-95). Außerdem baute Nouvel die Galeries Lafayette in Berlin (1992-96) und plante die 400 m hohe »Tour sans fins« in La Défense, Paris (1989), das Grand Stade für die Fußball-Weltmeisterschaft von 1998 in Paris (1994) und den Tenaga National Tower in Kuala Lumpur, Malaysia (1995), die aber alle nicht realisiert wurden. 1999 gewann er den Wettbewerb für das Musée de Quai Branly in Paris und für die Modernisierung des Reina Sofia Zentrums in Madrid, 1999.

Né en 1945 à Fumel, **JEAN NOUVEL** est admis à l'Ecole des Beaux-Arts de Bordeaux en 1964. En 1970, il crée une première agence avec François Seigneur. Son premier projet vraiment remarqué est l'Institut du Monde Arabe, à Paris (1981-87, avec Architecture Studio). Parmi ses autres réalisations : les immeubles d'habitation Nemausus, à Nîmes (1985-87), les bureaux de l'agence de publicité CLM/BBDO (Issy-les-Moulineaux, 1988-92), l'Opéra de Lyon (1986-93), le Vinci Centre International de Congrès (Tours, 1989-93), le centre commercial Euralille (Lille, 1991-94), la Fondation Cartier (Paris, 1991-95), les Galeries Lafayette (Berlin, 1992-96). Parmi ses projets non réalisés : une tour de 400 m (« Tour sans fins », La Défense, Paris, 1989), le Grand Stade de la Coupe du Monde de football 1998, (Paris, 1994), la Tenaga National Tower (Kuala Lumpur, Malaisie, 1995). Son dernier grand projet est le Centre de Congrès et de Musique de Lucerne (Suisse, 1992-99). En 1999, il a remporté le concours du Musée des Arts et Civilisations (Paris) et le concours pour la restructuration-extension du Centre Reina Sofia (Madrid, 1999).

LAW COURTS

Nantes, France, 1997-2000

Planning: 2/1995-6/97. Construction: 7/1997-6/2000.
Client: Ministère de la Justice. Total floor area: 20 000 m².
Usable floor area: 15 000 m². Budget: FF 230 000 000.

Set on a very visible site across from the old town of Nantes on the banks of the Loire River, Jean Nouvel's **LAW COURTS** are both ample and impressive. Part of a large effort to renovate the French courts that has led to buildings being designed in Bordeaux by Richard Rogers, and in Grasse by Christian de Portzamparc, the Nantes building covers a floor area of 15 000 m² and had a budget of 230 million FF. A sloping area paved with cobblestones leads up to the high black structure, whose most prominent feature is a public entrance hall 113 m long and 15 m high. The highly polished Zimbabwean black granite floor reflects the sky and even the city opposite, but does not really relieve the impression of gravity or even severity intended by Nouvel. The courtrooms are set in three 12 m-high black cubes, whose reddish and slightly claustrophobic interiors allude to the significance of the judicial process. A footbridge designed by the architects Barto & Barto is scheduled to be completed in June 2001, making the largely undeveloped site more accessible, in view of further construction, to include a planned school of architecture nearby.

Der weitläufig angelegte **GERICHTSHOF,** der weithin sichtbar gegenüber der Altstadt von Nantes am Ufer der Loire liegt, ist eindrucksvoll gestaltet. Er ist Teil eines umfassenden Programms zur Erneuerung französischer Gerichtsgebäude, in dessen Rahmen bereits Richard Rogers in Bordeaux und Christian de Portzamparc in Grasse tätig waren. Das Gerichtsgebäude in Nantes hat eine Nutzfläche von 15 000 m² und wurde mit einem Budget von 230 Millionen FF errichtet. Über einen leicht ansteigenden, mit Kopfstein gepflasterten Weg gelangt man in eine 113 m lange und 15 m hohe Eingangshalle, die das hohe, in schwarz gehaltene Bauwerk beherrscht. In ihrem Boden aus hochglanzpoliertem schwarzem Simbabwe-Granit spiegeln sich der Himmel und die Silhouette der gegenüberliegende Stadt, was jedoch den von Nouvel beabsichtigten Eindruck von Ernst und Strenge kaum mildert. Die Gerichtssäle wurden in drei 12 m hohe, dunkle kubische Räume verlegt, deren rötlich schimmerndes und leicht klaustrophobisch wirkendes Interieur auf die Bedeutung des Gerichtsprozesses anspielt. Eine von den Architekten Barto & Barto entworfene Fußgängerbrücke, die vorraussichtlich im Juni 2001 fertiggestellt wird, soll das zur Zeit größtenteils noch unbebaute, angrenzende Gelände, für das weitere Gebäude wie eine Architekturschule geplant sind, erschließen.

Implanté sur un terrain très exposé en bordure de Loire, face au vieux centre ville, ce **PALAIS DE JUSTICE** est à la fois vaste et impressionnant. Dans le cadre d'un important programme de rénovation des bâtiments judiciaires auquel ont participé Richard Rogers à Bordeaux ou Christian de Portzamparc à Grasse, le bâtiment nantais de 15 000 m² a été édifié pour un coût de 230 millions de F. Un plan incliné en galets conduit au bâtiment intégralement noir dont l'élément le plus caractéristique est un hall d'entrée de 113 m de long et 15 de haut. Le sol en granit noir poli du Zimbabwe reflète le ciel et même la ville, sans pour autant atténuer l'impression de gravité ou même de sévérité voulue par Nouvel. Les salles des tribunaux sont installées dans des cubes noir de 12 m de haut, dont l'intérieur rougeâtre et l'atmosphère claustrale illustrent le processus de la justice. Une passerelle dessinée par les architectes Barto et Barto devrait être achevée en juin 2001 pour rendre plus accessible le site qui devrait bientôt compter une école d'architecture.

Nouvel's Law Courts are intended to give a rather severe impression of the judiciary system. Black, a favorite color of the architect, dominates the vast entrance hall (right).

Wie von Nouvel beabsichtigt, vermittelt das Gerichtsgebäude einen Eindruck von der Strenge des Justizsystems. In der riesigen Eingangshalle (rechts) dominiert Schwarz, die Lieblingsfarbe des Architekten.

Le Palais de justice de Nouvel donne une impression plutôt sévère du système judiciaire. Le noir, couleur favorite de l'architecte, domine le vaste hall d'entrée (à droite).

The courtrooms are housed in three cubical volumes set at the rear of the cavernous black entrance hall. A rigorous grid system is used to determine all of the dimensions of the structure.

Die Gerichtssäle sind in drei kubischen Baukörpern untergebracht, die sich auf der Rückseite der höhlenartigen, in schwarz gehaltenen Eingangshalle (rechts) befinden.

Les salles des tribunaux sont logées dans trois volumes cubiques au fond du hall d'entrée dont le noir évoque une caverne. La trame rigoureuse s'impose à l'ensemble de la construction.

POLSHEK PARTNERSHIP

Polshek Partnership Architects, UP
320 West 13th Street
New York, NY 10014-1278
United States

Tel.: +1 212 807 7171
Fax: +1 212 807 5917
Email: info@polshek.com
Web: www.polshek.com

JAMES STEWART POLSHEK was born in Akron, Ohio, in 1930. He attended Case Western Reserve University (Cleveland, Ohio), graduating in 1951. He received his M.Arch. degree from Yale in 1955 and established his own practice in New York in 1963. Recent projects include the renovation of Carnegie Hall (New York), the Center for the Arts Theater at Yerba Buena Gardens (San Francisco, 1993), a Government Office Building (Chambery-le Haut, France, 1994), the Skirball Institute for Biomolecular Medicine and Residence Tower at New York University Medical Center (1993), the Seamen's Church Institute in the South Street Seaport Historic District (New York, 1991) and the renovation and expansion of the Brooklyn Museum of Art (New York). Recent projects include the Rose Center for Earth and Space, American Museum of Natural History (1997-2000) with his co-Design Principal on this project **TODD H. SCHLIEMANN**, the Cooper Hewitt National Design Museum renovation, and the Manhattan Supreme Court Criminal Courts Building, all in New York, and the National Museum of the American Indian Cultural Resources Center in Suitland, Maryland. James Stewart Polshek was Dean of the Graduate School of Architecture, Columbia University, New York (1972-1987) until Bernard Tschumi succeeded him in that post.

JAMES STEWART POLSHEK, geboren 1930 in Akron, Ohio, schloss 1951 sein Studium an der Case Western Reserve University in Cleveland ab. 1955 erwarb er seinen Master of Architecture an der Yale University und gründete 1963 sein eigenes Architekturbüro in New York. Zu Polsheks neueren Projekten zählen die Renovierung der Carnegie Hall in New York, das Center for the Arts Theater in den Yerba Buena Gardens in San Francisco (1993), ein Regierungsgebäude im französischen Chambery-le Haut (1994), das Skirball Institute for Biomolecular Medicine und ein Wohnturm im New York University Medical Center (1993), das Seamen's Church Institute im South Street Seaport Historic District in New York (1991) sowie die Renovierung und Erweiterung des Brooklyn Museum of Art in New York. Zu seinen jüngsten Arbeiten gehören das hier vorgestellte Rose Center for Earth and Space am American Museum of Natural History (1997-2000), zusammen mit **TODD H. SCHLIEMANN**, die Modernisierung des Cooper Hewitt National Design Museum und das Manhattan Supreme Court Criminal Courts Building alle in New York, sowie das National Museum of the American Indian Cultural Resources Center in Suitland, Maryland. Von 1971 bis 1987 war James Stewart Polshek Dekan der Graduate School of Architecture an der Columbia University in New York, bis Bernard Tschumi ihm auf diesem Posten nachfolgte.

JAMES STEWART POLSHEK naît à Akron, Ohio, en 1930. Il suit les cours de la Case Western Reserve University (Cleveland, Ohio) dont il est diplômé en 1951. Il passe son Master en architecture à Yale (1955) et crée sa propre agence à New York en 1963. Parmi ses réalisations : la rénovation de Carnegie Hall (New York), le Center for the Arts en Yerba Buena Gardens (San Francisco, 1993), un immeuble administratif en France (Chambéry-le-Haut, 1994), le Skirball Institute for Biomolecular Medicine and Residence Tower à la New York University Medical Center (1993), le Seamen's Church Institute du South Street Seaport Historic District (New York, 1991), la rénovation et l'extension du Brooklyn Museum of Art (New York). Plus récemment, il a réalisé avec **TODD H. SCHLIEMANN** le Rose Center for Earth and Space, American Museum of Natural History (1997-2000), la rénovation du Cooper Hewitt National Design Museum et le Manhattan Supreme Court Criminal Courts Building à New York, le National Museum of the American Indian Cultural Resources Center à Suitland, Maryland. James Stewart Polshek a été doyen de la Graduate School of Architecture, Columbia University, New York (1972-87), poste dont Bernard Tschumi a pris la succession.

ROSE CENTER FOR EARTH AND SPACE

*Frederick Phineas and Sandra Priest Rose Center for
Earth and Space, American Museum of Natural History
New York, NY, USA, 1997-2000*

*Client: American Museum of Natural History. Floor area of the sphere: 3 045 m².
Volume of the cube: c. 53 930 m³. Costs: $210 million.*

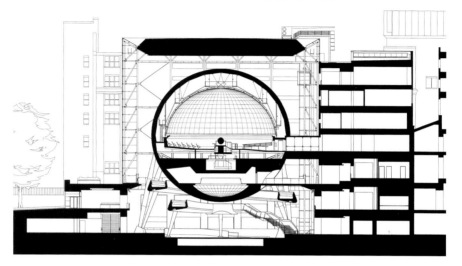

Located on the Upper West Side of Manhattan, at the northern extremity of the **AMERICAN MUSEUM OF NATURAL HISTORY, THE ROSE CENTER** is a seven-story complex of 30 000 m², built at a cost of $210 million. Set near Central Park on 81st Street, the spectacular 29 m-high glass building encloses the 27 m-diameter sphere housing the Hayden Planetarium. The original Hayden Planetarium, built in 1935, was considered a historic landmark by New Yorkers, and Polshek's plan to "blow it up and build a planetarium for the 21st century" caused initial opposition. The building's spherical form brings to mind historical precedents such as Etienne-Louis Boullée's cenotaph to Isaak Newton, or Claude-Nicolas Ledoux's Maison des gardes agricoles and his cemetery of the Saline de Chaux. More recently, Itsuko Hasegawa's Shonandai Cultural Center (Fujisawa, Kanagawa, 1987-90), and Adrien Fainsilber's Géode at La Villette in Paris. The new Rose Center, calling on the most sophisticated technology of astronomy and architecture, brings the public experience of the universe up to date in a most spectacular manner and, at that, in the heart of New York.

Das **ROSE CENTER** liegt an der Upper West Side von Manhattan, am nördlichen Ende des **AMERICAN MUSEUM OF NATURAL HISTORY** und ist ein siebengeschossiger, insgesamt 30 000 m² umfassender Komplex, der für 210 Millionen Dollar erbaut wurde. Das nahe dem Central Park in der 81. Straße errichtete spektakuläre Gebäude ist 29 m hoch und schließt eine Kugel mit einem Durchmesser von 27 m ein, die das Hayden Planetarium beherbergt. Dieses Planetarium wurde 1935 erbaut und gilt unter New Yorkern als historisches Baudenkmal, weshalb Polsheks Plan, »es in die Luft zu jagen und ein Planetarium für das 21. Jahrhundert zu errichten« für Widerstand sorgte. Die Kugelform des Gebäudes erinnert an historische Vorläufer wie Étienne-Louis Boullées Kenotaph für Isaac Newton oder das Maison des Gardes Agricoles und den Friedhof von Saline de Chaux von Claude-Nicolas Ledoux. Jüngere Beispiele für die Verwendung dieser geometrischen Grundform sind Itsuko Hasegawas Shonandai Cultural Center in Fujisawa, Kanagawa (1987-90) oder Adrien Fainsilbers Géode im Pariser La Villette. Das neue, mit modernster astronomischer und architektonischer Technologie konzipierte Rose Center bringt der Öffentlichkeit auf beeindruckende Weise das Erlebnis des Universums nahe, und das im Herzen von New York.

Situé dans le quartier de l'Upper West Side à Manhattan, à l'extrémité nord du **MUSEUM D'HISTOIRE NATURELLE, LE ROSE CENTER** est un complexe de sept niveaux et de 30 000 m² édifié pour un budget de $210 millions. Sur 81st Street, en bordure de Central Park, ce spectaculaire bâtiment de verre de 296 m de haut enferme une sphère de 27 m de diamètre qui abrite le Hayden Planetarium. Le Hayden Planetarium d'origine, construit en 1935, était considéré comme un monument par les New-yorkais, c'est pourquoi l'intention de Polshek de « l'exploser et de construire un planétaire pour le XXIe siècle » rencontra d'abord une vive opposition. La forme sphérique du bâtiment rappelle des projets comme le cénotaphe pour Isaak Newton de Etienne-Louis Boullée ou la maison des gardes agricoles et le cimetière des Salines de Chaux de Claude-Nicolas Ledoux, ainsi que plus récemment, le centre culturel Shonandai de Itsuko Hasegawa (Fujisawa, Kanagawa, 1987-90) ou la géode d'Adrien Fainsilber à la Cité des Sciences de la Villette à Paris. Le nouveau Rose Center qui fait appel aux technologies les plus sophistiquées en matière d'astronomie et d'architecture, il propose au public une des plus spectaculaires expérimentations de l'univers à ce jour, et ce en plein cœur de New York.

Where Santiago Calatrava chose the image of an eye for his Planetarium in Valencia, Polshek has preferred to use the sphere as a metaphor for the earth or other celestial bodies.

Während Santiago Calatrava die Form eines Auges für sein Planetarium in Valencia wählte, zog Polshek die Kugel als Metapher für die Erde und andere Himmelskörper vor.

Alors que Calatrava choisissait la forme d'un œil pour son Planétarium de Valence, Polshek a préféré celle de la sphère, métaphore de la terre et des planètes.

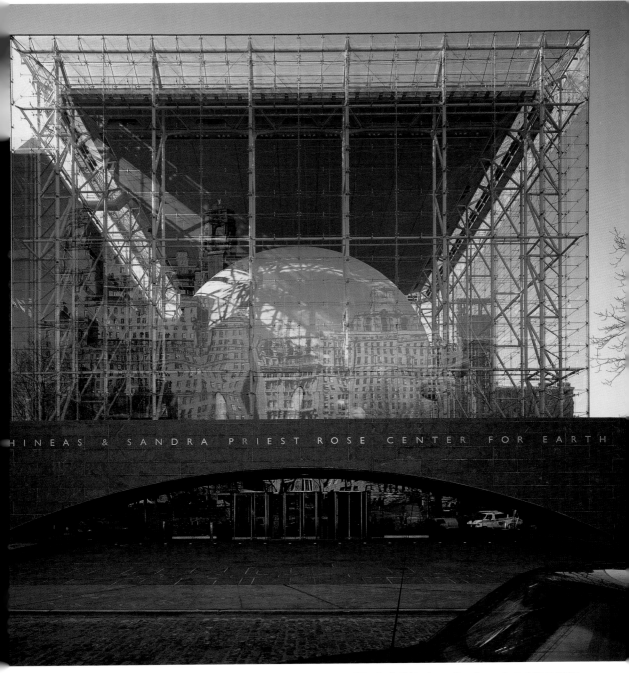

HINEAS & SANDRA PRIEST ROSE CENTER FOR EARTH

The external envelope reveals the inner sphere, if not the full complexity of the structure as seen in the drawing above left.

Die äußere Hülle gibt die Sicht auf den inneren Baukörper frei. Die Komplexität des Gebäudes wird erst im Aufriß (oben links) deutlich.

L'enveloppe externe révèle la sphère intérieure, mais non la complexité de la structure que montre le dessin ci-dessus à gauche.

Around the central sphere, the theme of the solar system is carried through to areas efficiently designed to receive the very large number of daily visitors drawn to the building.

Das Thema des Sonnensystems wird in allen Bereichen aufgegriffen und diese so gestaltet, dass sie die großen Besuchermengen gut bewältigen können.

Autour de la sphère centrale, le thème du système solaire se poursuit à travers les halls et les circulations conçus pour un grand nombre de visiteurs.

LVMH Tower ▶

CHRISTIAN DE PORTZAMPARC

Atelier Christian de Portzamparc
1, rue de l'Aude
75014 Paris
France

Tel: +33 1 4064 8000
Fax: +33 1 4327 7479
e-mail: studio@chdeportzamparc.com

CHRISTIAN DE PORTZAMPARC was born in Casablanca, Morocco in 1944. He studied at the École des Beaux-Arts, Paris (1962-69). Built projects include a Water Tower (Marne-la-Vallée, 1971-74), Les Hautes Formes public housing, (Paris, 1975-79), Nexus World housing (Fukuoka, Japan, 1989-91), extension for the Bourdelle Museum (Paris, 1988-92), the Cité de la Musique (Paris, 1984-95), the housing complex ZAC Bercy (Paris, 1991-94), and the Crédit Lyonnais Tower (Euralille, Lille, France, 1991-95, built over the new Lille-Europe railway station). He was awarded the 1994 Pritzker Prize. Recent work includes the LVMH Tower on 57th Street in New York (1996-99) published here, an extension to the Palais des Congrès Porte Maillot in Paris (1994-99), a tower for the Bandai Toy Company in Tokyo (1995-), a courthouse for Grasse in southern France (1993-2000), and the French Embassy in Berlin, due to be completed in 2002.

CHRISTIAN DE PORTZAMPARC, geboren 1944 in Casablanca, Marokko, studierte von 1962 bis 1969 an der École des Beaux-Arts in Paris. Zu seinen realisierten Projekten gehören der Water Tower in Marne-la-Vallée (1971-74), die Wohnanlage Les Hautes Formes in Paris (1975-79), die Nexus World-Wohnanlage im japanischen Fukuoka (1989-91), die Erweiterung des Museums Bourdelle in Paris (1988-92), die Cité de la Musique in Paris (1984-95), die ZAC Bercy-Wohnsiedlung in Paris (1991-94) und der über dem neuen Euralille-Bahnhof errichtete Crédit Lyonnais Tower in Lille (1991-1995). 1994 wurde Portzamparc mit dem Pritzker Prize ausgezeichnet. Zu seinen jüngsten Arbeiten zählen der hier vorgestellte LVMH Tower in New York (1996-99), ein Anbau für den Palais des Congrès Porte Maillot in Paris (1994-99), ein seit 1995 im Bau befindlicher Turm für die Spielzeugfabrik Bandai in Tokio, ein Gerichtsgebäude im südfranzösischen Grasse sowie die Französische Botschaft in Berlin, deren Fertigstellung für 2002 geplant ist.

Né à Casablanca en 1944, **CHRISTIAN DE PORTZAMPARC** étudie à l'Ecole des Beaux-Arts de Paris (1962-69). Parmi ses réalisations : un château d'eau (Marne-la-Vallée, 1971-74), l'immeuble de logements économiques Les Hautes Formes (Paris, 1975-79), un immeuble d'appartement, Nexus World (Fukuoka, Japon, 1989-91), l'extension du Musée Bourdelle (Paris, 1988-92), la Cité de la Musique (Paris, 1984-95), un immeuble d'habitation dans la ZAC de Bercy (Paris, 1991-94) et la tour du Crédit Lyonnais (Euralille, Lille, 1991-95), au-dessus de la gare de Lille-Europe. Il obtient en 1994 le Pritzker Prize. Il a récemment réalisé la tour LVMH, 57th Street, à New York (1996-99) publiée ici, l'extension du Palais des Congrès Porte Maillot (Paris, 1994-99), le Palais de justice de Grasse, France (1993-2000), une tour pour la Bandai Toy Company à Tokyo (1995-) et l'ambassade de France à Berlin, qui devrait être achevée en 2002.

LVMH TOWER

New York, NY, USA, 1995-99

Planning: 1995-97. Construction: 1997-99. Client: LVMH Corporation.
Floor area: 8 683 m². Costs: withheld.

By using New York City zoning regulations very efficiently, the architect managed to translate the setbacks in the facade into extra height – used for the three-story "Magic Room" at the top of the structure.

In sehr geschickter Umsetzung der New Yorker Bauvorschriften gelang es dem Architekten durch das Zurückstufen der Fassade (rechts) zusätzliche Höhe zu gewinnen, die er für die Anlage des dreistöckigen »Magic Room« (oben) als Bekrönung des Gebäudes nutzte.

Par une interprétation habile de la réglementation du zoning new-yorkais, l'architecte a mis à profit des retraits pour augmenter la hauteur de la tour et créer sa "Magic Room" de trois étages de haut, au sommet de l'édifice.

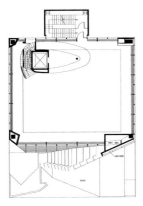

23th floor

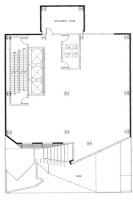

19th floor

3th floor

Set near the corner of 57th Street and Madison Avenue, the **LVMH TOWER** represents a shift in the design of tall buildings. Rather than the more common un-differentiated facade generally seen in Manhattan, this 23-story office building represents a complex Saint Gobain glass facade designed to avoid direct reflections of the black IBM Tower just across 57th Street. By carefully studying New York's complex zoning laws after a series of setbacks, the architect managed, through the use of a sophisticated design, to increase the overall height of his building, even edging out the neighboring Chanel Tower. This gave him the possibility of creating the so-called "Magic Room" atop the tower – a spectacular three-story room with views on three sides onto 57th Street, and toward Central Park. Portzamparc's contribution to the tower is in good part limited to this room and the facade, since the design of the offices, and of the boutiques on the ground floor, is the work of other architects. A sophis-ticated lighting system inserted into a "fault" line running up the facade gives the building a real night-time identity in the cityscape.

Der nahe der Kreuzung von 57. Straße und Madison Avenue gelegene 23-geschossige **LVMH TOWER** stellt mit seiner komplexen Fassade aus Saint Gobain-Glas eine Neuerung in der Hochhausarchitektur dar. Die Fassade, die sich deutlich von dem üblichen Erscheinungsbild der Hochhäuser in Manhatten absetzt, ist so strukturiert, dass eine direkte Spiegelung des genau gegenüberliegenden schwarzen IBM-Turms vermieden wird. In Umgehung der komplizierten New Yorker Baugesetze durch den Einsatz eines raffinierten Entwurfs, ist es dem Architekten gelungen, die Gesamthöhe seines Bürogebäudes so zu vergrößern, dass es nun sogar den benachbarten Chanel Tower überragt. Dies gab Portzamparc die Möglichkeit, den sogenannten »Magic Room« an die Turmspitze zu setzen – einen spektakulären dreigeschossigen Raum mit freiem, dreiseitigem Ausblick auf die 57. Straße und den Central Park. Portzamparcs Beitrag zur Gestaltung des Hochhauses beschränkt sich im Wesentlichen auf diesen Raum und die Fassade, die Büros und die im Erdgeschoß befindlichen Geschäfte wurden von anderen Architekten entworfen und ausgeführt. Eine kunstvolle Beleuchtung, die in einer an der Fassade verlaufenden »Bruchlinie« eingesetzt wurde, verleiht dem Gebäude auch bei Nacht eine unverkennbare Identität.

Dressée presque à l'angle de la 57th Street et de Madison Avenue, la **TOUR LVMH** marque une évolution dans la conception des immeubles de grande hauteur. Au lieu de ces façades plus ou moins différenciées que l'on voit d'habitude à Manhattan, cette tour de bureaux de 23 étages arbore une complexe façade en verre de Saint Gobain conçue pour éviter la réflexion directe de l'énorme tour noire d'IBM qui se dresse de l'autre côté de la rue. Après avoir étudié attentivement la réglementation com-pliquée du zoning de la ville de New York, Portzamparc a réussi, au moyen d'une série d'habiles retraits, à augmenter la hauteur totale de l'immeuble, jusqu'à dépasser sa voisine, la Tour Chanel. Ceci lui a permis de créer, au sommet, la « Magic-Room », une spectaculaire salle de trois étages de haut qui offre des vues sur trois côtés et sur Central Park. La contribution de l'architecte s'est pour une bonne part limitée à la façade et à cette salle, car l'aménagement des bureaux et des boutiques a été confiée à d'autres intervenants. Un système sophistiqué d'éclairage a été inséré dans une « faille » qui court verticalement sur la façade ce qui, la nuit, confère à l'immeuble sa forte identité.

Christian de Portzamparc concentrat-ed his efforts on the facade, and the Magic Room. His responsibility did not extend to interior decoration or to the ground level Christian Dior boutique designed by Peter Marino.

Christian de Portzamparc konzentrier-te sich in seiner Gestaltung auf die Fassade und den »Magic Room«. Er war weder für die Innenraumausstat-tung noch für die im Erdgeschoss liegende und von Peter Marino ent-worfene Christian Dior Boutique zuständig.

Christian de Portzamparc a concentré ses efforts sur la façade et la "Magic Room". Il n'a été chargé ni des amé-nagements intérieures ni du magasin Christian Dior du rez-de-chaussée, œuvre de Peter Marino.

ELIZABETH DE PORTZAMPARC

Elizabeth de Portzamparc
Architecte d'Intérieurs-Mobilier
77/79, rue du Cherche Midi
75006 Paris
France

Tel: + 33 1 5363 3232
Fax: + 33 1 5363 3239
e-mail: elizabeth.deportzamparc@wanadoo.fr
web: www.elizabethdeportzamparc.com

Born in Brazil, **ELIZABETH DE PORTZAMPARC** has been active in design and architecture in Paris since 1975, when she did a study of the urban development of the Elancourt-Maurepas area of Saint-Quentin en Yvelines. She was Director of the Urban Planning Atelier of the city of Antony from 1977 to 1980. From 1988 to 1992, she created and directed the design gallery Mostra in Paris. She worked on the interior design of the Grasse Law Courts (1996-99), and is presently designing the interiors of the future French Embassy in Berlin (with Christian de Portzamparc). She was selected to design the station stops for the new Bordeaux tramway line, and is creating not only the interior design and furniture for The Munt, a multiple-screen movie theater in Amsterdam, but also the interiors for the Musée de la Bretagne in Rennes. She completed the Espionne boutique at the Palais des Congrès in Paris (1999), and the Café de la Musique, also in Paris (1995), as well as numerous apartments.

Die in Brasilien geborene **ELIZABETH DE PORTZAMPARC** ist seit ihrer 1975 entstandenen Studie über die Stadtentwicklung des Elancourt-Maurepas Bezirks von Saint-Quentin en Yveline als Designerin und Architektin in Paris tätig. Von 1977 bis 1980 war sie Leiterin des Ateliers für Stadtplanung der Stadt Antony und von 1988 bis 1992 gestaltete und leitete sie die Design Galerie Mostra in Paris. Sie entwarf die Innenausstattung des Gerichtsgebäudes in Grasse (1996-99) und arbeitet derzeit zusammen mit ihrem Mann Christian de Portzamparc an der Innenarchitektur der zukünftigen Französischen Botschaft in Berlin. Aktuell ist sie mit der Gestaltung der Haltestellen für eine neue Straßenbahnlinie in Bordeaux beauftragt und entwirft die Innenraumgestaltung und Einrichtung für The Munt (ein Multiplex-Kino in Amsterdam) und die Interieurs des Musée de la Bretagne in Rennes. Abgeschlossene Projekte sind die Boutique Espionne im Palais des Congrès in Paris (1999), das ebenfalls in Paris liegende Café de la Musique (1995) sowie zahlreiche Privatwohnungen.

Née au Brésil, **ELIZABETH DE PORTZAMPARC** est active dans les domaines de l'architecture et du design à Paris depuis 1975, date de son étude sur le développement de la zone d'Elancourt-Maurepas à Saint-Quentin-en-Yvelines. Elle dirige l'atelier d'urbanisme de la ville d'Antony de 1977 à 1980. De 1988 à 1992, elle a créé et animé la galerie de design Mostra à Paris. Elle conçoit les aménagements intérieurs du palais de justice de Grasse (1996-99) et l'intérieur de la future ambassade de France à Berlin (avec Christian de Portzamparc). Elle a été sélectionnée pour les arrêts de la nouvelle ligne de tramway de Bordeaux, les aménagements intérieurs et le mobilier de De Munt (une salle de cinéma multiplex à Amsterdam) et ceux du Musée de la Bretagne à Rennes. Elle a réalisé la boutique Espionne au Palais des Congrès de Paris (1999), le Café de la Musique, toujours à Paris (1995), ainsi que de nombreux appartements.

LES GRANDES MARCHES
RESTAURANT

Paris, France, 2000

*Planning: 11/1999-4/2000. Construction: 06-09/2000. Client: FLO Prestige.
Floor area: 1000 m². Costs: FF 13 million (not including the kitchen).*

In the large, deep volume of the ground floor, Elizabeth de Portzamparc has installed a spectacular spiraling staircase. She specifically designed the furniture for this restaurant as well.

Elizabeth de Portzamparc setzte eine spektakulär geschwungene Treppe in das sich weiträumig in die Tiefe erstreckende Erdgeschoss. Sie hat auch die Möbel speziell für dieses Restaurant entworfen.

Dans le vaste et profond rez-de-chaussée, Elisabeth de Portzamparc a implanté un spectaculaire escalier en spirale. Elle a également dessiné l'ensemble du mobilier de ce restaurant.

Built in the ground floor of an annex of the Bastille Opera in Paris (designed by Carlos Ott), **LES GRANDES MARCHES RESTAURANT** is set in a space whose previous decor was truly banal. Elizabeth de Portzamparc reworked the ground and first floor of the space (a total of 1 000 m², with 650 m² open to the public) around a sweeping new monumental staircase, whose steps are referred to in the restaurant's name. The upper level offers carefully framed views of the Bastille Square. The facility, which can seat 220 people, was built in just three months (June 5 to September 6, 2000). Many of the curving, sensuous wall surfaces have a metallic appearance achieved through the use of sprayed titanium particles. Elizabeth de Portzamparc designed not only the basic volumes of the restaurant, but also its furniture, and facilities such as the bar or toilets, giving a sense of coherence to the whole that is rarely achieved in a chain restaurant (Les Grandes Marches belongs to the Flo brasserie chain). Christian de Portzamparc designed a glazed structure for the restaurant's terrace, but the interior is very much in the spirit of his wife's work, in particular her Café de la Musique in the Villette area of Paris.

Das im Erdgeschoss eines von Carlos Ott entworfenen Anbaus der Pariser Opéra de la Bastille gelegene **RESTAURANT LES GRANDES MARCHES** entstand als Umbau von ursprünglich eher unspektakulär gestalteten Räumlichkeiten. Das Zentrum der Räume im Erdgeschoss und dem ersten Stock (mit einer Gesamtnutzfläche von 1 000 m², von denen 650 m² der Öffentlichkeit zugänglich sind) bildet eine monumentale, weit ausschwingende Treppe, die dem Restaurant seinen Namen gab. Im oberen Stockwerk bieten sich dem Besucher sorgfältig gerahmte Ausblicke auf den Place de la Bastille. Das Restaurant mit 220 Sitzplätzen wurde in nur drei Monaten, von Juni bis September 2000, fertiggestellt. Die sinnlich gewölbten Wandoberflächen sind teilweise mit Titanpartikeln besprüht, was ihnen eine metallische Wirkung verleiht. Elizabeth de Portzamparc ist nicht nur für die Innenarchitektur des Restaurants verantwortlich, sondern entwarf auch die Möbel sowie verschiedene Nebenräume wie die Bar und die Toiletten. Dies verleiht dem Ganzen einen in sich stimmigen Eindruck, der in zu einer Kette gehörenden Restaurants (Les Grandes Marches gehört zur Flo Brasserie-Gruppe) selten anzutreffen ist. Das Restaurant-Interieur ist ein charakteristisches Beispiel für den Stil von Elizabeth de Portzamparc, der auch in anderen ihrer Arbeiten, insbesondere im Café de la Musique im Pariser Viertel Villette, zum Ausdruck kommt. Der verglaste Bauteil für die Restaurant-Terrasse stammt von ihrem Mann Christian de Portzamparc.

Aménagé au rez-de-chaussée d'un bâtiment annexe de l'Opéra Bastille de Paris (Carlos Ott), le **RESTAURANT LES GRANDES MARCHES** est implanté dans un volume dont le décor était banal. Elisabeth de Portzamparc a retravaillé ses deux niveaux (1 000 m², dont 650 ouverts au public) autour d'un nouvel escalier monumental en courbe, dont les marches évoquent le nom de l'établissement. Le niveau supérieur donne sur la place de la Bastille avec des vues soigneusement cadrées. L'ensemble de 220 places a été réalisé en trois mois (5 juin-6 septembre 2000). Les courbes sensuelles des murs présentent un aspect métallique dû à la projection de particules de titane. Elisabeth de Portzamparc a conçu à la fois les volumes, le mobilier et les équipements, comme le bar ou les toilettes, pour arriver à une cohérence que l'on trouve rarement dans un restaurant de chaîne (Flo en l'occurrence). Pour la terrasse, Christian de Portzamparc a dessiné une structure de métal et de verre, dans l'esprit du travail de son épouse, qui avait déjà créé le café de la Musique à la Villette.

A view of the restaurant area (above) and the bar (right) on the upper level of the Grandes Marches Restaurant. Views toward the Place de la Bastille are combined here with a refinement in both color schemes and lighting patterns.

Blick in den Restaurantbereich (oben) und die Bar (rechts) in der oberen Etage des Grandes Marches Restaurants. Die Aussicht auf den Place de la Bastille wird hier mit einer raffinierten Farbzusammenstellung und Lichtgestaltung kombiniert.

Vue de la salle de restaurant (en haut) et du bar (à droite) à l'étage du Restaurant des Grandes Marches. Les vues sur la place de la Bastille participent au raffinement des propositions chromatiques et de l'éclairage.

RICHARD ROGERS

Richard Rogers Partnership
Thames Wharf
Rainville Road
London W6 9HA
England

Tel: +44 207 385 1235
Fax: +44 207 385 8409
e-mail: enquiries@richardrogers.co.uk
Web: www.richardrogers.co.uk

Born in 1933 in Florence, Italy, of British parents, **RICHARD ROGERS** studied at the Architectural Association in London (1954-59). He received his M.Arch. degree from the Yale University School of Architecture in 1962, and created partnerships with his wife Su Rogers, Norman and Wendy Foster (Team 4, London, 1964-66), and with Renzo Piano in London, Paris and Genoa (1971-77). In 1977, he founded Richard Rogers Partnership in London. He has taught at Yale, and has been Chairman of the Trustees of the Tate Gallery, London (1981-89). His main buildings include the Centre Georges Pompidou (Paris, with Renzo Piano, 1971-77), the Lloyd's of London Headquarters (1978-86), Channel 4 Television Headquarters (London, 1990-94), the European Court of Human Rights (Strasbourg, France, 1989-95), the Daimler Benz Offices and Housing (Potsdamer Platz, Berlin, 1994-98), and the Law Courts (Bordeaux, France, 1993-98).

RICHARD ROGERS, 1933 als Sohn britischer Eltern in Florenz geboren, studierte von 1954 bis 1959 an der Architectural Association in London. Seinen Master of Architecture erwarb er 1962 an der Yale University School of Architecture. Mit seiner Frau Su sowie Norman und Wendy Foster gründete er 1964 in London das Büro Team 4, das bis 1966 bestand. Von 1971 bis 1977 arbeitete er in Partnerschaft mit Renzo Piano in London, Paris und Genua. 1977 gründete er Richard Rogers Partnership in London. Rogers hat in Yale gelehrt und war von 1981 bis 1989 Vorstand des Kuratoriums der Tate Gallery in London. Zu seinen wichtigsten Bauten gehören das Centre Georges Pompidou in Paris (mit Renzo Piano, 1971-77), die Hauptverwaltung von Lloyd's of London (1978-86), die Zentrale von Channel 4 in London (1990-94), der Europäische Gerichtshof für Menschenrechte in Straßburg (1989-95), die Büros und Wohnungen für Daimler-Benz am Potsdamer Platz in Berlin (1994-98) sowie das Palais de Justice in Bordeaux (1993-98).

Né à Florence, Italie, en 1933 de parents britanniques, **RICHARD ROGERS** étudie à l'Architectural Association de Londres (1954-59). Diplômé d'architecture de la Yale University School of Architecture en 1962, il fonde une agence avec son épouse Su Rogers, Norman and Wendy Foster (Team 4, Londres, 1964-66), puis avec Renzo Piano à Londres, Paris et Gènes (1971-77). Il crée Richard Rogers Partnership à Londres en 1977. Il a enseigné à Yale et a été président du Conseil d'administration de la Tate Gallery, (Londres, 1981-89). Parmi ses principales réalisations : le Centre Georges Pompidou (Paris, avec Renzo Piano, 1971-77), le siège des Lloyd's of London (Londres, 1978-86), le siège de Channel 4 (Londres, 1990-94), la Cour européenne des droits de l'homme (Strasbourg, France, 1989-95), le Palais de justice de Bordeaux (1993-98), ainsi que des bureaux et des logements pour Daimler Benz (Potsdamer Platz, Berlin, 1994-98).

MILLENNIUM DOME

London, England, 1996-99

Competition: 2/96. Planning: 5/96-5/97. Construction: 6/97-9/99.
Client: The New Millennium Experience Company Limited. Total floor area: 250 000 m².
Costs: £43 000 000.

The structure of Richard Rogers' **MILLENNIUM DOME** is based on a network of cable netting suspended from twelve 100-m masts, covered by a 100,000-m² canopy of PTFE-coated glass fiber. This project is by any definition massive; the site structures and associated infrastructure cost no less than £43 million. Despite its size, the Millennium Dome appears in a sense as little more than a large tent. At that, its overall height gives visitors the impression that the structure is in fact less imposing than it really is. The interior pavilions have very little to do with the design of the dome itself, since they are each the work of other architects. Rogers' technological approach is evident in the masts and the freestanding blocks that provide climatic control or electrical power for the complex. Heavily criticized for its cost and infrastructure failures, the Dome nonetheless marked the turn of the century more clearly than any other building erected elsewhere in the world.

Richard Rogers' **MILLENNIUM DOME** besteht aus einem an zwölf 100 m hohen Masten aufgehängten Stahlkabelgeflecht, das von einem 100 000 m² großen Schutzdach mit Teflon PTFE (Polytetrafluorethylen) beschichteter Glasfaser überdeckt wird. Dieses in jeder Hinsicht riesige Projekt hat alles in allem die Summe von 43 Millionen Pfund verschlungen. Trotz seiner enormen Größe wirkt der Millennium Dome eher wie ein überdimensionales Zelt, und auch seine Gesamthöhe macht auf ankommende Besucher einen weitaus weniger imposanten Eindruck als erwartet. Die im Inneren verteilten Ausstellungspavillons haben sehr wenig mit der Gestaltung des Bauwerks selbst zu tun, da sie alle von unterschiedlichen Architekten ausgeführt wurden. Rogers sehr technisch geprägter Entwurf zeigt sich an den Masten und freistehenden Baukörpern, die zur Regulierung von Temperatur und Luftfeuchtigkeit bzw. der Stromversorgung dienen. Obgleich der Millennium Dome wegen seiner Kosten und aufgetretener infrastruktureller Pannen heftig kritisiert wurde, markierte er die Jahrhundertwende eindrucksvoller als jedes andere Bauwerk.

La structure du **DOME DU MILLÉNAIRE** de Richard Rogers est tenue par un réseau de câbles suspendus partant de 12 mâts de 100 m de haut. Elle est recouverte d'une toile de 100 000 m² en fibre de verre enduite de PTFE. Ce projet est gigantesque à tous égards. Rien que les aménagements du site et les infrastructures ont coûté £43 millions. Malgré sa taille, le dôme n'est guère plus imposant qu'une immense tente. Vu de loin, sa hauteur relativement faible par rapport à sa circonférence donne aux visiteurs l'impression qu'il est moins gigantesque qu'en réalité. Les pavillons intérieurs ont peu de rapport avec le dôme lui-même, puisque chacun d'entre eux a été confié à un architecte différent. L'approche technologique de Rogers se reconnaît aux mâts et aux blocs techniques indépendants qui conditionnent l'air et fournissent l'électricité à l'ensemble. Très critiqué pour son coût et les problèmes posés par certains défauts d'infrastructures, le dôme néanmoins a marqué davantage le changement de millénaire que n'importe quel bâtiment érigé à cette occasion dans le monde.

Seen from almost any angle, the Dome does not give a real sense of its immensity, because of the flat curve of the roof.

Die flache Wölbung des Daches verschleiert die eigentliche Größe des Millennium Dome.

La courbe aplatie du toit empêche de percevoir l'immensité du dôme, quel que soit l'angle de vue.

The carnival or circus atmosphere beneath the Dome was of course not at all the architect's responsibility, but the Dome itself remains tainted in England by the failure of its attractions.

Obwohl der Architekt für die zirkusartige Atmosphäre im Inneren des Doms nicht verantwortlich war, hat sein Gebäude auch wegen des Misserfolgs seiner Attraktionen in England erheblich an Ansehen verloren.

L'atmosphère de carnaval ou de cirque de l'intérieur du dôme ne doit rien à l'architecte. L'échec du projet tient au manque d'attractivité de son contenu.

SCHMIDT, HAMMER & LASSEN

Schmidt, Hammer & Lassen K/S
Mønsgade 8
Postbox 13
8000 Århus C
Denmark

Tel: +45 86 201900
Fax: +45 86 184513
e-mail: info@shl.dk
Web: www.shl.dk

Extension of the Royal Library of Denmark ►

MORTEN SCHMIDT was born in 1956. Joint Managing Director of SHL, he graduated from the School of Architecture in Århus (1982). He is in charge of the company's international projects. **BJARNE HAMMER** was born in 1955, and is also a Joint Managing Director of the firm. He graduated from the Århus School of Architecture in 1982, and is in charge of projects for the Danish government, municipalities and service businesses. **JOHN F. LASSEN,** born in 1953, also graduated from the Århus School (1983) ,and is in charge of housing projects for SHL. The fourth Joint Managing Director is **KIM HOLST JENSEN**, born in 1964. Current work for the firm includes a new headquarters for NCC Denmark (under construction), new headquarters for Andersen Consulting near the Copenhagen Harbor (1998-2001), and 700 housing units for NCC Polska in Warsaw, currently under construction.

MORTEN SCHMIDT, geboren 1956, schloß 1982 sein Studium an der Architekturschule in Århus ab. Gegenwärtig ist er als Kodirektor von SHL für die Durchführung der internationalen Firmenprojekte verantwortlich. **BJARNE HAMMER** wurde 1955 geboren und machte ebenfalls 1982 seinen Abschluß an der Architekturschule in Århus. Auch er ist Kodirektor von SHL; sein Aufgabengebiet umfaßt die Betreuung von Projekten für die dänische Regierung sowie für Stadtbehörden und Dienstleistungsunternehmen. **JOHN LASSEN**, geboren 1953, studierte bis 1983 an der Architekturschule in Århus und betreut derzeit die Wohnbauprojekte von SHL. Vierter Kodirektor der Firma ist der 1964 geborene **KIM HOLST JENSEN**. Zu den jüngsten Projekten von SHL gehören neue Hauptverwaltungen für NCC Dänemark (im Bau) und für Andersen Consulting in der Nähe des Kopenhagener Hafens (1998-2001) sowie die derzeit im Bau befindlichen 900 Wohneinheiten für NCC Polska in Warschau.

Né en 1956, **MORTEN SCHMIDT** est codirecteur de l'agence SHL et chargé des projets internationaux. Il est diplômé de l'Ecole d'architecture de Århus (1982). **BJARNE HAMMER**, né en 1955 et également codirecteur, est chargé des projets pour l'Etat danois, les municipalités et les entreprises de service. Il est diplômé de l'Ecole d'architecture de Århus (1982). **JOHN LASSEN**, né en 1953, a fait ses études au même endroit (diplômé en 1983), il est responsable de projets pour le secteur du logement. Le quatrième codirecteur est **KIM HOLST JENSEN**, né en 1964. Parmi leurs projets en cours : le nouveau siège de NCC Danemark, le siège de Andersen Consulting, près du port de Copenhague (1999-2001) et 900 appartements pour NCC Polska à Varsovie, actuellement en construction.

EXTENSION OF THE ROYAL LIBRARY OF DENMARK

Copenhagen, Denmark, 1993-99

Planning: 1993-95. Construction: 1995-99. Client: The Danish Ministry of Culture/The Royal Library.
Floor area: new building ca. 21 000 m², rebuilding ca 6 500 m². Costs: DKK 370 000 000.

This **EXTENSION OF THE ROYAL LIBRARY OF DENMARK** founded in 1653 on the island of Slotsholmen in historical Copenhagen, near the Christiansborg Palace and the Copenhagen Stock Exchange, adds to the space 21 000 m² and increases its shelf capacity on open shelving to 200 000 volumes. A slanted seven-story black granite cube, the new building includes five exhibition galleries, a restaurant and a cafe, a store, an auditorium seating 600 people, and space for the National Folklore Archives, a Danish Literature Information Center and other cultural facilities. A dramatic sandstone-clad atrium looks out on the water, and escalators lead up to the first-floor reading rooms. The architects write that the atrium is "the organic interior of the building. The wavy design of the walls refers to the human, the body and the inner world of the soul." A transparent 18 m-long bridge connects to the original building above Christians Brygge from the main (C level) floor, emphasizing the proximity of the old city and underlining the openness of the new structure in contrast to its apparently closed black facades.

Der **ERWEITERUNGSBAU DER KÖNIGLICHEN BIBLIOTHEK VON DÄNEMARK** befindet sich in der Nähe des Christiansborg Palasts und der Kopenhagener Börse. Er fügt der Fläche der 1653 auf der Insel Slotsholmen im historischen Kopenhagen gegründeten Bibliothek etwa 21 000 m² hinzu und vergrößert die Regalfläche auf ein Fassungsvermögen von 200 000 Bände. Das neue Gebäude besteht aus einem siebengeschossigen Kubus aus schwarzem Granitstein und enthält fünf Ausstellungsräume, ein Restaurant und Café, ein Geschäft, ein Auditorium mit 600 Sitzen sowie Räume für das Nationale Volkskundearchiv, ein Informationszentrum zum Thema dänische Literatur und andere kulturelle Einrichtungen. Ein dramatisch wirkendes, mit Sandstein verkleidetes Atrium ist zum Wasser hin ausgerichtet, Rolltreppen führen zu den Lesesälen im ersten Stock. Die Architekten schreiben: »Das Atrium ist das organische Zentrum des Gebäudes. Das wellenförmig verlaufende Muster der Wände soll den Menschen, seinen Körper und die Innenwelt seiner Seele symbolisieren.« Durch eine transparente, 18 m lange Brücke, die das neue mit dem alten Gebäude verbindet, wird die Nähe der Altstadt spürbar und die Offenheit des neuen Bauteils im Kontrast zu seiner scheinbar geschlossenen schwarzen Außenfassade unterstrichen.

L'EXTENSION DE LA BIBLIOTHÈQUE ROYALE DU DANEMARK fondée en 1653 sur l'île de Slotsholmen dans le Copenhague historique, à proximité du palais de Christianborg et de la Bourse, augmente la surface jusqu'alors disponible de 210 000 m² et la capacité de stockage de 200 000 volumes. Un cube incliné, en granit s'élève sur 7 étages contenant cinq galeries d'exposition, un restaurant, une cafétéria, une boutique, un auditorium de 600 places, un espace pour les archives du folklore national, un centre d'information sur la littérature danoise et d'autres équipements culturels. Un spectaculaire atrium habillé de grès donne sur un plan d'eau. De là, des escaliers mécaniques conduisent aux salles de lecture du premier étage. Les architectes expliquent que l'atrium « est le cœur organique du bâtiment. En forme de vague, le dessin des murs renvoie à l'être humain, au corps et au monde intérieur de l'âme. » Une passerelle transparente de 18 m de long au-dessus de Christians Brygge relie l'extension au niveau principal (C) du bâtiment historique, ce qui renforce le lien avec la vieille ville et fait ressortir le caractère ouvert de cette nouvelle construction, qui contraste avec ses façades noires apparemment fermées.

Like Moneo's Kursaal Auditorium, the extension of the Royal Library has an angled, geometric monolithic quality that does not immediately identify any specific function.

Der Erweiterungsbau der Königlichen Bibliothek besitzt, ebenso wie Moneos Kursaal-Auditorium, schräge, strengmonolithisch wirkende Fassaden, die zunächst keine bestimmte Funktion erkennen lassen.

Comme dans le Kursaal de Moneo, l'extension de la Royal Library se présente sous forme d'un monolithe incliné qui n'exprime pas directement sa fonction spécifique.

Openings and passageways permit
visitors both to penetrate into the
monolith and to move about its inner
space more freely than might be
expected on the basis of the rather
austere façade.
Here, the mystery gives way to
an inner light, like a closed book
opening to its reader.

Zahlreiche Öffnungen und Durchgän-
ge erlauben den Besuchern, sich im
Inneren des Bauwerks freier zu bewegen (links), als es seine eher strenge,
geschlossene Außenfassade (oben)
erwarten lässt. Hier weicht das ge-
heimnisvolle Dunkel einer inneren
Helligkeit, wie bei einem Buch, das
sich seinem Leser öffnet.

Des ouvertures et des passages permettent aux visiteurs de pénétrer
dans le bâtiment monolithique et de
se déplacer à l'intérieur plus aisé-
ment que son austère façade ne le
laisse supposer. Le mystère fait place
à une sorte de lumière intérieure,
comme un livre fermé s'ouvrant sous
les yeux d'un lecteur.

The basic fragility of the book is here contrasted with the powerful materiality of a dark solid block of matter. Although some technical elements are visible, on the whole priority has been given to volume and movement over exposure of the workings of the building.

Die Fragilität des Buchs kontrastiert mit dem kraftvollen Materialcharakter der dunklen, massiven Stein- und Metallblöcke. Obwohl einige technische Details sichtbar sind, besaßen die Raumwirkung und Offenheit insgesamt Priorität vor einer funktionalen Ausdrucksweise.

La fragilité intrinsèque du livre contraste ici avec la puissante présence de ce bloc massif. Bien que certains éléments techniques restent visibles, dans l'ensemble, la priorité a été donnée aux espaces et au mouvement plutôt qu'à la mise en valeur de la structure du bâtiment.

Overlapping passageways and stairs give an almost Piranesian quality to this interior view (left), while a view of the same space from a different angle (right) emphasizes the opening toward the light and water of the exterior.

Einander überschneidende Übergänge und Treppen verleihen der Innenansicht eine an Piranesis Phantasiearchitektur erinnernde Raumwirkung (links). Dagegen wird in der Ansicht desselben Raums aus einem anderen Blickwinkel (rechts) die Öffnung nach außen, hin zu Licht und Wasser deutlich.

Des passages couverts et des escaliers superposés confèrent une qualité quasi piranèsienne à cette vue intérieure (à gauche), tandis qu'une vue du même espace sous un angle différent (à droite) met en valeur l'ouverture vers la lumière et l'eau, à l'extérieur.

ÁLVARO SIZA

Álvaro Siza – Arquitecto, LDA.
Rua do Aleixo, 53-2°
4150-043 Porto
Portugal

Tel: +351 22 616 7270
Fax: +351 22 616 7279

Serralves Foundation ▶

Born in Matosinhos, Portugal, in 1933, **ÁLVARO SIZA** studied at the University of Porto School of Architecture (1949-55). He created his own practice in 1954, and worked with Fernando Tavora from 1955 to 1958. Since 1976 he has been Professor of Construction at the University of Porto, receiving the European Mies van der Rohe Prize in 1988, and the Pritzker Prize in 1992. He built a large number of small-scale projects in Portugal, and more recently has worked on the reconstruction of the Chiado (Lisbon, Portugal, since 1989), the Meteorology Center (Barcelona, Spain, 1989-92), the Vitra Furniture Factory (Weil am Rhein, Germany, 1991-94), the Porto School of Architecture at Porto University (1986-95), and the University of Aveiro Library (Aveiro, Portugal, 1988-95). His latest projects are the Portuguese Pavilion for Expo '98 (Lisbon, 1998), and the Serralves Foundation (Porto, 1996-99) published here.

ÁLVARO SIZA, geboren 1933 in Matosinhos, Portugal, studierte von 1949 bis 1955 Architektur an der Universität Porto. 1954 gründete er sein eigenes Büro, in dem er von 1955 bis 1958 mit Fernando Tavora zusammenarbeitete. Seit 1976 lehrt Siza als Professor für Bauwesen an der Universität Porto. 1988 wurde ihm der Mies-van-der-Rohe-Preis der Europäischen Gemeinschaft verliehen, 1992 erhielt er den Pritzker Prize. In Portugal hat er viele kleinere Bauten ausgeführt, und seit 1989 arbeitet er am Wiederaufbau des Lissabonner Chiado-Viertels. Neuere Bauten sind das Meteorologische Zentrum in Barcelona (1989-92), die Möbelfabrik Vitra in Weil am Rhein (1991-94), die Architekturschule der Universität Porto (1986-95) und die Bibliothek der Universität Aveiro (1988-95). Seine jüngsten Projekte sind der Portugiesische Pavillon für die Expo '98 in Lissabon (1998) und die hier vorgestellte Stiftung Serralves in Porto (1996-99).

Né à Matosinhos, Portugal, en 1933, **ALVARO SIZA** étudie à l'Ecole d'architecture de l'Université de Porto (1949-55). Il crée sa propre agence en 1954 puis collabore avec Fernando Tavora de 1955 à 1958. Il est professeur de construction à l'Université de Porto depuis 1976. Il obtient le Prix Mies van der Rohe de la Communauté Européenne en 1988 et le Prix Pritzker en 1992. Il réalise un grand nombre de projets de petites dimensions au Portugal, puis travaille à la restructuration du quartier du Chiado, à Lisbonne (1989-). Réalisations récentes : le centre de météorologie, Barcelone, Espagne (1989-92) ; l'usine de meubles Vitra, Weil-am-Rhein, Allemagne (1991-94) ; l'Ecole d'architecture de Porto, Université de Porto (1986-95) ; la bibliothèque de l'Université d'Aveiro, Portugal (1988-95). Parmi ses derniers projets : le pavillon portugais pour Expo '98 à Lisbonne (1998) et la Fondation Serralves (Porto, 1996-99), publiée dans ces pages.

SERRALVES FOUNDATION

Porto, Portugal, 1991-99

Planning: 1991-99. Construction: 1996-99. Client: Serralves Foundation.
Landscape: Global – João Gomes da Silva and Erika Skabar. Floor area: 15 000 m².

The **SERRALVES FOUNDATION,** specializing in contemporary art, was created through a joint venture of the Portuguese government and 50 private investors. Established in the Quinta de Serralves, a large property including the main house built in the 1930s, it is located not far from the center of Porto. Siza's new structure, located in the park of the Foundation, is both substantial in size and ambitious in scope. Using a suspended ceiling system similar to the one he devised for the Galician Center of Contemporary Art, Siza created a number of large, flexible galleries, intended for temporary art shows. Interior courtyards and numerous windows permit the visitor to remain in contact with the attractive park environment (of which Siza designed three hectares).

Die auf zeitgenössische Kunst spezialisierte **STIFTUNG SERRALVES** wurde durch die Zusammenarbeit der portugiesischen Regierung mit 50 Investoren aus der Privatwirtschaft begründet. Ihr in der Quinta de Serralves gelegener Sitz mit dem in den 1930er Jahren erbauten Haupthaus befindet sich auf einem großen Gelände unweit des Zentrums von Porto. Sizas neues Gebäude, das in dem zur Stiftung gehörenden Park errichtet wurde, ist sowohl von seiner Größe als auch seinem Anspruch her ein großangelegtes Unternehmen. Der Architekt schuf unter Verwendung einer Hängedeckenkonstruktion, wie er sie in ähnlicher Form bereits für das Galicische Zentrum für Zeitgenössische Kunst entworfen hat, eine Reihe großer, flexibler Galerien, in denen Wechselausstellungen gezeigt werden sollen. Innenhöfe und zahlreiche Fenster erlauben dem Besucher einen ständigen Ausblick auf die reizvolle, umgebende Parklandschaft (von der Siza 3 ha gestaltet hat).

La **FONDATION SERRALVES** d'art contemporain est née d'un partenariat entre l'Etat portugais et 50 mécènes privés. Installée dans la Quinta de Serralves, vaste propriété où se trouvait déjà une belle demeure des années 1930, elle est située à proximité du centre de Porto. Le nouveau bâtiment de Siza, édifié dans le parc de la Fondation, est de taille et de propos ambitieux. A partir d'un système de plafonds suspendus ressemblant à celui mis au point pour le Centre d'art contemporain de Galice, Siza a créé plusieurs vastes galeries d'expositions temporaires. Des cours intérieures et de nombreuses ouvertures permettent au visiteur de conserver le contact avec un parc magnifique (dont 3 ha ont été conçus par Siza).

Set at some distance from the old city of Porto, the new building of the Serralves Foundation does not give a very open impression from the exterior (above) but its complex forms allow ample light into the appropriate galleries, as well as views out toward the park (right).

Das neue Gebäude der unweit der Altstadt von Porto gelegenen Stiftung Serralves macht von außen einen eher abweisenden Eindruck (oben). Seine komplexen Formen lassen jedoch viel natürliches Licht in die einzelnen Ausstellungsräume und geben immer wieder Ausblicke auf den Park frei (rechts).

Non loin de la vieille ville de Porto, le nouveau bâtiment de la Fondation Serralves semble très peu ouvert sur l'extérieur (ci-dessus), mais ses formes complexes laissent pénétrer une généreuse lumière dans ses galeries, et découvrir des perspectives sur le parc (à droite).

Siza is a master of the subtle
manipulation of light and materials,
here to the benefit of the art works
that are placed in spaces whose
architecture and lighting can be
modified to accommodate specific
types of installation.

Siza ist ein Meister der subtilen
Gestaltung mit Licht und Material.
Im Vordergrund stehen dabei die
Kunstwerke, die in Räumen präsentiert werden, deren Innenausstattung
und Lichtdesign je nach Art der Ausstellung verändert werden können.

Siza est un des maîtres de la manipulation subtile de la lumière et des
matériaux, ici au bénéfice d'œuvres
d'art disposées dans des espaces
dont l'architecture et l'éclairage peuvent être modifiés selon les types de
présentations.

EDUARDO SOUTO DE MOURA

Souto Moura Arquitectos Lda
Rua do Aleixo, 53-1°A
4150-043 Porto
Portugal

Tel: +351 2 618 7547
Fax: +351 2 610 8092
e-mail: souto.moura@mail.telepac.pt

EDUARDO SOUTO DE MOURA was born in Porto, Portugal, in 1952. He graduated from the School of Architecture of Porto in 1980. He was an Assistant Professor at the Faculty of Architecture in Porto from 1981 to 1991. From 1974 to 1979 he worked in the office of Álvaro Siza and established his own practice the following year. Recent work includes row houses in the Rua Lugarinho (Porto, Portugal, 1996), the renovation of the Municipal Market in Braga (1997), the Silo Norte Shopping building published here, a house and wine cellar (Valladolid, Spain, 1999), and the Portuguese Pavilion, Expo 2000 (Hanover, Germany, with Álvaro Siza, 1999). Current work includes the conversion of the building of the Carvoeira da Foz (Porto) and a project for the Braga Stadium.

EDUARDO SOUTO DE MOURA, geboren 1952 im portugiesischen Porto, schloß 1980 sein Studium an der Architekturschule der Universität Porto ab. Von 1981 bis 1991 lehrte er am Fachbereich Architektur der Universität Porto. Bevor er sich 1980 mit einem eigenen Büro selbständig machte, arbeitete er von 1974 bis 1979 im Büro von Álvaro Siza. Zu seinen neueren Projekten gehören eine Reihenhausanlage in der Rua Lugarinho in Porto (1996), die Modernisierung des städtischen Marktplatzes in Braga (1997) und das hier vorgestellte Gebäude im Einkaufszentrum Silo Norte in Portugal, ein Wohnhaus und Weinkeller in Valladolid, Spanien (1999) und, in Zusammenarbeit mit Álvaro Siza, der Portugiesische Pavillon für die Expo 2000 in Hannover (1999). Gegenwärtig arbeitet er am Umbau des Gebäudes der Carvoeira da Foz in Porto und an einem Projekt für das Stadion in Braga.

Né à Porto, Portugal, en 1952, **EDUARDO SOUTO DE MOURA** est diplômé de l'Ecole d'architecture de Porto (ESBAP, 1980). Il a été Professeur assistant à la faculté d'architecture de Porto (FAUP) de 1981 à 1991. Après avoir travaillé auprès d'Álvaro Siza de 1974 à 1979, il a fondé sa propre agence en 1980. Parmi ses réalisations récentes : une succession de maisons rua Lugarinho (Porto, 1996), la rénovation du marché municipal de Braga (1997), le centre commercial de Silo Norte publié ici, une maison et un chais (Valladolid, Espagne, 1999) et le projet du pavillon portugais d'Expo 2000 (Hanovre, Allemagne, avec Álvaro Siza, 1999). Il travaille actuellement à la reconversion de l'immeuble de la Carvoeira da Foz (Porto) et à un projet de stade à Braga, au Portugal.

SILO NORTE SHOPPING

Matosinhos, Portugal, 1998

Planning and construction: 1998. Client: IMOR-R.
Floor area: 226 m². Costs: withheld.

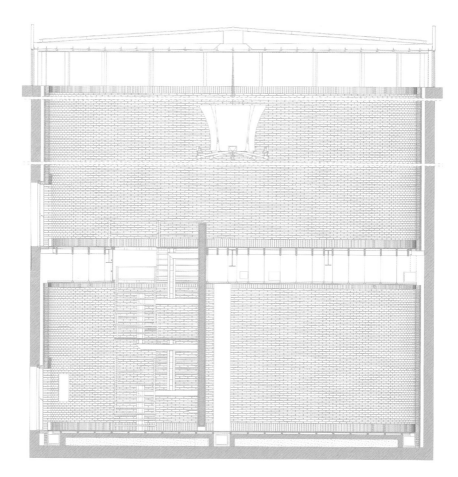

Located in the rather ugly, industrial
Porto suburb of Matosinhos, birth-
place of Álvaro Siza, this facility
demonstrates the architect's ability
to reuse a very specific building type
for an entirely different purpose.

Dieser Bau, der in dem tristen In-
dustrievorort von Porto, Matosinhos,
gelegen ist, demonstriert Souto de
Mouras Talent, einen spezifischen
Bautyp für einen vollkommen
anderen Zweck zu adaptieren.

Situé dans l'assez laide banlieue
industrielle de Matosinhos, lieu de
naissance d'Alvaro Siza, cette intervention montre la capacité de l'architecte à réutiliser un type de bâtiment
destiné à un autre usage.

The architect was asked to create an exhibition gallery and an auditorium inside a spiral ramp that gives access to a parking area. The available space was thus defined in terms of a 22 m-high, 12 m-diameter cylinder, with the auditorium placed on the ground level. The architect lined the cylinder with adobe brick to reduce reverberations, and placed the gallery space above the auditorium to obtain some natural light. With its wooden floors and street lamps used for internal night lighting, the space reflects the sober, powerful style of Souto de Moura. Although **SILO NORTE SHOPPING** was a difficult space to work with, the architect succeeded in making it seem coherent with the relatively elegant external concrete spiral of the parking access ramp.

Eduardo Souto de Moura wurde beauftragt, innerhalb einer spiralförmig verlaufenden Rampe, die den Zugang zu einem Parkkomplex bildet, eine Kunstgalerie und ein Auditorium zu entwerfen. Der verfügbare Raum ist als 22 m hoher Zylinder mit einem Durchmesser von 12 m definiert, in dessen Erdgeschoss das Auditorium untergebracht wurde. Um den Widerhall zu vermindern, kleidete der Architekt den Zylinder mit Lehmziegeln aus. Die Galerie wurde zur Nutzung der natürlichen Lichtverhältnisse über dem Auditorium angelegt. Sowohl die Straßenlaternen, die für eine Innenbeleuchtung bei Nacht sorgen, als auch die Holzböden spiegeln den nüchternen, kraftvollen Stil von Souto de Moura. Obwohl **SILO NORTE SHOPPING** als Raum schwierig zu gestalten war, gelang dem Architekten ein harmonisches Zusammenspiel von Innenraum und äußerer Betonspirale.

Le problème posé était de concevoir une galerie d'exposition et un auditorium à l'intérieur d'une rampe en spirale donnant accès à un parking. Le volume disponible consistait donc en un cylindre de 12 m de diamètre et 22 de haut, l'auditorium étant implanté en sous-sol. Souto de Moura a doublé le cylindre de briques de terre pour réduire la réverbération du bruit et place la galerie au-dessus de l'auditorium pour bénéficier de la lumière naturelle. Avec ses sols en bois et son éclairage de type urbain, l'espace crée incarne le style sobre et puissant de l'architecte. Dans cet espace de **SILO NORTE SHOPPING** difficile à traiter, l'architecte a réussi à trouver une cohérence entre l'intérieur et l'élégante spirale en béton.

Souto de Moura typically suspends an apparently solid wall on a sliced I-beam, raising some doubt as to where solidity and weight actually lie in this structure.

Charakteristisch für Souto de Moura ist das Einhängen einer scheinbar massiven Wand in Doppel-T-Träger, was den Betrachter im Unklaren darüber lässt, wo bei dieser Konstruktion die Masse und das Gewicht liegen.

A sa manière très personnelle, Souto de Moura fait reposer un mur apparemment massif sur une IPN, si bien que le visiteur se demande ce qui porte le poids et la masse de la construction.

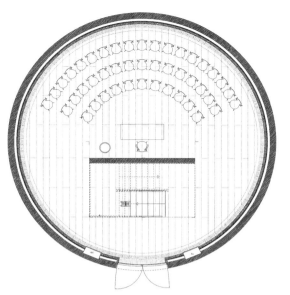

Creating architectural surprise inside such a restricted volume is a measure of the designer's ability to redefine existing space.

Architektonische Überraschungen dieser Art in einem so begrenzten Baukörper sind ein Maßstab für die Fähigkeit des Architekten, einen bestehenden Raum neu zu definieren.

La création de surprises architecturales dans un volume aussi réduit donne la mesure du talent de ce concepteur qui redéfinit admirablement un espace existant.

PHILIPPE STARCK

Philippe Starck
27, rue Pierre Poli
92130 Issy-les-Moulineaux
France

Tel: +33 1 4108 8282
Fax: +33 1 4108 9665

PHILIPPE STARCK was born in Paris in 1949, and attended the École Nissim de Camondo there. He is of course best known as a designer of objects such as chairs or lamps. He has always had an interest in architecture, however. His architectural and interior design projects include the Café Costes (Paris, 1984), the Royalton Hotel (New York, 1988), the Laguiole Knife Factory (France, 1988), the Paramount Hotel (New York, 1990), the Nani Nani Building (Tokyo, 1989), the Asahi Beer Building (Tokyo, 1989), the Teatriz Restaurant (Madrid, 1990), and his Baron Vert Building in Osaka, Japan (1990). He has worked on a number of hotels with Ian Schrager, including the St. Martin's Lane Hotel published here and the Sanderson Hotel, both in London.

PHILIPPE STARCK, geboren 1949 in Paris, studierte an der École Nissim de Camondo in Paris. Obwohl er vor allem als Designer von Einrichtungsgegenständen bekannt geworden ist, zeigte er immer auch ein aktives Interesse an Architektur. Zu seinen baulichen und innenarchitektonischen Projekten gehören das Café Costes in Paris (1984), das Royalton Hotel (1988) und das Paramount Hotel (1990), beide in New York, die Messerfabrik in Laguiole, Frankreich (1988), das Nani Nani-Gebäude (1989) und das Gebäude der Asahi-Brauerei (1989), beide in Tokio, das Restaurant Teatriz in Madrid (1990) sowie das Baron Vert Building in Osaka (1990). Darüber hinaus hat Starck in Zusammenarbeit mit Ian Schrager eine Reihe von Hotels gestaltet, so das hier vorgestellte St. Martin's Lane Hotel und das ebenfalls in London befindliche Sanderson Hotel.

PHILIPPE STARCK, né à Paris en 1949, suit les cours de l'Ecole Camondo. Il est surtout connu comme designer d'objets (sièges, luminaires, etc.) mais s'est toujours intéressé à l'architecture. Parmi ses projets d'architecture et d'aménagements intérieurs : le café Costes (Paris, 1984), le Royalton Hotel (New York, 1988), l'usine de coutellerie (Laguiole, France, 1988), le Paramount Hotel (New York, 1990), l'immeuble Nani Nani (Tokyo, 1989), l'immeuble de la brasserie Asahi (Tokyo, 1989), le restaurant Teatriz (Madrid, 1990) et l'immeuble Baron vert (Osaka, Japon, 1990). Il est intervenu sur plusieurs hôtels pour Ian Schrager, dont le récent St. Martin's Lane Hotel, publié ici, et le Sanderson Hotel, tous deux à Londres.

ST. MARTIN'S LANE HOTEL
London, England, 1999

Opening date: September 1999. Client: Ian Schrager London Limited.

Set on St. Martin's Lane not far from Trafalgar Square, the first **HOTEL** to be opened in London by the American Ian Schrager, in collaboration with the French designer Philippe Starck, is nothing if not a success. Starck's unexpected combinations of giant flower vases, outsized chess pieces, Louis XV-style armchairs, and stools shaped like golden molars combined with Schrager's marketing talent are what is required to bring the rich and the fashionable together in one place. The place is a revamped modernist office building whose facade remains remarkably uncluttered by such inconvenient items as the hotel's name. Clearly, you don't belong in this hotel if you don't know that you have arrived. This is a successful combination of a renovated modernist architecture with Starck's theatrical sense of space and design.

Das in der St. Martin's Lane unweit des Trafalgar Square gelegene, von dem Amerikaner Ian Schrager eröffnete und in Zusammenarbeit mit dem französischen Designer Philippe Starck gestaltete **HOTEL** ist zweifellos ein Erfolg. Starcks ungewöhnliche Kombinationen von riesigen Blumenvasen, überdimensionalen Schachfiguren, Sesseln im Louis XV-Stil und Stühlen in Form goldener Backenzähne, ergeben zusammen mit Schragers Marketing-Talent die erforderlichen Zutaten, um die Hautevolee anzuziehen. Das Haus ist ein renoviertes modernes Bürogebäude, dessen Fassade auffallend frei ist von Banalitäten wie dem Namenszug des Hotels. Alles in allem stellt dieses Projekt eine gelungene Mischung aus moderner Architektur und Starcks theatralischer Auffassung von Raum und Form dar.

En bordure de St. Martin's Lane, non loin de Trafalgar Square, ce premier **HÔTEL** ouvert à Londres par l'Américain Ian Schrager en collaboration avec le designer français Philippe Starck est un grand succès. Le bizarre assemblage starckien de vases pour fleurs géants, de pièces d'échec surdimensionnées, de fauteuils de style Louis XV et de tabourets dorés en forme de molaires ainsi que le vigoureux marketing de Schrager correspondent aux attentes d'une clientèle riche et sensible à la mode. Il s'agit en fait de la restructuration d'un immeuble de bureaux moderniste dont la façade se passe de toute enseigne : vous ne méritez pas de descendre ici si vous n'en connaissez pas l'adresse. Combinaison réussie d'architecture moderniste revisitée et d'un sens théâtral de l'espace et du design à la Starck.

The enormous revolving doors on St. Martin's Lane lead to the entrance foyer, which opens out into a bar and restaurant.

Die riesige Drehtür auf der an der St. Martin's Lane gelegenen Gebäudeseite führt in die Hotelhalle, die sich zu einer Bar und einem Restaurant erweitert.

Les énormes portes pivotantes qui donnent sur St. Martin's Lane conduisent au hall d'entrée qui s'ouvre à son tour sur un bar et un restaurant.

A view of the dining room.

Ansicht des Restaurants.

Vue de la salle-à-manger.

The ground-level bar, located at the rear of the entrance foyer, features these small vertical tables. Well suited to bar use, they, typically for Philippe Starck, challenge existing furniture typology.

Die Bar an der Rückseite der Hotelhalle ist mit kleinen, auf überproportional langen Beinen stehenden Tischen ausgestattet, die auf eine für Starck charakteristische Weise die bestehende Typologie für Einrichtungsgegenstände in Frage stellt.

Le bar du rez-de-chaussée, situé à l'arrière du hall d'entrée, est équipé de petites tables perchées. Bien adaptées à l'utilisation dans un bar, elles sont fideles aux principes de Starck qui remet en question la typologie classique du mobilier.

YOSHIO TANIGUCHI

*Taniguchi and Associates
Yamakatsu Building
4-1-40 Toranomon, Minato-ku
Tokyo 105-0001
Japan*

*Tel: +81 3 3438 1506
Fax: +81 3 3438 1248*

YOSHIO TANIGUCHI was born in Tokyo in 1937. He received a Bachelor's degree in Mechanical Engineering from Keio University in 1960 and his M.Arch. degree from the Harvard Graduate School of Design in 1964. He worked in the practice of Kenzo Tange from 1964 to 1972. In 1979 he established Taniguchi and Associates. His built work in Japan includes the Tokyo Sea Life Park (Tokyo, 1989), the Marugame Genichiro-Inokuma Museum of Contemporary Art, and the Marugame City Library (Marugame, Japan, 1991), the Toyota Municipal Museum of Art (Toyota City, 1995), the Tokyo Kasai Rinkai Park View Point Visitors Center (Tokyo, 1995), and the Tokyo National Museum Gallery of Horyuji Treasures (Tokyo, 1997-99) published here. Yoshio Taniguchi is currently working on the complete renovation and expansion of the Museum of Modern Art in New York.

YOSHIO TANIGUCHI, geboren 1937 in Tokio, erwarb 1960 sein Diplom in Maschinenbau an der Keio-Universität und 1964 seinen Master of Architecture an der Harvard Graduate School of Design (GSD). Von 1964 bis 1972 arbeitete er im Büro von Kenzo Tange. 1979 gründete er Taniguchi and Associates. Zu seinen Bauten in Japan gehören der Sea Life Park in Tokio (1989), das Genichiro-Inokuma Museum für zeitgenössische Kunst in Marugame und die Stadtbibliothek von Marugame (1991), das Städtische Museum für Kunst in Toyota City (1995), das Kansai Rinkai Park View Point Visitors Center in Tokio (1995) und die hier vorgestellten Ausstellungsräume der Horyuji Schatzkammern im Nationalmuseum in Tokio (1997-99). Gegenwärtig arbeitet Taniguchi an der Renovierung und Erweiterung des Museum of Modern Art in New York.

Né à Tokyo en 1937, **YOSHIO TANIGUCHI** est diplômé d'ingénierie mécanique de l'Université Keio (1960) et Master of Architecture de la Harvard Graduate School of Design (1964). Il travaille dans l'agence de Kenzo Tange de 1964 à 1972, et crée Taniguchi et Associés en 1979. Parmi ses réalisations au Japon : le parc marin de Tokyo (Tokyo, 1989), le Musée d'art contemporain Genichiro-Inokuma et la bibliothèque municipale de Marugame (Japon, 1991), le Musée d'art municipal Toyota (Toyota City, 1995), le Centre d'accueil des visiteurs du parc de Kasai Rinkai (Tokyo, 1995) et la galerie des Trésors Horyuji du Musée national (Tokyo, 1997-99), publié ici. Il travaille actuellement à la rénovation intégrale et à l'extension du Museum of Modern Art de New York.

TOKYO NATIONAL MUSEUM, GALLERY OF HORYUJI TREASURES

Tokyo, Japan, 1994-99

Planning: 4/1994-3/95. Construction: 4/1995-3/99.
Client: Ministry of Education and Ministry of Construction.
Total floor area: 4 031 m².

Set in the grounds of the **TOKYO NATIONAL MUSEUM** in Ueno Park in Tokyo, this new structure by Taniguchi was designed to house a number of treasures from the Horyuji Temple in Nara. The building covers an area of 1 934 m² and has a total floor area of 4 031 m². It is a four-story structure built of reinforced concrete with a steel frame. Inspired by the wooden boxes used to protect precious art objects in Japan, the design includes a high metal canopy, a glazed entrance area and a completely darkened exhibition area in the interior. Open on two sides to the garden environment with a shallow basin marking the entrance area, the building's construction has a jewel-like precision. It is a masterpiece in itself, worthy of one of the finest architects currently working in Japan.

Yoshio Taniguchi entwarf für das **TOKIOTER NATIONAL MUSEUM** in Ueno Park einen Bau zur Präsentation von Kunstwerken, die ursprünglich dem Horyuji Tempel in Nara gehörten. Die viergeschossige Stahlbetonkonstruktion – ein mit Stahlbeton ummanteltes Stahlskelett – hat eine Grundfläche von 1 934 m² und eine Gesamtnutzfläche von 4 031 m². Inspiriert von den in Schichten aufgebauten Holzkisten, die im alten Japan zum Schutz kostbarer Kunstgegenstände verwendet wurden, beinhaltet die Gestaltung ein hohes, überhängendes Schutzdach aus Metall, einen verglasten Eingangsbereich und einen vollständig abgedunkelten Ausstellungsbereich. Im Eingangsbereich ist das Gebäude nach zwei Seiten zum umgebenden Garten und einem flachen Wasserbecken hin geöffnet. Mit seinen präzisen und kostbaren Formen kann dieser Bau mit Recht ein Meisterwerk genannt werden, würdig eines der besten japanischen Architekten unserer Tage.

Sur les terrains du **MUSÉE NATIONAL DE TOKYO**, dans le parc Ueno, cette nouvelle réalisation de Taniguchi a été spécialement construite pour recevoir un certain nombre d'œuvres qui se trouvaient à l'origine dans le temple Horyuji de Nara. Pour une surface au sol de 1 934 m², le musée dispose de 4 031 m² de planchers sur quatre niveaux. Il est en béton armé sur ossature d'acier. Inspiré des boîtes en bois qui servaient à protéger les objets précieux au Japon, il possède un auvent en métal surplombant, une zone d'entrée vitrée entourée d'un bassin et une aire d'exposition centrale sans ouverture. Donnant de deux côtés sur le parc, il a été construit avec une précision d'horloger. Ce chef d'œuvre est à l'image du travail de Taniguchi, l'un des architectes le plus raffinés travaillant actuellement au Japon.

The extreme rigor and geometric clarity of Taniguchi's architecture is visible in these images of the main approach path to the museum (left) and in the entrance foyer (below).

Der Hauptzugangsweg zum Museum (links) und das Foyer (unten) machen die extreme Strenge und geometrische Klarheit von Taniguchis Baukunst augenfällig.

La rigueur extrême et la pureté géométrique du travail de Taniguchi sont évidentes dans ces vues de l'accès principal du musée (à gauche) et du foyer d'entrée (ci-dessous).

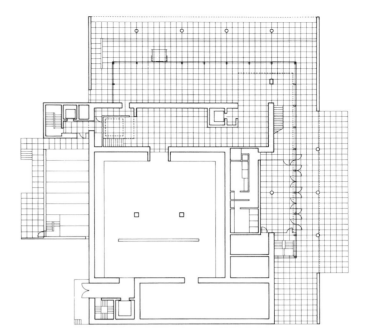

The visitor progresses from the light entrance areas to the almost total darkness of the main exhibition hall, where the extraordinary Buddhist relics of the Temple are displayed.

Die Besucher gelangen von dem hellen Eingangsbereich in den ab-gedunkelten Ausstellungssaal, wo die kostbaren Reliquien des Tempels präsentiert werden.

Partant de la zone d'entrée très lumi-neuse, le visiteur pénètre dans l'obs-curité quasi totale de la principale salle d'exposition où sont présentées d'extraordinaires reliques du temple.

Lerner Hall Student Center ▶

BERNARD TSCHUMI

Bernard Tschumi Architects
227 West 17th Street
New York, NY 10011
United States

Tel: +1 212 807 6340
Fax: +1 212 242 3693
e-mail: nyc@tschumi.com
Web: www.tschumi.com

7 rue Pecquay
75004 Paris
France
Tel: +33 1 5301 9070
Fax: +33 1 5301 9079
e-mail: bernard.tschumi.architectes@wanadoo.fr

BERNARD TSCHUMI was born in Lausanne, Switzerland, in 1944. He studied in Paris and at the ETH, Zurich. He taught at the Architectural Association, London (1970-79), and at Princeton (1976 and 1980). He has been Dean of the Graduate School of Architecture, Planning and Preservation of Columbia University in New York since 1988. He opened his own office, Bernard Tschumi Architects (Paris, New York), in 1981. Major projects include: Parc de la Villette (Paris, France, 1982-98), second prize in the Kansai International Airport Competition (1988), Glass Video Gallery (Groningen, Netherlands, 1990, recently made part of the Groninger Museum, the Fresnoy National Center for the Contemporary Arts (Tourcoing, France, 1991-98), Lerner Hall Student Center, Columbia University (New York, 1994-99), School of Architecture (first phase, Marne-la-Vallée, France, 1994-99) published here, and the Interface Flon Transport System in Lausanne, Switzerland (1988-2001).

BERNARD TSCHUMI, geboren 1944 in Lausanne in der Schweiz, studierte in Paris und an der Eidgenössischen Technischen Hochschule in Zürich. Von 1970 bis 1979 lehrte er an der Architectural Association in London und von 1976 bis 1980 in Princeton. Seit 1988 ist er Dekan der Graduate School of Architecture, Planning and Preservation der Columbia University in New York. 1981 eröffnete er sein eigenes Büro, Bernard Tschumi Architects, mit Niederlassungen in Paris und New York. Zu seinen wichtigsten Projekten gehören: der Parc de la Villette in Paris (1982-98), ein Wettbewerbsbeitrag für den internationalen Flughafen Kansai (1988), der den zweiten Preis erhielt, die Glass Video Galerie in Groningen, Niederlande, die kürzlich in das Groninger Museum eingegliedert wurde (1990), das staatliche Zentrum für zeitgenössische Kunst Le Fresnoy in Tourcoing, Frankreich (1991-98) sowie das Interface Flon Transport System in Lausanne (1988-2001). Das Lerner Hall Student Center der Columbia University in New York (1994-99) und die Architekturschule in Marne-la-Vallée (erster Bauabschnitt 1994-99) werden beide hier vorgestellt.

Né à Lausanne, Suisse, en 1944, **BERNARD TSCHUMI** étudie à Paris et à l'Institut fédéral de technologie de Zurich (ETH). Il enseigne à l'Architectural Association (Londres, 1970-79) et à Princeton (1976 et 1980). Il est doyen de la Graduate School of Architecture, Planning and Preservation de Columbia University, New York, depuis 1988. Il a ouvert son agence, Bernard Tschumi Architects en 1981 (New York et Paris). Parmi ses principaux projets : le Parc de la Villette (Paris, 1982-98), le second prix du concours pour l'aéroport international de Kansai (1988), la Glass Video Gallery (Groningue, Pays-Bas, 1990 ; récemment intégrée au Musée de Groningue), le Centre National pour les Arts contemporains du Fresnoy (Tourcoing, France, 1991-98), le Lerner Hall Student Center, Columbia University (New York, 1994-99) et l'Ecole d'Archi-tecture de Marne-la-Vallée, (1ère phase, 1994-99), publiée dans ces pages, ainsi que l'Interface Flon Transport System à Lausanne (1988-2001).

LERNER HALL STUDENT CENTER

Columbia University, New York, NY, USA, 1994-99

Planning: 1994-95. Construction: Fall 1996 – Summer 1999.
Client: Columbia University. Floor area: 20 903 m². Costs: $85 000 000.

The $85 million 20 903-m² **LERNER HALL STUDENT CENTER** is built (in collaboration with Gruzen Samton Architects) in large part of precast concrete, brick and cast-stone masonry with cast-in-place concrete columns. One of its most surprising features is the bank of ramps set just behind a structural glass wall on the side of the building facing the campus. This skewed space is used incidentally to house some 6 000 student mailboxes, but it is also a device to bring students together into a common space, while solving the structural questions related to the uneven terrain of the site. Indeed, the glass facade of the building stands out as being surprisingly different than the opposite (Broadway) side of the building, which had to fit into the plan for the campus alignments and building design of McKim, Mead and White of 1890. As Dean of the Columbia School of Architecture, Bernard Tschumi thus leaves a lasting mark on the university.

Das für 85 Millionen $ in Zusammenarbeit mit Gruzen Samton Architects erbaute, 20 903 m² große Alfred **LERNER HALL STUDENT CENTER** besteht überwiegend aus Betonfertigteilen, einer Kombination von Ziegel- und Kunststeinmauerwerk, Aluminium, Glas und vor Ort gegossenen Betonstützen. Um die Unebenheiten des Geländes auf der dem Campus zugewandten Gebäudeseite auszugleichen, wurden im mittleren Bauteil hinter einer Fassade aus Glas Rampen angelegt. Diese verbinden die auf unterschiedlicher Höhe liegenden Geschosse der angrenzenden Bauten, darüber hinaus wird der Bereich hinter der Fassade als Treffpunkt und zur Unterbringung von fast 6 000 Briefkästen für die Studenten genutzt. Die Glasfassade unterscheidet sich stark von der am Broadway liegenden Seite des Gebäudes, die sich in den Generalplan für den Campus einfügen musste, den McKim, Mead and White 1890 entwickelt hatte. Damit hat Bernard Tschumi, Dekan der Columbia School of Architecture, eine bleibende Spur an seiner Universität hinterlassen.

Le **LERNER HALL STUDENT CENTER** de 20 903 m² (budget: $85 millions) est en grande partie construit (en collaboration avec Gruzen Samton Architects) en éléments de béton préfabriqués, brique et pierre moulée. L'une de ses caractéristiques les plus surprenantes est la succession de rampes implantée juste derrière une façade en verre donnant sur le campus. Cet espace « en biais » sert éventuellement à abriter les quelques 6 000 boîtes aux lettres des étudiants, mais correspond aussi à la volonté de réunir les étudiants dans un espace commun tout en résolvant les problèmes de structure posés par un terrain inégal. Cette façade de verre est étonnement différente de celle qui donne sur Broadway contrainte de respecter l'alignement et le plan de masse de McKim, Mead and White de 1890. Doyen de la Columbia School of Architecture, Bernard Tschumi aura laissé une marque durable sur son université.

The architect approached the problem of the difference in levels of the street and campus sides of the building by using a system of inclined ramps.

Der Architekt löste das Problem der unterschiedlichen Höhe von Campus und straßenseitigen Gebäudeteilen durch ein System geneigter Rampen.

L'architecte a traité la différence de niveaux entre la rue et le campus au moyen d'un système de rampes inclinées.

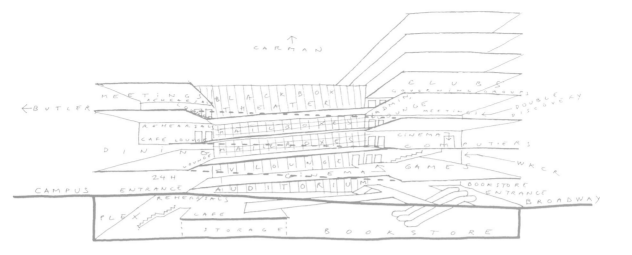

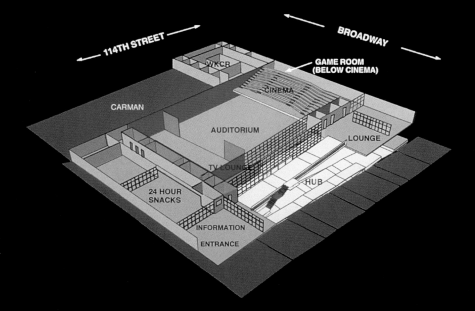

114TH STREET

BROADWAY

WKCR

GAME ROOM
(BELOW CINEMA)

CINEMA

CARMAN

AUDITORIUM

LOUNGE

TV LOUNGE

24 HOUR
SNACKS

HUB

INFORMATION

ENTRANCE

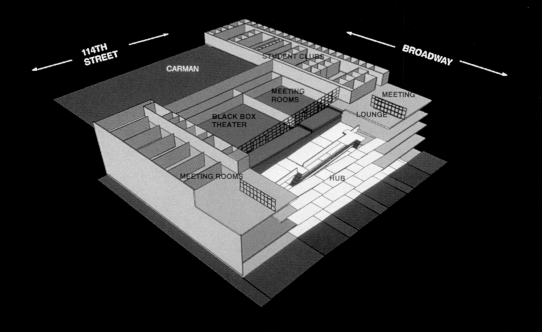

114TH
STREET

BROADWAY

STUDENT CLUBS

CARMAN

MEETING
ROOMS

MEETING

BLACK BOX
THEATER

LOUNGE

MEETING ROOMS

HUB

The tilting of the access ramps gives an unexpected image of a building that is fundamentally very practical and intended for use by large numbers of students.

Die geneigten Erschließungsrampen verleihen dem sehr funktional gestalteten Gebäude, das von einer großen Zahl von Studenten genutzt wird, eine überraschende Note.

L'inclinaison des rampes d'accès donne une image étrange à ce bâtiment très pratique, conçu pour être utilisé par un grand nombre d'étudiants.

UN STUDIO

UN Studio Van Berkel & Bos BV
Stadhouderskade 113
1073 AX Amsterdam
Netherlands

Tel: +31 20 570 2040
Fax: +31 20 570 2041
e-mail: info@unstudio.com
web: www.unstudio.com

Bascule Bridge and Bridgemaster's House ▶

BEN VAN BERKEL was born in Utrecht in 1957, and studied at the Rietveld Academie in Amsterdam and at the Architectural Association (AA) in London, receiving the AA Diploma with honors in 1987. After working briefly in the office of Santiago Calatrava, he established his practice in Amsterdam with **CAROLINE BOS** in 1988. He was visiting professor at Columbia University, New York, and visiting critic at Harvard University (1994). Diploma Unit Master, AA, London (1994-95). UN Studio Van Berkel & Bos has built the Karbouw (1990-92) and ACOM office buildings (1989-93), and the REMU electricity station (1989-93), all in Amersfoort, housing projects and the Aedes East Gallery for Kristin Feireiss (now Director of the Netherlands Architecture Institute, Rotterdam) in Berlin, as well as the Erasmus Bridge in Rotterdam (inaugurated in 1996). More recent projects in the Netherlands include the Möbius House ('t Gooi, 1993-97), the Museum Het Valkhof (Nijmegen, 1995-99), and renovation and extension of Rijksmuseum Twente (Enschede, 1992-96). Current work includes the MuMuTh Music Theater (Graz, 1998-2002), and the electrical substation Umspannwerk Mitte (Innsbruck, 1996-2000), both in Austria.

BEN VAN BERKEL, geboren 1957 in Utrecht, studierte an der Rietveld-Akademie in Amsterdam und an der Architectural Association (AA) in London, wo er 1987 sein Diplom mit Auszeichnung erwarb. Nach kurzer Tätigkeit bei Santiago Calatrava gründete er 1988 mit **CAROLINE BOS** ein eigenes Büro in Amsterdam. 1994 war van Berkel Gastprofessor an der Columbia University in New York und Gastkritiker in Harvard, von 1994 bis 1995 erwarb er das Diploma Unit Master an der AA in London. Außer der 1996 eröffneten Erasmus-Brücke in Rotterdam hat das Architekturbüro UN Studio Van Berkel & Bos die Bürogebäude Karbouw (1990-92) und ACOM (1989-93) sowie das Elektrizitätswerk REMU (1989-93), alle im niederländischen Amersfoort, ausgeführt. In Berlin entstanden Wohnbauten und die Galerie Aedes East für Kristin Feireiss (der jetzigen Leiterin des Niederländischen Architekturinstituts in Rotterdam). Zu den jüngsten Projekten in den Niederlanden gehören das Möbius-Haus in 't Gooi (1993-97), das Museum Het Valkhof in Nijmegen (1995-99) und die Modernisierung und Erweiterung des Rijksmuseum Twente in Enschede (1992-96). UN Studio realisiert derzeit zwei Bauten in Österreich: das Musiktheater MuMuTh in Graz (1998-2002) und das Umspannwerk Mitte in Innsbruck (1996-2000).

BEN VAN BERKEL naît à Utrecht en 1957. Il étudie à la Rietveld Academie d'Amsterdam et à l'Architectural Association (AA) de Londres, dont il sort diplômé avec mention en 1987. Après avoir brièvement travaillé dans l'agence de Santiago Calatrava en 1988, il ouvre son agence à Amsterdam, et s'associe avec **CAROLINE BOS**. En 1994, il est professeur invité à la Columbia University, New York, et critique invité à Harvard puis Diploma Unit Master à l'AA, Londres en 1994-95. Outre le pont Erasme à Rotterdam (inauguré en 1996), UN Studio Van Berkel & Bos a construit les immeubles de bureaux Karbouw (1990-92), ACOM (1989-93) et la centrale électrique REMU (1989-93), tous à Amersfoort en Pays-Bas, ainsi que des projets de logements et la galerie Aedes East à Berlin pour Kristin Feireiss (actuellement directrice de l'Institut néerlandais d'architecture de Rotterdam). Parmi leurs projets les plus récents, la maison Möbius ('t Gooi, 1993-97) ; le musée Het Valkhof (Nimègue, 1995-99) ; la rénovation et l'extension du Rijksmuseum Twente (Enschede, 1992-96) toutes dans les Pays-Bas; le complexe consacré à la musique MuMuTh (Graz, Autriche, 1998-2002) et le Umspannwerk Mitte (Innsbruck, Autriche, 1996-2000)

BASCULE BRIDGE AND BRIDGEMASTER'S HOUSE

Purmerend, Netherlands, 1995-98

Planning: 4/95-4/96. Construction: 12/96-3/98. Client: City of Purmerend.
Floor area ground floor bridgemaster's house: 36 m². Costs: ca. Hfl 14 000 000.

Ben van Berkel often works at the border between industry, architecture and engineering, as his Electrical Substation in Amersfoort or the Erasmus Bridge in Rotterdam prove. In what he calls "bridge for an ordinary place" in the north of the Netherlands, the three decks of the **BASCULE BRIDGE** open and close asynchronously "imitating the movement of playing fingers." A 12-m-high **BRIDGEMASTER'S HOUSE** controls the movement of the bridge. A concrete core covered with perforated steel plates reveals some of its inner workings, but also gives a mysterious appearance to this unique object. As van Berkel points out, redesigning such apparently banal elements requires new "non-hierarchical relationships between architects and engineers."

Ben van Berkels Entwürfe bewegen sich häufig an der Grenze zwischen Industrie, Architektur und Maschinenbaukunst, wie sein Elektrizitätswerk in Amersfoort oder seine Erasmus-Brücke in Rotterdam beweisen. Bei der im Norden Hollands gelegenen **HEBEBRÜCKE**, die van Berkel als »Brücke für einen alltäglichen Ort« bezeichnet, öffnen und schließen sich drei Plattformen auf asynchrone Weise, wodurch sie »die Bewegung spielender Finger nachahmen«. Von dem 12 m hohen Gebäude der **BRÜCKENWACHT** werden die Aktivitäten der Hebebrücke gesteuert. Ein mit perforierten Stahlplatten umhüllter Betonkern lässt einen Teil seiner inneren Mechanik sichtbar werden und verleiht diesem einzigartigen Bauwerk gleichzeitig ein geheimnisvolles Aussehen. Wie van Berkel betont, erfordert die Gestaltung solch scheinbar alltäglicher Gebäude neue »nicht-hierarchische Formen der Zusammenarbeit zwischen Architekten und Ingenieuren«.

Ben van Berkel travaille souvent aux frontières de l'industrie, de l'architecture et de l'ingénierie, comme le montrent sa station électrique d'Amersfoort, Pays-Bas (1994) ou le pont Erasme à Rotterdam. L'ouvrage qu'il qualifie de « pont pour un lieu ordinaire », au Nord des Pays-Bas présente trois tabliers du **PONT BASCULANT** qui s'ouvrent et se ferment de façon asynchrone « reprenant le mouvement de doigts qui pianotent. » Un petit bâtiment de 12 m de haut sert de **POSTE DE CONTRÔLE**. Le noyau de béton, couvert de plaques d'acier perforé révèle une partie des mécanismes intérieurs, mais donne également un aspect mystérieux à cet objet architectural original. Comme le fait remarquer van Berkel, concevoir des éléments apparemment aussi banalisés demande d'inventer de nouvelles « relations non hiérarchiques entre les architectes et les ingénieurs. »

Using unusual surface treatments and skewed building forms, Ben van Berkel challenges the very staid model of the traditional bridgemaster's house, adding an element of movement and transparency.

Mit ungewöhnlicher Oberflächenbehandlung und schrägen Flächen stellt van Berkel der traditionellen Bauweise von Brückenwachtgebäuden mit eher statischer Wirkung hier Bewegung und Transparenz entgegen.

A partir de formes inclinées et de surfaces inhabituelles, Ben van Berkel remet en question la forme classique du poste de contrôle de batellerie et l'enrichit d'un élément de mouvement et de transparence.

The angled form of the bridge-master's house recalls the movement of the bridge itself, as the image below clearly demonstrates.

Die schräge Form der Brückenwacht nimmt Bezug auf die Bewegungsabläufe der Hebebrücke.

L'inclinaison de la forme penchée rappelle le mouvement et le profil du pont lui-même, comme le montre la vue ci-dessous.

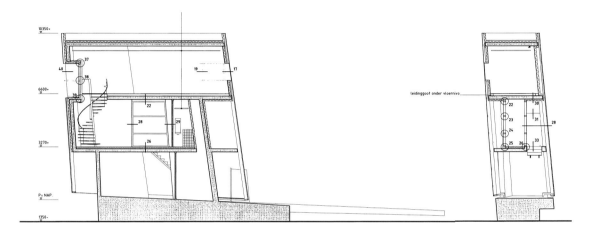

WILLIAMS AND TSIEN

Tod Williams Billie Tsien and Associates
222 Central Park South
New York, NY 10019
United States

Tel.: +1 212 582 2385
Fax: +1 212 245 1984
e-mail: twbta@network.net

TOD WILLIAMS was born in Detroit in 1943. He gained his B.A. degree (1965) and his M.F.A. degree (1967) from Princeton University. After six years as associate architect with Richard Meier in New York, he began his own practice there in 1974. He taught at Cooper Union for more than 15 years, as well as at Harvard, Yale, the University of Virginia, and the Southern California Institute of Architecture (SCI-Arc). He won the Prix de Rome in 1983. **BILLIE TSIEN,** born in Ithaca, New York, in 1949, gained her B.A. degree from Yale, and her M.Arch. from the University of California, Los Angeles (1977). A painter and graphic designer (1971-75), she has taught at Parsons School of Design, SCI-Arc, Harvard and Yale. Their built work includes the Feinberg Hall at Princeton University (New Jersey, 1986), the New College of the University of Virginia (Charlottesville, Virginia, 1992), and the renovation and extension of the Museum of Fine Arts in Phoenix, Arizona (1996). Current projects include an aquatic center for the Cranbrook Schools in Michigan, the Museum of American Folk Art in New York, and an amphitheater seating 25 000 in Guadalajara, Mexico.

TOD WILLIAMS, geboren 1943 in Detroit, erwarb 1965 den Bachelor of Arts und 1967 den Master of Fine Arts an der Princeton University. Nach sechsjähriger Mitarbeit im Büro von Richard Meier machte er sich 1974 in New York selbständig. Er lehrte an der Cooper Union, in Harvard und Yale, an der University of Virginia und am Southern California Institute of Architecture (SCI-Arc). 1983 wurde ihm der Prix de Rome verliehen. **BILLIE TSIEN**, geboren 1949 in Ithaca, New York, erwarb den Bachelor of Arts an der Yale University und 1977 den Master of Architecture an der University of California, Los Angeles. Von 1971 bis 1975 arbeitete sie als Malerin und Grafikerin. Außerdem lehrte sie an der Parsons School of Design, am SCI-Arc, in Harvard und Yale. Wichtige Bauten von Williams und Tsien sind die Feinberg Hall in Princeton, New Jersey (1986), das New College der University of Virginia in Charlottesville (1992), sowie der Umbau des Museum of Fine Arts in Phoenix, Arizona (1996). Zu ihren jüngsten Projekten gehören ein Zentrum für Wassersport für die Cranbrook Schulen in Michigan, das Museum of American Folk Art in New York und ein Amphitheater mit 25 000 Plätzen in Guadalajara, Mexiko.

TOD WILLIAMS, né à Detroit en 1943, Bachelor of Arts en 1965, Master of Fine Arts, 1967, Princeton University. Après six ans d'exercice comme architecte associé dans l'agence de Richard Meier (1967-73), il crée son agence à New York en 1974. Il enseigne pendant plus de 15 ans à la Cooper Union, à Harvard, Yale, à l'Université de Virginie et au Southern California Institute of Architecture (SCI-Arc). Prix de Rome en 1983. **BILLIE TSIEN**, née à Ithaca, New York, en 1949, Bachelor of Arts, Yale, Master of Architecture, UCLA, 1977. Elle a été peintre et graphiste de 1971 à 1975. Enseigne à la Parsons School of Design, SCI-Arc, à Harvard et à Yale. Parmi leurs réalisations : Feinberg Hall (Princeton, New Jersey, 1986), New College, University of Virginia (Charlottesville, Virginia, 1992) ; restauration complète et extension du Museum of Fine Arts de Phoenix, Arizona (1996). Parmi leurs projets actuels : un centre aquatique pour les Cranbrook Schools (Michigan), le Museum of American Folk Art (New York) et un amphithéâtre de 25 000 places à Guadalajara (Mexique).

RIFKIND HOUSE

Georgica Pond, Long Island, New York, USA, 1997-98

Construction: 1997-98. Client: Robert and Arleen Rifkind.
Floor area: 465 m² Costs: withheld

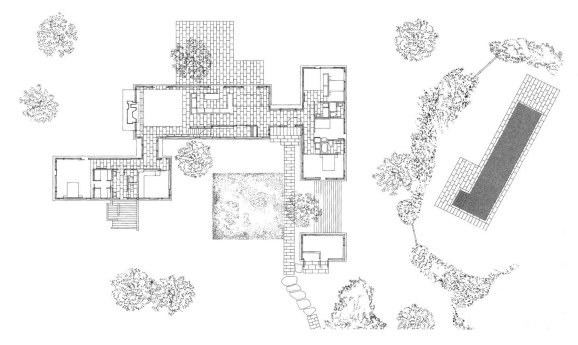

Set on a 1.5-hectare site on the edge of a large pond within view of the ocean, the **RIFKIND HOUSE** was intended to satisfy the client's specifications for "quiet serenity, an openness to the landscape and a sense of spaciousness without monumentality." It is, except for the slightly higher living room area, only about 3 m in height. It comprises four units – a planting and storage shed, a three-bedroom guest wing, a master bedroom area, and a "public" section. A wood-frame structure with cedar-siding, the house has ample glazing set in mahogany window frames, while inside floors are covered with Douglas fir and New York bluestone. Bookshelves, beds, dressers and furniture, also designed by the architects, are made of American cherry.

Das **RIFKIND HOUSE** ist auf einem 1,5 ha großen Grundstück mit Blick auf den Atlantik am Rand eines Teichs gelegen. Es sollte auf Wunsch des Bauherrn von »gelassener Heiterkeit, einer Offenheit für die Landschaft und einem Gefühl von Geräumigkeit ohne Monumentalität« geprägt sein. Das gesamte Gebäude ist, mit Ausnahme des leicht erhöhten Wohnraums, nur ca. 3 m hoch und setzt sich aus vier Einheiten zusammen: einer Kombination von Gewächshaus und Lagerschuppen, einem Gästetrakt mit drei Zimmern, einem großen Schlafraum und einem »öffentlichen« Bereich. Die aus einem mit Zedernholz verkleideten Holzgerüst bestehende Außenfassade des Hauses wird von großen Glasflächen mit Mahagoniholzrahmen durchbrochen, während die Böden im Inneren mit Douglasie und blauem Tonsandstein aus dem Hudsongebiet bedeckt sind. Die ebenfalls von den Architekten entworfenen Bücherregale, Betten, Kommoden und auch die anderen Möbel sind aus amerikanischem Kirschbaum gefertigt.

Située au bord d'un étang sur un terrain de 1,5 ha, la **MAISON RIFKIND** répond au souhait du client qui recherchait la « sérénité naturelle, l'ouverture sur le paysage et une impression d'espace sans monumentalité ». A l'exception du séjour, légèrement surélevé, la maison ne dépasse pas 3 m de hauteur. Elle se compose de quatre éléments – un hangar de stockage et de jardinage, une aile pour invités avec trois chambres, une partie réservée à la chambre du maître de maison et une zone « publique ». La structure en bois est bardée de cèdre. Les ouvertures en acajou sont vastes et les sols en pin de Douglas ou pierre bleue de New York. Les rayonnages pour les livres, les lits, les commodes et le mobilier sont en cerisier américain et ont été dessinés par les architectes.

Seen from two different angles, the house appears to be quite closed, with its horizontal cedar siding, or alternatively quite open, with the large vertical glass panels allowing views out toward the wooded site.

Während die mit Zedernholz verkleideten Wände auf der einen Seite des Gebäudes einen eher geschlossen Charakter vermitteln, wirken die großen Glasflächen, die den Blick auf das bewaldete Grundstück freigeben, sehr offen.

Selon les angles de vue, la maison semble plutôt fermée derrière son habillage de cèdre ou très ouverte par ses hauts panneaux de verre qui donnent sur le terrain boisé.